D1825400

HAWKER HURRICANE SURVIVORS

A COMPLETE CATALOGUE OF
EVERY EXISTING
HURRICANE WORLDWIDE

Gordon Roy

19th Sept 2015

@Geoffrey Hullett

HAWKER HURRICANE SURVIVORS

A COMPLETE CATALOGUE OF
EVERY EXISTING
HURRICANE WORLDWIDE

GORDON RILEY

Grub Street • London

Published by
Grub Street
4 Rainham Close
London
SW11 6SS

Copyright © Grub Street 2015
Copyright text © Gordon Riley 2015

A CIP record for this title is available from the British Library

ISBN-13: 9-781-909808-34-8

Printed and bound by Finidir, Czech Republic

NB: Whilst the author and publisher have made every effort to ensure
the accuracy of the information presented in this book as at the date of
publication, they can accept no liability for any loss, damage or expense
resulting from reliance on such information. Anyone seeking to enter into any
financial or commercial transaction in respect of any of the aircraft described
should rely exclusively on their own inspection and enquiries.

CONTENTS

ACKNOWLEDGEMENTS

In any work such as this the author has to rely upon the help of many contributors who have supplied information, photographs and other details. In the case of photographs the photographer is credited next to their images. I would particularly like to thank the following individuals for their help in compiling this book:

Peter R Arnold, Steven Atkin, Ken Beanlands, Guy Black, Paul Blackah, Andrew Boehly, Don Bradshaw, Gary Brown, Craig Charleston, Brian Davis, Richard de Boer, Peter Dimond, Tony Ditheridge, Tom Dolezal, Ken Duffey, Tony Dyer, Richard Edgeler, Lynn Garrison, Carl Geust, Benjamin Gilbert, Arne Hansen, Mike Henniger, Greg Herrick, Colin Higgs, Ken Hopper, Lee Howard, Daniel Hunt, Jerry Jagen, Robs Lamplough, Antti Lappalainen, Birger Larsen, Phillip Lawton, Jon Leake, Norman Malayney, Ken McBride, Dave McDonald, Malcolm McLeod, Chris Michell, Heather Norman, Michael Oakey, Boris Osetinskiy, Gordon Page, Ross Pay, Col Pope, Winston G Ramsey, Geoff Rayner, Juha Ritaranta, Andy Robinson, Paul Rogers, Peter Rushen, Andy Saunders, Bob Schneider, Mark Sheppard, Steven Smart, Kjell Sørensen, Kari Stenman, Nick Stroud, William Tassell, Peter Teichman, Julian Temple, Peter Vacher, Jerry Vernon, Frédéric Vormezeele, Rem Walker and Kermit Weeks.

Very special thanks must also be extended to my wife Jacqueline for her understanding and patience – which was frequently tried – during the months that it took to produce this book.

FOREWORD

It would take me weeks to read and absorb all Gordon's words, but what I have read reveals a world beyond my imagination. The depth of his research will surely bring the spotlight back onto a great aircraft.

In telling the story not just of the Hurricane but of specific Hurricanes, Gordon treats each plane as an individual. In this he echoes the way we each related to our own plane. We pilots have had a chance to tell our stories so it's gratifying to be able to read the stories of our silent partners. Gordon's thorough research will surely bring the spotlight back onto a great aircraft.

First into battle, it served in virtually every theatre of war. Upstaged, it merely changed its role. Its robustness and simplicity of build allowed it to be quickly patched up and restored to service. An aircraft without vice, it served me well in its various forms – at home in 1940-41, off HMS *Argus* into Russia in 1941, off CAM ships in 1942 and later in the Far East.

I am delighted to think that my JX-O, a flamer in August 1940, is to be 'recreated'. And it is just conceivable that the shadow of my GO-31 might find its way home from Russia to be reunited with its fellow fighters.

Wg Cdr J F D (Tim) Elkington

PREFACE

With 2015 being the 75th anniversary of the Battle of Britain – arguably the Hawker Hurricane's 'finest hour' – it seemed appropriate to tell the story of each of the surviving Hurricanes from around the world. Building on research originally started 30 years ago, when the total number was thought to be around 20 aircraft, this book catalogues every known survivor as of 2015, with the number now more than three times that.

The oldest Hurricane in existence, L1592, is a veteran of both the British Expeditionary Force to France in 1939 and the Battle of Britain and is displayed in the Science Museum, London, whilst the youngest, PZ865 – the very last Hurricane ever built – is still flying with the RAF Battle of Britain Memorial Flight, to which it was delivered in 1972, having never been taken on charge by the RAF when it was built at Langley in the summer of 1944.

Each aircraft is documented from the day it left the factory up to the present day, some have incredible histories whereas others served in very mundane, but still essential, second-line roles until they were disposed of. Where possible each aircraft is illustrated with a present-day photograph together with others taken throughout its life.

The relatively recent discoveries of many Hurricanes in the former Soviet Union, together with examples found across Canada in the 1970s and 1980s, has led to a number of aircraft being restored to fly in private hands around the world and the author has been privileged to have been granted access to several workshops – including that of Hawker Restorations Ltd, the acknowledged leader in Hurricane restorations.

In any work such as this there will be contradictions with aircraft appearing in lists in magazine articles, books or websites for which there is little or no hard evidence that they exist. The same mistakes get repeated over and over again and eventually acquire a veneer of truth simply due to that repetition. The aircraft detailed in this book all exist, the author has either seen them personally or corresponded or spoken with somebody closely associated with the aircraft who can vouch for its existence.

The nature of the subject matter is such that by the time the book is published it will already be slightly dated as aircraft take to the air following restoration or appear in new colour schemes. Nevertheless, this book is testimony to Sir Sydney Camm's masterpiece in the year of its 80th birthday and to the bravery of its pilots, on which this nation depended 75 years ago.

Gordon Riley, July 2015

INTRODUCTION

Having entered RAF service with No. 111 Sqdn at Northolt in December 1937, the Hurricane had a relatively short operational life which peaked during the Battle of Britain when a total of 1,715 Hurricanes saw service – more than all other British fighters combined. The last front-line squadrons in the European Theatre gave up their Hurricanes in 1943, although others soldiered on in South East Asia Command and Palestine until No. 6 Sqdn retired its last two examples in January 1947. The Hurricane's metal tubular fuselage structure, with its mix of wooden formers, stringers and fabric covering, could absorb a lot of punishment and was loved by both pilots and ground crews, who could carry out damage repairs in the field. It was this very structure which limited both its performance and development potential; Hawkers realised this and produced both the Typhoon and Tempest, using stressed-skin monocoque construction techniques for the rear fuselage, as successors to the Hurricane, with the result that the last of the 14,533 Hurricanes built – PZ865 – rolled out of the Langley factory in July 1944. Having been purchased by Hawkers in 1945 it survives in flying condition with the RAF Battle of Britain Memorial Flight 70 years later, having been civilianised as G-AMAU in May 1950 to become a company demonstrator, high-speed taxi and part-time racing aircraft. It was maintained in flying condition by Hawkers for over 20 years, first at Langley and then at Dunsfold, before being gifted to the Royal Air Force in 1972.

As early as 1944, The Air Historical Branch had the foresight to designate a number of historic airframes for post-war preservation, including two early Hurricane Mk Is, L1592 and P2617, both of which survive, the first in the Science Museum, London, and the second in the Royal Air Force Museum, London. The former is unique as the only Hurricane to survive with the original fabric-covered wings still fitted. Although Hurricanes were supplied to a variety of overseas air forces in the immediate post-war period, most were rapidly replaced with more modern equipment and were swiftly consigned to the scrapyard. The RAF found little use for the venerable Hurricane – even as

In July 1951 there were only two flyable Hurricanes in the UK, a situation which remained the same until 1967 when Bob Diemert's Mk XIII was imported from Canada for use in the film *The Battle of Britain*. Here LF363 peels away with PZ865 about to follow it during filming of *Angels One Five*; the remaining three were loaned by the Portuguese Air Force. *(W G Ramsey/After the Battle)*

a ground instructional airframe – as its construction was considered antiquated for the new generation of fitters who would be servicing the jet fighters then entering service. The Hurricane's fabric-covered fuselage was not particularly suited to outdoor display in the British climate so very small numbers were used as gate guardians, the all-metal Spitfire being a far better candidate for such duties.

Bob Diemert rebuilt RCAF 5377 at Carmen, Manitoba, and flew it as CF-SMI. It was brought to the UK in 1967 to be used in *The Battle of Britain*. *(Bryan Gibbins)*

By mid-1947 there was a single airworthy Hurricane on RAF charge, LF363, which had been delivered to No. 63 Sqdn at Turnhouse in March 1944 before finding its way onto the Station Flight at Middle Wallop where it came to the notice of Air Vice-Marshal Sir Stanley Vincent, the only RAF pilot to have shot down enemy aircraft in both World Wars. Vincent had been station commander at Northolt in 1940 from where, at the height of the Battle of Britain, he had flown a Hurricane in combat, claiming five Dornier Do 17s and two Bf 109s – the latter two on 30 September 1940.

A replica of his Hurricane was installed as a gate guardian at RAF Northolt on 15 September 2010. Between 1945 and 1948 Vincent was senior air staff officer of RAF Fighter Command, moving on to air officer commanding No. 11 Group between 1948 and his retirement in 1950. It was during this time that he led the 1949 Battle of Britain Flypast over London in LF363. Thanks to a combination of patronage by high-ranking officers and sheer good luck, LF363 managed to survive in airworthy condition – although examination of its Form 700 records might throw doubt on its degree of 'airworthiness' at points in its post-war career! It joined the embryonic RAF Battle of Britain Memorial Flight at Biggin Hill in 1957 and – despite a catastrophic flying accident in 1991 – it was rebuilt and returned to service at Coningsby in 1998 where it is based as the longest-serving individual aircraft in the history of the RAF.

By the time that the film *Angels One Five* was made at RAF Kenley in 1951 only LF363 and Hawker's G-AMAU/PZ865 were available in the UK for flying use in the film so several Hurricanes were supplied by the Portuguese air force for use in the flying sequences. The Air Historical Branch loaned both L1592 and P2617 for ground sequences and at least one other was used for studio shots. As with most other operators, the Portuguese scrapped their last Hurricanes in 1954 and the Portuguese Air Force Museum now has to make do with a fibre-glass full scale model.

LF363 and PZ865 were the only known airworthy

During filming of *The Battle of Britain* the world's three airworthy Hurricanes flew together for the first time, PZ865, LF363 and CF-SMI/G-AWLW bringing up the rear. *(Peter Sargent via Peter R Arnold)*

examples of the type until they were joined by a Canadian-built Hurricane Mk XII which had been assembled by a Canadian pilot and engineer, Bob Diemert, from parts found on farms in Manitoba and restored to fly as CF-SMI in 1966. This aircraft was air-freighted to the UK in 1967, re-registered G-AWLW and joined the cast being assembled for the film *The Battle of Britain* in which all three Hurricanes flew together from Duxford, North Weald and elsewhere during the summer of 1968. The shortage of Hurricanes meant that several of the Hispano Buchons were painted in RAF camouflage to make up the numbers, the Hurricanes always appearing nearest the camera ship. With the film over G-AWLW was acquired by Samuelson Film Services Ltd of Elstree and then sold to Sir William Roberts in 1969 to become part of his Strathallan Aircraft Collection until repatriated by the Canadian Warplane Heritage of Hamilton, Ontario, as C-GCWH in 1984 – only to be destroyed in a hangar fire on 15 February 1993.

It was Bob's restoration of this Hurricane which started a movement amongst North American enthusiasts who started scouring Canadian farms, scrapyards and crash sites for Hurricanes and other warplanes which had been sold as surplus in the late 1940s and were ripe for recovery and restoration. Several were restored, either to fly or as static museum exhibits, from the multitude of major parts collected, most using a combination of the best components collected from several different airframes. It is known that one centre section – from RCAF 5409 – was cut in two and shared by two different restorers and Jack Arnold of Brantford, Ontario, collected over 20 Hurricane hulks, which he sold as 'restoration packages'. Unfortunately Jack Arnold and others did not understand the way in which the Canadian constructors' numbers matched with the aircraft serials and this led to many mis-identifications which the present author has attempted to unravel.

One must appreciate that in the 1970s and 1980s the collectors and restorers had no real interest in tracing the identity of the components that they were exchanging. The Hurricane hulks were seen as no more than sources of parts, their identities were irrelevant and frequently not recorded or only vaguely remembered. Despite the help of specialist historians Norman Malayney, Jerry Vernon and Dr Jon Leake the job of tracing the full backgrounds of some of the Canadian examples has been virtually impossible.

The former Soviet Union has proved a very fertile location for the recovery of crashed Hurricanes, like these two in St Petersburg in 1991. *(Peter R Arnold Collection)*

More recently, the collapse of the former Soviet Union has unleashed another batch of recovered relics onto the Hurricane world. Once again, the habit of the Russian wreck collectors of making up a 'package' from the best parts of several wrecks has not helped when attempting to discover the identities and histories of these aircraft.

Although Bob Diemert, Paul Mercer, Peter Rushen, Neil Rose, Harry Whereatt, Geoff Rodwell and others were successful in restoring Hurricanes to fly, it was the establishment of a specialist Hurricane restoration company – Hawker Restorations Ltd – by Tony Ditheridge and Sir Tim Wallis, first at Earls Colne in Essex and latterly at Milden in Suffolk, which resulted in a veritable squadron of Hurricanes taking to the air once again. To date Tony's company has restored seven airworthy Hurricanes together with a small number of static museum examples. They have also provided kits of components to other restoration companies such as Phoenix Aero Services at Thruxton, Hants, who completed the rebuild of a Hurricane to airworthy condition. Airframe Assembles Ltd of Sandown on the Isle of Wight, well-known for their Spitfire restorations, have manufactured several sets of brand-new wings but the Bournemouth facility of Bob Cunningham is the specialist Hurricane wing workshop whilst Eye Tech Engineering Ltd and Retro Track and Air Ltd are mainly responsible for the Merlin engines.

At the other end of the scale are groups of enthusiasts and individuals who have valiantly collected parts from several

Hawker Restorations Ltd is the foremost company responsible for the restoration of Hurricanes to flying condition; here are P3717 (left) and P2902 (right) in their workshop in June 2013. *(Darren Harbar Photography)*

Hurricanes – often from crash-sites or using cast-offs from other projects – in order to fashion complex composite static Hurricanes which will eventually become lovingly restored museum exhibits to preserve the memory of Sir Sydney Camm's masterpiece for generations to come. Other groups, such as the Tangmere Aviation Museum, have recovered and conserved substantial crash-site remains which are included in this book, although the many displays of smaller components recovered from crash sites, mainly in the 1970s, have not been included.

The book is divided into two main sections, followed by four appendices. The first section deals with the British-built Hurricanes, the second with the Canadians whilst the appendices cover unidentified but extant aircraft, projects & relics, rumours and the ones that got away. Although it is tempting to list aircraft by mark number and then by

serial, the way in which the contracts were fulfilled meant that some aircraft were re-manufactured and changed their mark number while the serials tend to jump back and forth between the marks so the aircraft are simply listed in serial number order no matter what mark they were.

When the present author and the late Graham Trant originally considered writing a book on the surviving Hurricanes in the mid-1980s we decided that we would have to cover all surviving Hawker types as there were so few Hurricanes known to exist. How times have changed!

BRITISH-BUILT HURRICANES

The prototype Hurricane, K5083, was built in the Experimental Shop at Canbury Park Road, Kingston upon Thames, and taken by road to Brooklands where it was assembled and test flown for the first time on 6 November 1935. Space for production was then made available at Kingston by sub-contracting other work to Westland Aircraft Ltd at Yeovil (Hectors) and General Aircraft Ltd at Hanworth (Fury II, Harts and Hinds). A total of 24,000 sq ft of space was thus made available at Kingston with a further 14,000 at Brooklands to be used for final assembly and testing. Hawkers were also in the process of establishing another production facility – with its own aerodrome – at Langley, west London. The plan was to switch all Hurricane production to Langley by 1939 but in the event production continued at Kingston and Brooklands for some time and major sub-contracts were given to the Gloster Aircraft Company Ltd at Brockworth whilst the Austin Motor Company built a batch – almost exclusively for delivery to Russia – at its factory at Longbridge, Birmingham.

The surviving British-built Hurricanes include examples of the Mks I, II and IV and they are listed by serial number. Any entry with an asterisk denotes that the serial cannot be proven.

Mark I	Initially powered by the Merlin II driving a fixed-pitch, two-bladed, Watts wooden propeller and armed with eight .303 inch Browning machine guns. Metal stressed-skin wings appeared on production aircraft in March 1939 and the Watts propeller was replaced by a de Havilland, two-position, all-metal, three-bladed propeller. The Merlin III introduced a universal propeller shaft which allowed the fitting of either the all-metal de Havilland or the composite bladed Rotol three-bladed variable pitch propeller.
Mark IIA Series 1	Essentially the same as a Mk I airframe, the Mk IIA Series I featured the Merlin XX engine with a two-speed supercharger. The increased length of the engine required a modified engine bearer and cowlings together with a deeper air scoop to accommodate the enlarged radiator and oil cooler. At least 100 Mk Is were converted to this configuration, many by Rolls-Royce at Hucknall.
Mark IIA Series 2	In order to increase the hitting power of the Hurricane it was decided to install two extra Brownings per wing, bringing the count up from eight to 12. The additional guns were fitted outboard of the undercarriage and protruded from the leading edge as the chord is reduced at that point.
Mark IIB	As the 12-gun wing became standard the designation was changed to Hurricane Mk IIB. Many of these were fitted with bomb racks and became known as 'Hurribombers'. When fitted with these racks the third gun out from the wing root was deleted as the bolt heads for the racks occupied the space normally used by the gun, thus 'Hurribombers' featured a 10-gun wing and two 250 lb GP bombs.

Mark IIC	Following tests with both Oerlikon and Hispano Mk I 20mm cannon, the cannon-armed Hurricane IIC entered service in March / April 1941. Further developments led to the rocket or 40mm cannon-armed Mk IID which had striking success in the Western Desert but none of these survive.
Mark IV	The last development of the Hurricane, the Mk IV, featured the so-called 'Universal' wing which was first proposed in 1941. Full service clearance was issued on 1 June 1943 and permitted the carriage of 250 lb or 500 lb bombs; two, four or eight three-inch RPs; one or two 40mm Vickers 'S' anti-tank guns, one or two 44 gallon drop tanks or asymmetric combinations of these. The only store not permitted to be loaded asymmetrically was the 88 gallon ferry tank. Additional armour was fitted to protect the engine and the radiator and a single .303 inch Browning was installed in each wing to be loaded with tracer ammunition for sighting purposes.

L1592
Hawker Hurricane Mk I

The Science Museum, South Kensington

L1592 is the oldest surviving Hurricane, having been built by Hawkers at Brooklands against Contract No. 527112/36 which had been placed in May 1936. The contract called for 600 aircraft, which were to carry serials in the range L1547–L2146. This aircraft was the 45th to be built and was powered by a 1,030 hp Rolls-Royce Merlin II driving a Watts two-bladed wooden propeller. L1592 was fitted with fabric-covered metal wings (common to the first 430 Hurricanes in the batch) and is unique as the only Hurricane to have survived with the fabric-covered wings intact – although there is no evidence to suggest that they are those fitted during construction.

Taken on RAF charge on 19 May 1938, L1592 was delivered to No. 56 Sqdn at North Weald, Essex, on 3 June 1938 where the squadron was converting from Gloster Gauntlets. It remained on strength until 27 July 1939 when it was transferred to No. 17 Sqdn, now also based at North Weald instead of its pre-war home at Kenley. Its RAF Movement Record (Form 78) indicates that it was issued to No. 87 Sqdn, based at Merville, France, as part of the Air Component of the British Expeditionary Force (BEF) on 10 October 1939, followed by a posting to No. 43 Sqdn at Tangmere just four days later on 14 October. Although possible, this is thought to have been a clerical error and the aircraft probably moved directly to Tangmere.

Its time with 'The Fighting Cocks' was relatively short as just over a month later, on 16 November 1939, L1592 found its way back to No. 17 Sqdn, now based at Debden in Essex, a few miles north of its old base at North Weald. Here it remained until 16 February 1940 when it returned to No. 43 Sqdn, which had forsaken its traditional south coast base of Tangmere and moved north to Acklington, Northumbria, the previous November from where it was carrying out defence duties over Newcastle and the surrounding area. The squadron moved further north, to Wick, Scotland, on 26 February and it was from this base that L1592, by then coded

L1592 as displayed in the Science Museum, London, January 2015. *(Gordon Riley)*

Michael Dennison and John Gregson walk past L1592 during filming *Angels One Five* at Kenley in July 1951. *(Author's Collection)*

FT-C and being flown by F/O J D Edmonds of B Flight, shared in the destruction of a Heinkel He 111 which was shot down during a defensive patrol in the late afternoon of 10 April 1940. The other pilots were Flt/Lt Peter Townsend (L1742), F/O Folkes (N2585) and P/O Upton (L1725). By this time its Watts two-bladed propeller had been replaced with a de Havilland three-bladed unit which imparted a significant increase in performance.

As Operation Dynamo swung into action No. 43 Sqdn was recalled to Tangmere to assist in covering the evacuation beaches at Dunkirk, arriving at its pre-war home on 31 May 1940. The very next day P/O Anthony Woods-Scawen damaged two Bf 109s over Dunkirk before L1592 was hit in the cooling system and Woods-Scawen was forced to make a wheels-up landing back at Tangmere due to his rapidly overheating engine. The Hurricane was immediately allocated to No. 49 MU of No. 43 Salvage and Repair Group with the intention that it would be transferred to the de Havilland Aircraft Company for repairs. De Havilland was part of the 'Hurricane Repair Organisation' and repaired 138 Hurricanes at Hatfield during 1940. The aircraft was collected from Tangmere on 4 June and transferred to No. 10 MU at Hullavington on 27 June where it appears to have remained – possibly requiring further work – until 23 July when it was allocated to No. 615 'County of Surrey' Sqdn at Kenley, south of London.

No. 615 was part of 11 Group, which bore the brunt of the Luftwaffe attacks on the airfields around London, and its base at Kenley came under attack at 1322 hours on Sunday 18 August when between 30 and 50 Luftwaffe bombers attacked at medium level, whilst a further group of Dornier Do 17s, escorted by Bf 109s, came in at low level from the east. The damage was extensive with three hangars destroyed together with equipment stores, four Hurricanes and a Blenheim. Four further aircraft were damaged and there were 19 casualties – nine of them fatal. Nos 64 and 615 Sqdns were scrambled to counter the attack whilst No. 111 took off from nearby Croydon – resulting in the latter being undefended when a group of Do 17s attacked and managed to drop 19 bombs on the aerodrome. As the dust settled L1592 / KW-Z of No. 615 Sqdn approached Croydon at 1400 hours in a critical condition, having been badly damaged in combat with several Bf 109s over Sevenoaks. P/O D J Looker brought his burning aircraft in to land – only to find himself the target of the airfield ground defences, who proceeded to fire tracer bullets at him from all directions. Looker escaped from his Hurricane to be admitted to Croydon Hospital, suffering from severe shock and concussion, whilst an airfield official lodged a complaint against him for "… unannounced use of the landing facilities".

L1592 at an early post-war Battle of Britain Week display on Horse Guards Parade, London. *(Author's Collection)*

Despite the damage L1592 was deemed repairable and was collected by No. 13 MU, Henlow, where it was rebuilt and upgraded with a Rolls-Royce Merlin III of 1,310 hp which featured a universal propeller shaft, enabling it to be fitted with either de Havilland or Rotol propellers. As the aircraft retains its fabric-covered wings to this day it is something of a mystery as to why they were not replaced with metal-skinned wings during this major repair; the job normally

On Horse Guards Parade in 1953 L1592 had been repainted with Bob Stanford Tuck's 'DT-A' code. (© A Flying History Ltd.)

required only three hours to complete but it was noted that at Henlow the record for changing both mainplanes, fitting eight guns and loading them with ammunition was 1 hour and 55 minutes!

No. 13 MU generally took between 14 and 21 days to repair a badly damaged Hurricane but L1592 was not ready for transfer to No. 10 MU at Hullavington until 2 October 1940, following which it was dispatched to Christchurch, Hampshire, on 10 October to join the Station Defence Flight where it was coded ZQ-U. Christchurch had been a typical small civil aerodrome and flying school during the 1930s. When the war started it was taken over by the RAF and a shadow factory building the Airspeed Oxford was established. By the summer of 1940 the Special Duty Flight arrived at Christchurch from St Athan to support both the Telecommunications Research Establishment at Worth Matravers and the Air Defence Experimental Establishment at Christchurch. It was reinforced, by absorbing H Flight of No. 1 Anti-Aircraft Co-operation Unit and later a calibration flight, at which point it was renamed the Telecommunications Flying Unit. The flight was involved in many aspects of radar development including airborne interception radar for night fighters and air-to-surface radar for Coastal Command.

Christchurch airfield, like many others, had a small number of fighter aircraft provided as a local or Station Defence Flight. These were not part of the main fighter defences but would be scrambled to protect the airfield. The pilots would be present at Christchurch on other duties but

any who were qualified fighter pilots could be on standby to fly the Station Defence Flight Hurricanes. The pilots included S/Ldr P E Meagher and F/Lt D L Rayment; on several occasions these two pilots engaged enemy fighters and bombers, damaging several and each pilot shot down at least one bomber. F/Lt Rayment was flight commander of the Special Duty Flight and he was awarded the Air Force Cross on 1 July 1941. The venerable Hurricane suffered an undercarriage collapse at Christchurch on 28 April 1941 but was repaired on site and continued to serve there until August 1941 when, on the 22nd of the month, it was transferred to the re-named Telecommunications Flying Unit prior to leaving for No. 15 MU at Wroughton on 25 August.

At an unknown date in 1941, L1592 found itself at No. 9 Air Observers School, Penrhos, near Pwllheli, Gwynedd, Wales, where it remained until 21 April 1942 when it was issued to No. 5 (Pilots) Advanced Flying Unit at Ternhill, Shropshire, which had been established on 13 April by re-naming No. 5 Flying Training School and which was equipped with Hurricanes and Miles Masters. The life of an advanced trainer was a tough one and on 24 July 1942, L1592 came to grief with a Cat AC flying accident. It was allotted for Repair on Site (ROS) by a Civilian Repair Organisation on 2 August and was back on flying duties by 23 September, remaining at Ternhill for a few more weeks before transfer to No. 48 MU at Hawarden, near Chester, on 18 October. Here it was placed in store until 19 February 1943 when it was allocated to No. 9 (Pilots) Advanced Flying Unit based

L1592 seen at Dunsfold in May 1961 following restoration by Hawkers for the Science Museum. (BAE SYSTEMS)

at Errol, between Perth and Dundee, Scotland. Similarly equipped with Masters and Hurricanes, L1592 soldiered on until it was transferred to No. 22 MU at Silloth, Cumbria, on 8 October 1943.

In the spring of 1944 plans were put in place to preserve a selection of historically important aircraft for future generations. L1592 was one of those selected and on 6 August 1944 it was transferred to No. 52 MU at Pengham Moors, Cardiff for preparation for long-term storage – i.e. it was dismantled and crated. The Bellman hangar used for storage of the museum aircraft was requisitioned as a wood store in December 1944 and L1592 is next noted at No. 47 MU, Sealand, during 1945. It is however likely that it had been transferred to No. 76 MU at Wroughton – together with P2617 and other aircraft – in December 1944 prior to its arrival at Sealand.

Between 1945 and 1954, L1592 was officially on charge to the Air Historical Branch and it is thought to have been transferred to their storage centre at Stanmore Park, north London, in May 1947. From here it was periodically retrieved and exhibited on Horse Guards Parade, London, for Battle of Britain displays, being displayed in September 1950 in grey/green camouflage with the code letter 'I' behind the fuselage roundels – evidence of its last unit, No. 9 (P)AFU. In July 1951 it was taken to RAF Kenley for static use in the film *Angels One Five* about a Hurricane squadron during the Battle of Britain. The film company modified the paint-scheme by overpainting the rear fuselage sky band whilst the original code was replaced with those of No. 56 Sqdn; L1592 is known to have been coded 'US-D' and may also have carried 'US-N'. By the 1953 Battle of Britain Day display on Horse Guards Parade it had been repainted to represent Bob Stanford Tuck's Hurricane of No. 257 Sqdn with the code letters 'DT-A' (see previous page) and it continued to carry these markings after its allocation to the Science Museum, London, in November 1954, being transferred from Stanmore Park to the museum's store at Sydenham, south London, on 16 December 1954. Although some sources have suggested that it was used in the 1956 film *Reach for the Sky* this is thought to be unlikely and as far as can be proven it remained stored until 22 August 1960 when it was taken by road to Hawker's airfield at Dunsfold, Surrey, for restoration and repainting prior to being moved into the newly-constructed Aviation Gallery on the top floor of the Science Museum in Exhibition Road, South Kensington, in May 1961. The markings chosen were based on those which it would have carried when operating with No. 615 Sqdn from Kenley during the Battle of Britain, markings which it retains to this day.

L1639
Hawker Hurricane Mk I
Cambridge Fighter and Bomber Society, Little Gransden

L1639 was the 93rd Hurricane constructed by Hawkers at Brooklands against Contract No. 527112/36 which had been placed in May 1936. The contract called for 600 aircraft, which were to carry serials in the range L1547-L2146. Powered by a 1,030 hp Rolls-Royce Merlin II driving a Watts two-bladed wooden propeller, L1639 was fitted with fabric-covered metal wings (common to the first 430 Hurricanes in the batch) and was taken on RAF charge on 27 July 1938, being issued to No. 85 Sqdn at RAF Debden, Essex, on 30 August.

No. 85 had reformed at Debden on 1 June 1938 from A Flight of No. 87 Sqdn and was initially equipped with the Gloster Gladiator but these were soon replaced by Hurricanes. It remained based at Debden until it moved to France as part of the Air Component of the BEF on 9 September 1939. Once in France the squadron moved from base to base, relocating as the campaign progressed; its bases were: 9-29 September 1939, Rouen/Boos; 29 September-5 November 1939, Merville; 5 November 1939-10 April 1940, Lille/Seclin; 10-26 April 1940, Mons-en-Chaussée; 26 April-22 May 1940, Lille/Seclin.

L1639 remained on charge with No. 85 Sqdn until March 1940 when its records indicate that it was flown back to the UK for attention by Hawkers before being passed on to No. 20 MU at Aston Down, on 13 March where it was prepared for operational use once again and issued to No. 504 'County of Nottingham' Sqdn on 5 April. It may have been during either of these occasions that the two-bladed Watts propeller was replaced with a three-bladed Rotol variable-pitch unit. At that time No. 504 was based at RAF Debden, Essex, with

The reconstructed fuselage of L1639 at Little Gransden in August 2014. *(Gordon Riley)*

temporary detachments at Martlesham Heath on the Suffolk coast, but with the intensity of the Battle of France increasing No. 504 became one of the Hurricane units sent to France during May 1940. Initially based at Vitry-en-Artois it moved on to Lille/Marcq and Norrent-Fontes before retreating to Manston, Kent, and then back to its base at Debden.

With all of the confusion of the time it is hardly surprising to find that there are conflicting accounts of what happened to cause L1639 to crash but evidence gathered by the restoration team, including first-hand accounts by the late Joe Rogers – whose son Paul is spearheading the restoration project – indicates that on 14 May 1940 it was being flown by S/Ldr James Boyd Parnall, who was on temporary attachment to No. 504 Sqdn based at Lille/Marcq, France, having previously served with No. 85 Sqdn. Whilst on patrol in the Louvain area with three other Hurricanes, he encountered and attacked a group of Heinkel He 111 bombers. Bounced by Bf 109s from III./JG26, three of the Hurricanes were shot down and Parnall's aircraft crashed and he was killed. (Note: Parnall is buried in Belgium and is also reported to have been flying Hurricane L1941.)

Although the main wreckage was collected shortly after the crash, significant remains lay undisturbed and were forgotten until the surviving surface remnants were recovered following an account by the late Joe Rogers. Various components were retrieved from the crash site including the rudder pedals, controls and many identity plates, which will see original parts from L1639 make up

around 20 percent of the rebuilt airframe. Sadly Joe passed away in 1996.

In order to carry out the restoration work on L1639 the Cambridge Fighter and Bomber Society have located numerous other Hurricane airframes, wings and components, which have come from a wide variety of sources. The reconstructed airframe incorporates many original components which were sourced from two other Hurricanes, BD731 and BD736, shot down over northern Russia, together with detail parts from Canada and cast-offs from airworthy aircraft including LF363. A major part of the cockpit section is from Z4035 and components recovered from Z3055 (under restoration in Malta, q.v.) have also found their way into the reconstructed aircraft. The Rolls-Royce Merlin was rebuilt to running condition by using parts from seven different donor engines. Each had suffered different degrees of damage, but the team was able to restore one complete engine which was successfully run for the first time on 9 August 2009.

The group has the oldest and most complete set of Hawker-built, fabric-covered Hurricane wings in existence, outside of the Science Museum's L1592. These were found in Flowers' scrap yard, Chippenham, Wilts, under a pile of other debris and were rescued by Tim Moore of Skysport Engineering Ltd. Due to their historic significance they will be preserved and a new set is being built for L1639 utilising the originals as templates, although some original wing parts from other wrecks are being incorporated.

This Hurricane is being restored to original specifications, using engineering drawings from the period, right down to the Watts two-bladed, fixed-pitch wooden propeller. Paul Rogers, the chairman of the Cambridge Fighter and Bomber Society, estimates that it will be another nine years or so before the aircraft is complete and able to taxy under its own power once again. It will be painted in its original No. 85 Sqdn markings; during the Battle of France L1639 carried the squadron markings VY-Q and the rebuilt aircraft will be completed to look the same as it did during this period. The eventual plan is to have the aircraft put on display at an established museum in the United Kingdom or abroad whilst the society carries on with its next project – a Hawker Fury Mk I biplane fighter, K1928.

The late Joe Rogers running up L1639 with its new Rotol propeller. *(Paul Rogers/CFBS)*

L1866/RCAF 323
Hawker Hurricane Mk I / Two-Seater Mk II

Hawker Restorations Ltd, Milden, Suffolk, UK

L1866 was constructed by Hawkers against Contract No. 527112/36 which had been placed in May 1936. The contract called for 600 aircraft, which were to carry serials in the range L1547-L2146. Powered by a 1,030 hp Rolls-Royce Merlin II driving a Watts two-bladed wooden propeller, L1866 was fitted with fabric-covered metal wings (common to the first 430 Hurricanes in the batch) but was not delivered to the RAF.

The RCAF had made initial enquiries regarding the supply of Hurricanes during 1937 but these had been turned down on the grounds that deliveries to the RAF were not to be disrupted. Further pressure was mounted through the Dominion Chiefs of the Air Staff Committee, at the time of the Munich Crisis in 1938, which resulted in a batch of 20 Hurricanes being taken from the Kingston production lines and delivered to the RCAF. At the same time it was agreed to set up a production line under licence to the Canadian Car and Foundry Company of Montreal.

Although the aircraft had already been allocated RAF serials they were manufactured using their RCAF serials, RCAF 310-330, and the first five left the UK for Canada in October 1938. These were L1759-L1763 which were built as RCAF 310-314. The next batch was shipped during February and March 1939, L1866 leaving the factory as RCAF 323 in March and was the last fabric-winged Hurricane produced by Hawkers, L1867/RCAF 324 being the first production Hurricane to feature the all-metal stressed-skin wing. All of the Canadian aircraft were fitted with Watts two-bladed, fixed-pitch, wooden propellers.

RCAF 323 was taken on charge at RCAF Station Dartmouth, NS, on 17 May 1939 where it was issued to No. 1 (F) Sqdn which had been formed as a fighter unit at Trenton, Ontario on 21 September 1937 equipped with Armstong-Whitworth Siskin biplanes. The nucleus of the members had come from the Fighter Flight of No. 3 (Bomber) Squadron

and the squadron moved to Calgary, Alberta, in August 1938 before it re-equipped with its first Hurricanes in February 1939. Following the outbreak of war the squadron was mobilised at St Hubert, Quebec, on 10 September 1939, and on 5 November it moved to Dartmouth, Nova Scotia. Its first operational mission was carried out on 20 November when a Hurricane (believed to be 324) took off from Dartmouth on a naval co-operation sortie (diving practice on naval vessels) in Bedford Basin near Halifax, NS. Its final operational mission before embarking for the UK was on 24 April 1940 when two Hurricanes took off from Dartmouth on a 50-mile radius local reconnaissance flight. On 28 May 1940 it absorbed No. 115 (Fighter) Squadron of the Auxiliary Air Force, which had been based at Montreal, before leaving for the UK on 8 June 1940 – bringing its Hurricanes with it – to arrive at Middle Wallop on 21 June.

RCAF 323 was not amongst the aircraft which left Montreal in June 1940 as it had suffered a Category B accident at 1432 hours on 14 March 1940 whilst being flown by F/O

Work under way on L1866 at Milden in March 2015 showing the rear seat in position in the cockpit area of the airframe. It is being recomfigured as a two-seat Mk II. (*Gordon Riley*)

When delivered to Canada L1866 / RCAF 323 would have looked like this, RCAF 315. *(Author's Collection)*

John Kerwin of Belleville, Ontario. He was not injured in the accident but 323 was shipped to CCF at Fort William under Requisition Number CD.WII64 and repaired at a cost of $6,452.18. It was transferred to the RCAF's Eastern Air Command on 1 April 1940 before transfer to CCF on 5 May and, with the repairs completed, it was reallocated to No. 1 (F) Sqdn on 27 June 1940.

By the time it caught up with its unit the rest of the aircraft had either been exchanged for more modern Hurricanes or had been brought up to UK standards with VP propellers and current camouflage and markings, the work being carried out at Croydon to which the squadron was transferred on 4 July. The squadron was allocated the unit code 'YO' and 323 – as far as can be proven – is the only example which continued to serve under its Canadian serial and was given the code 'YO-D'. The Canadians were attached to No. 111 Sqdn at Northolt for training in combat techniques and whilst there the CO, S/Ldr 'Ernie' McNab, DFC, destroyed a Dornier Do 215 over Westgate-on-Sea, Kent, on 15 August.

The squadron moved to Northolt on 17 August and became fully operational; on its second patrol on 26 August it came across a force of between 25-30 Dorniers and was credited with three destroyed and three damaged in the ensuing combat. On 5 October 1940 RCAF 323 was being flown by F/Lt Paul Pitcher of Montreal, Quebec, and destroyed a Bf 109 and damaged a Bf 110. Shortly

afterwards, on 11 October the squadron was moved to Prestwick for a 'rest' period performing coastal patrols over the Clyde approaches. 323 found itself being transferred to No. 615 (County of Surrey) Sqdn, RAuxAF, which was moving south from Prestwick to take up residence at Northolt so it is very probable that the aircraft remained in situ whilst the personnel moved from Northolt to Prestwick and vice versa.

During a squadron patrol on 6 November 1940 RCAF 323, flown by Sgt Jack Hammerton, was last seen at 25,000 feet, leaving the formation, apparently in pursuit of enemy aircraft. The 25-year-old Hammerton was killed when the aircraft crashed in bad visibility near the railway line at Noahs Ark, Kemsing, near Sevenoaks, Kent. The crash site was excavated during the 1980s and some of the remains of the aircraft, including the brass maker's plate showing both the c/n 41H101908 and the RCAF serial '323' were displayed in the Shoreham Aircraft Museum, Kent, for many years. These were acquired by Craig Charleston and are to become the identity associated with the two-seat Mk II currently under construction by Hawker Restorations.

L1988
Hawker Hurricane Mk I

Norwegian Aviation Museum, Bodø, Norway

L1988 was another of the first batch of Hurricanes constructed by Hawkers at Brooklands against Contract No. 527112/36, which had been placed in May 1936. The contract called for 600 aircraft, which were to carry serials in the range L1547-L2146. Powered by a 1,030 hp Rolls-Royce Merlin III (No. 4921-119636), L1988 was taken on RAF charge on 25 May 1939 when it was allocated to No. 17 Sqdn, which had moved from Kenley to North Weald and was in the process of re-equipping from the Gloster Gauntlet II to the Hurricane Mk I. For some reason it was re-allocated

to 11 Group and transferred to No. 56 Sqdn at North Weald on 14 June. This may have been a mere paper exercise as No. 17 took over a number of 56 Sqdn's older Hurricanes during this time and the factory-fresh L1988 may have been issued to No. 56 as a replacement.

It remained on strength with No. 56, moving between its two bases at North Weald and Martlesham Heath, until it was transferred to No. 229 Sqdn on 11 March 1940. This squadron had reformed at Digby in Lincolnshire on 6 October 1939 as a Blenheim-equipped fighter squadron

The Merlin, forward fuselage and other parts from L1988 following recovery from the crash site in June 2000. *(Arne Hansen)*

The radiator and oil cooler are clearly visible in this photo of the centre section in situ at the crash site. (*Arne Hansen*)

and had begun shipping protection patrols on 21 December 1939. During this period the squadron was also used for radar trials and underwent night training but in March 1940 the unit converted to Hurricanes and the night-flying training came to naught. In May 1940 the squadron sent one flight to reinforce the BEF Hurricane squadrons which were attempting to stem the German offensive; it remained in France for eight days before being forced to retreat to southern England.

L1988 was transferred to No. 46 Sqdn, also based at Digby, on 1 May 1940 but a few days later, on 9 May 1940, the squadron's 18 Hurricanes were craned on board HMS *Glorious* and, after a few false starts, the carrier left the Clyde for Norway on 14 May to provide support to ground forces fighting in the Narvik area. *Glorious* left Scotland on 14 May but had to anchor off Vesterålen from 18 May until the airfield at Skånland was ready for use.

By 26 May everything was ready and at 2030 hours the Hurricanes departed *Glorious,* the ship making 30 kts into the wind to assist their take-off run. S/Ldr Kenneth 'Bing' Cross was the first to land but his Hurricane (P2632/PO-X) nosed over in soft ground and damaged the prop. The next five landed without problems but when F/Lt Stewart touched down, his Hurricane turned over and was destroyed. Three more landed successfully but Cross ordered the remaining eight aircraft to divert to Bardufoss and land there. (AVM Sir Kenneth Cross, KCB, CBE, DSO, DFC died on 18 June 2003.)

Three days later, on 29 May, F/O J W 'Jack' Lydall was flying L1988 as part of a group of nine Hurricanes on patrol near Narvik when they encountered a force of 26 Luftwaffe bombers approaching Vestfjorden. They attacked three He 111s from KG 100 and KG 26 north of Lødingen. Heinkel He 111 6N+BA, flown by Oblt Wolfgang Metzke, crash-landed at Ulvsvåg on Hamarøy, two crew were killed but Metzke and Gruppenkommandeur Hptm Artur von Casimir were taken prisoner. Another He 111 was attacked by Lydall and made a forced landing at Dverberg on Andøya but Lydall himself was shot down by a Bf 110 of Stab I/ZG 76, his Hurricane crashing in flames.

Jack Lydall was buried in the cemetery in Bodø but after the war his body was moved to the cemetery at Narvik. The substantial remains of his Hurricane lay where it had crashed until they were recovered from Bardufoss by a team from the Norwegian Aviation Museum and No. 339 Sqdn of the Royal Norwegian Air Force on 28 June 2000 and moved to Bodø where they remain stored.

N2394/HC-452
Hawker Hurricane Mk I

Aviation Museum of Central Finland, Luonetjarvi AB, Tikkakoski

Built at Brooklands as a Merlin III-powered Hurricane Mk I, N2394 was originally ordered against Contract No. 751458/38 which called for a total of 300 aircraft to be given serials in the range N2318-N2729. This particular aircraft was built in 1939 and formed part of the second serial block, N2380-N2409, and according to its Aircraft Movements Card (Form 78) it was delivered directly to No. 20 MU at Aston Down, arriving on 3 November. The late Frank Mason listed this as one of 10 aircraft which had been selected for sale to Poland in the summer of 1939 and which were in transit when Germany invaded on 1 September 1939. The crated aircraft were then returned to the UK and stored at No. 5 MU, Kemble, and No. 20 MU, Aston Down, from where they were selected when the Finnish government placed an order for 12 Hurricanes, to be fulfilled from RAF

stocks, in early 1940; they were then assembled and flown to St Athan. The final note on its RAF record card is that it was sold to the Gloster Aircraft Company Ltd on 2 February 1940.

A group of Finnish pilots, under the command of Lt Jussi Räty, took a commercial flight from Helsinki to Stockholm and continued their journey to London via Copenhagen and Amsterdam. From London they travelled to RAF St Athan where they arrived on 5 February 1940. At St Athan the group – known as 'Detachment Räty' – was divided into three flights A, B and C, under the overall command of S/Ldr Tom Pinkham. Training commenced on Link Trainers before progressing on to the North American Harvard and then finally the Hurricanes. Bad weather prevented any flying until 9 February, when the unit was visited by King

N2394/HC-452 following conservation work as displayed in the Aviation Museum of Central Finland in December 2014. *(Antti Lappalainen/Finnish Air Force Museum)*

George VI and Queen Elizabeth, but training progressed well and on 21 February the first three Hurricanes (HC-451, HC-452 and HC-455) were ready for collection from Gloster's Brockworth aerodrome where they had been repainted in Finnish Air Force markings and prepared for delivery. (Note: When delivered to St Athan the Hurricanes all carried serials in the HU- range but this was changed to HC- following their arrival in Finland.)

Räty decided to carry out the ferry flight to Finland as two batches of six aircraft; the first, including HC-452/N2394, left St Athan on 25 February accompanied by a short-nose Bristol Blenheim Mk I, flown by S/Ldr Roger Bushell of 'Great Escape' fame, as an escort. The first leg took them north over Wales, passing to the west of Liverpool and 2½ hours later they landed at Grangemouth northwest of Edinburgh. After refuelling the aircraft headed to Wick, where they stayed the night.

The following day the Hurricanes took off at 1115 hours and set course for Stavanger, Norway. They were accompanied by two Lockheed Hudsons and a Sunderland flying boat, the job of the Sunderland being to pick up the pilots from the sea if any had to ditch. During the middle part of the crossing the weather deteriorated and they had to fly at less than 100 ft above the waves for 15-20 minutes, but despite problems keeping in contact with the lead Hudson the group maintained formation. After 2½ hours they crossed the coast near Stavanger but when the lead Hudson didn't give the disengagement signal (wing rock) the Hurricanes broke and landed at Sola airfield. Bad weather meant that they did not reach Västerås Hässlö airfield until 29 February and it was decided to stay there for a week before continuing the flight.

HC-452/N2394 was one of the first group of Hurricanes to depart Västerås Hässlö airfield on the morning of 7 March; the pilot was Ensign Nissinen – who had flown it from St Athan. Bad weather forced them to return, having only made it as far as Stockholm, but a second attempt that afternoon saw them land at the Morane-Saulnier MS 406 fighter base on a frozen lake at Säkylä.

'Detachment Räty' remained at Säkylä with No. 28 Sqdn supporting the air defence of Turku (Åbo) with the Morane fighters. The Winter War was about to end and no interception tasks were given to the aircraft. At times the Hurricanes were flown to Hollola base, where a new squadron was formed with Brewster Buffaloes and Fiat G 50s. The plan was to use the new fighters in combat over the Bay of Viipuri, but no such missions were flown and on 10 March the Hurricanes returned to Säkylä to defend Turku but the Winter War ended on 13 March 1940.

N2394/HC-452 in September 1941. *(Kari Stenman)*

The Hurricanes were maintained on standing alert until 23 March, when they returned to peacetime readiness and on 27 March the detachment was ordered to move to Hollola to be attached to LeLv 24 (No. 24 Sqdn) and they flew there on the 30th. Because of the poor runway at Hollola the Hurricanes moved to Malmi airport at Helsinki on 4 April. No. 24 was based there with their Brewster Buffaloes and some of the Hurricanes were kept on alert at Helsinki. The Hurricanes and the MS 406s moved to Turku on 15 May and performed alert duties from Artukainen airfield.

Following Lt Räty's transfer to Tampere to head the Flight Test Centre with the rank of captain, the 'Detachment Räty' was disbanded and attached to LeLv 28 (No. 28 Sqdn) as a flight. When the Continuation War started in 1941 new pilots were trained for the remaining eight Hurricanes and the previous Hurricane pilots were retrained to fly the MS 406s. The temporary peace with the Soviet Union, between 1940–41, proved hard for the few remaining Hurricanes and by the time that the Continuation War started they were decidedly weary and proved to be less agile than the Buffaloes. The Hurricane flight was attached to LeLv 32 (later LeLv 10) during the Continuation War as 'Detachment Kalaja' but only achieved 5½ 'kills' during the war.

HC-452 was delivered to LeLv 28 on 27 May 1940

N2394 / HC-452 in July 1943, fitted with the rudder from HC-455 which it still carries today. *(Kari Stenman)*

and served until 29 August 1940 when it was transferred to LeLv 30. It remained with this unit until 18 June 1941 when it was transferred to 1/LeLv 30 and assigned to 2Lt Esko Ruotsila as its regular pilot; Ruotsila was to become the most successful Hurricane pilot of the Continuation War. On 1 July 1941 Ruotsila delivered it to Os. Kalaja / LeLv 32 and on 19 August 1941 to 1/LeLv 10. On 19 September 1941 it was taxied into soft ground at Tiiksjärvi and slowly went up on its nose, the pilot, SSgt Lauri Suominen, escaped without injuries.

On 23 September 1941 newly-promoted 1Lt Ruotsila delivered HC-452 to LeLv 32 and it remained with the unit until 23 June 1942 when it was delivered to 2/LeLv 26. On 25 September 1942 the starboard main undercarriage leg collapsed on landing at Immola damaging the propeller and starboard wing tip but the pilot, SSgt Lauri Jutila, escaped without injury. On 21 October 1942 it was delivered to the state aircraft factory for repairs. On 16 February 1943 fresh camouflage was applied with light blue-grey undersides. On 1 March 1943 HC-452 was delivered to 2/LeLv 26 and on 26 July 1943 it was placed in store at the air depot with 208 hours 15 mins logged, being finally struck off charge on 9 August 1944. During its service career HC-452 scored 2½ 'kills' all in the hands of Lt Esko Ruotsila of LeLv 32 and all Polikarpov I-153s of 7 IAP. The first two engagements took place on 3 and 15 July 1941 and the third was on 8 January 1942.

HC-452 was stored at Vesivehmaa Air Base where it was kept dismantled for nearly 40 years before being brought out and exhibited at the Aviation Museum of Central Finland, which also acts as the Finnish Air Force Museum, at Luonetjarvi AB, Tikkakoski near Jyväskylä. During 2004 it was on temporary display at Helsinki/Vantaa Airport for the 'Air Defence Victory 1944' exhibition. An extensive programme of conservation began in 2010 which saw the Hurricane repaired and renovated whilst keeping as much original structure and paintwork as possible in order to retain its late wartime paint.

P2617
Hawker Hurricane Mk I

RAF Museum, Hendon

P2617 was built by the Gloster Aircraft Company Ltd (a subsidiary of the Hawker Aircraft Ltd) as part of a batch of 500 Hurricanes ordered against Contract No. 962371/38. The aircraft bore serials between P2535-P3264, with P2617 forming part of the second block (P2614-2653). Powered by a 1,280 hp Merlin III (engine number 119697) and fitted with a Rotol three-bladed propeller it would have been flown from Brockworth to No. 20 MU at nearby Aston Down between 13-19 January, 1940.

It was then ferried to No. 6 MU at Brize Norton, which accepted it on 24 February, and it was probably here that it was prepared for service prior to being allocated to its first operational unit, No. 615 (County of Surrey) Sqdn, RAuxAF, which was based at Abbeville, France, where it was in the process of converting from Gladiators to Hurricanes. The filing clerk was busy on 14 April as P2617 was issued to both No. 615 Sqdn and to No. 1 R&SU (Repair and Salvage Unit) on the same day and the next day re-allocated to No. 607 (County of Durham) Sqdn, RAuxAF – which was also based at Abbeville. As both squadrons were part of the BEF and both re-equipping with Hurricanes it is quite possible that they either pooled aircraft between them or that No. 615 had a greater need than No. 607. We will never know.

It is believed that P2617 served with A Flight of No. 607 Sqdn carrying the codes AF-F and these are the markings to which it has been restored. The German *Blitzkrieg* on France commenced on 10 May and No. 607 Sqdn was immediately in action against scattered formations of unescorted enemy

P2617 displayed in the Battle of Britain Hall, RAF Museum, Hendon, in February 2015. *(Gordon Riley)*

On display on Horse Guards Parade, London, in the 1950s, '14' was its code when serving with No. 9 (P)AFU at Hullavington. *(Gary Brown Collection)*

bombers over the Belgian frontier. On 19 May some 20 German divisions exploited a gap that effectively split the Allied armies in two and No. 607 Sqdn moved to Norrent-Fontes (between Lille and Le Touquet) and operated throughout the day from there.

The following day, as the Germans continued to advance towards Amiens and Arras, the squadron was ordered to abandon all equipment and move the short distance to Boulogne. P2617 flew at least two sorties on 20 May: P/O Humphreys flying it on a patrol between 0600–0700 hours while P/O Bromley carried out a further patrol between 1040–1140 hours. It was flown home to Croydon later that day as the squadron was ordered to evacuate and return to the UK to regroup, having claimed 72 enemy aircraft during those 11 hectic days.

Whilst based at Croydon P2617 suffered Cat B damage (beyond repair on site) but luckily No. 4 MU was available, in the form of Rollason's of Croydon, who rapidly fixed the damage and the aircraft was test-flown by F/O Irving for 15 mins the following day. Further test flights were performed by S/Ldr B A Hitchings on 9 & 10 June. Between June and September the squadron was rested at its home base at Usworth near Sunderland and on 15 August it repelled a mixed force of 40/60 He 111s and Do 17s claiming eight destroyed, six probables and five damaged.

With the Battle of Britain now raging across southern England the squadron was re-assigned to 11 Group and flew south to Tangmere on the Sussex coast, flying its first sorties on 8 September. It is known from logbooks that P2617 was flown operationally by F/Lt James M Bazin on 11 September.

As hostilities became quieter No. 607 returned north, this time to Turnhouse near Edinburgh, and on 26 October P2617 was re-allocated to No. 1 (Canadian) Squadron – later to become No. 401 Sqdn RCAF – which was based at nearby Prestwick and was flying patrols over the Clyde approaches. It was whilst serving with this squadron, now based at Castletown on the Pentland Firth, that at 1545 hours on 20 November failing oil pressure forced F/O Watson to make a wheels-up forced landing in a field near Saltcoats, Stevenston, Ayrshire.

P2617 was allocated for repairs by the Gloster Aircraft Company Ltd the following day and it was presumably returned to Brockworth where it remained until 29 March 1941 when it was delivered to No. 15 MU at Wroughton for storage. After a few weeks it was flown to No. 5 MU at nearby Kemble on 4 May for preparation for service and delivered to No. 9 Service Flying Training School at Hullavington on 31 July.

Kenneth More sliding off the wing of P2617 at Kenley during filming *Reach for the Sky* in 1955. *(W G Ramsey/ After The Battle)*

Within a week it had suffered its first accident, the undercarriage collapsing on landing at the relief landing ground at Babdown, Wilts, on 5 August. The incident was put down to structural failure, probably brought on

By June 1968 P2617 had been refurbished and was on display at Abingdon for the 50th Anniversary of the formation of the RAF. (*Chris England*)

by previous heavy landings and no blame was associated with the pilot. Its next major incident – caused by hitting some wooden stakes after a precautionary landing in a field at 1945 hours on 24 September – was however blamed on the pilot. On this occasion he was considered to have been at fault by showing poor judgement when proceeding with a flight under adverse weather conditions, resulting in the landing south of Ruddington between Nottingham and Loughborough.

The aircraft was dispatched to de Havilland on 1 October for repairs to be carried out – whether this was at Hatfield or Whitney is not known but the company was part of the Hurricane Repair Organisation and repaired 12 at Hatfield and 17 at Whitney during 1941. It was noted as awaiting collection on 31 December and on 8 January 1942 it was allocated to No. 8 Service Flying Training School (SFTS) at Montrose, Scotland, where it resumed its training role. Two months later, on 9 March, it was re-allocated to No. 9 (Pilots) Advanced Flying Unit back at its old stamping ground of Hullavington in Wiltshire and on 9 May it suffered another accident, Cat AC (beyond unit capacity) and was issued to a party from Hawker Aircraft Ltd for repairs on site on 14 May, returning to its unit on the 23rd. P2617 served at Hullavington for a further 14 months, until 21 August 1943, on which date it was transferred to No. 22 MU at Silloth, Cumbria, where it was placed in store.

As luck would have it, the Air Historical Branch was selecting historic aircraft for long-term preservation and as a Battle of Britain veteran P2617 fitted the bill perfectly so on 3 April 1944 it was chosen (along with L1592, qv) to be preserved for posterity. It was ready for transfer by road to No. 82 MU at Lichfield, Staffs, on 14 May and on 6 August it was allocated to the Packing Unit at No. 52 MU, Cardiff. As with L1592 it was initially stored in a Bellman hangar but this was needed for wood storage in December 1944 and the crated museum aircraft were dispersed, P2617 finding its way to No. 76 MU at Wroughton, Wilts, before being relocated to No. 47 MU at Sealand, Flintshire, where it was recorded on 1 February 1946. It probably remained there until May 1947 when it is thought to have been transferred to Stanmore Park, north London, along with six other preserved aircraft – which were to be used for various static displays on Horse Guards Parade, London, in the late 1940s and early 1950s.

July 1951 saw both P2617 and its stablemate L1592 taken to Kenley, Surrey, where they were used as static Hurricanes in the film *Angels One Five* starring Jack Hawkins and John Gregson. The film company modified the paint-scheme by overpainting the rear fuselage sky band and the original code was replaced with those of No. 56 Sqdn. Although several authors have suggested that it was taxied and possibly even flown in the film this is not the case. Careful examination of

When the RAF Museum opened in November 1972 P2617 was displayed in plain camouflage without squadron codes. (*Gordon Riley*)

the film shows that the aircraft shown taxying with the serial P2617 is actually LF363 (qv). Following filming P2617 was returned to Stanmore Park and with the temporary paint removed it reappeared on Horse Guards Parade in grey/green camouflage and bearing the code '14' behind the fuselage roundels – evidence of its final unit, No. 9 (P)AFU at Hullavington (see page 29).

On 12 August 1955 it was seen on a Queen Mary trailer at Croydon Airport, probably when the driver took a break whilst delivering it to Kenley once more, this time for static use in the film *Reach for The Sky* starring Kenneth More as Douglas Bader. It is believed that the film company changed markings several times to give the impression of more aircraft – using different codes and serials on each side of the fuselages – and P2617 is thought to have been marked as T4107/SD-P, SD-W and SD-X (see page 29). Following filming it was taken by road direct to Horse Guards Parade in September 1955 and was seen to be back in its original markings but with traces of the US-P codes from *Angels One Five* still visible.

Where it went following the Battle of Britain Week display of 1955 is unclear but by July 1957 it was stored with No. 15 MU at Wroughton, Wilts, and during 1958 it was seen at Rufforth, Yorkshire, before finally reaching No. 71 MU at Bicester, Oxfordshire, later that year. Here it was given a thorough overhaul and repaint in preparation for its role as a travelling exhibit, appearing on Horse Guards Parade in September 1959 resplendent in the codes of No.

607 Sqdn as AF-T. These markings were retained, despite several repaints, until May 1967 when it was transferred by road to Henlow, Bedfordshire, to be prepared for use in the film *The Battle of Britain*. Although it has been suggested that it was restored to taxying condition by 8 February 1968 and noted as H3426/MI-C and H3427/MI-S this seems unlikely as it left Henlow in April 1968, returning to No. 71 MU at Bicester, where it was restored as AF-T and took part in the RAF 50th Anniversary Royal Review at Abingdon on 14 June that year.

Between 1968 and 1972, P2617 carried on with its RAF Exhibition Flight role being exhibited at a variety of venues around the UK but in May 1972 it was allocated to the newly-established Royal Air Force Museum and transferred to Hendon, north London, where it was seen to have been restored in early-1940 camouflage with silver and black undersides but no squadron codes as at that time its Battle of France provenance had not been established. Initially displayed in the Sir Sydney Camm Memorial Hall (long-since redeveloped and lost) it was given the serial 8373M on 5 September 1973.

With the opening of the Battle of Britain Hall in 1978, P2617 was moved into one of the replica E Pens and repainted as AF-F with the port wing underside painted black. Some 20 years later, on 3 August 1998, it was officially donated to the RAF Museum by the Ministry of Defence. It remains displayed at Hendon.

P2902
Hawker Hurricane Mk I

R A Roberts, Milden, Suffolk, UK

P2902 was built at Brockworth by the Gloster Aircraft Company Ltd (a subsidiary of Hawker Aircraft Ltd) as part of a batch of 500 Hurricanes ordered against Contract No. 962371/38. The aircraft bore serials between P2535-P3264, with P2902 forming part of the second block (P2900-2924). Powered by a 1,280 hp Merlin III (engine number 144641) and fitted with a Rotol three-bladed propeller it was allocated to No. 20 MU at Aston Down, Glos, as a reserve aircraft on 25 April 1940 and taken on charge on 13 May.

The wreckage of P2902 being lifted from the beach at Leffrinckoucke in 1989 – the wings were stolen that night! (*Francky Turquet*)

With the Battle of France raging it was issued almost immediately to B Flight of No. 245 Sqdn on 19 May and took up the code DX-R – known as 'R for Robert'. The unit was based at Drem, Scotland but A Flight was sent to France during that month, returning on the 20th, and further detachments were made to Hawkinge, Kent, in order to fly patrols over Dunkirk and the English Channel during Operation Dynamo – the BEF evacuation from Dunkirk.

P2902 had only eight hours flying time recorded on 31 May when it took off from Hawkinge in the hands of a 19-year-old Scottish pilot, Kenneth McGlashan – 'Mac' to those who knew him. Mac was leading the rear section of three Hurricanes in a Vic formation, covering the forward nine aircraft of the squadron. Sgt Alan Hedges soon had to return to base due to fluctuating oil pressure, leaving Mac alone with Sgt Geoff Howitt on his right wing. A group of German bombers was spotted en route to attack Dunkirk and the leading nine aircraft dived into the attack with Mac and Howitt bringing up the rear. As he prepared to attack a pair of Bf 109s, which were flying below him, his offensive patrol came to an abrupt end when he was attacked from the rear by a group of five Bf 109s. Wounded and temporarily partially blinded by oil and glycol splashing into his eyes, Mac had heard that the 109 was not good at pulling out of a steep dive so he put the Hurricane into one and by the time his sight came back he was very low. He pulled out of the dive, blacked out and when he came to he found himself travelling very fast and low along a beach.

Safely tucked away in Craig Charleston's workshop on 29 April 1994. (*Craig Charleston*)

The rebuilt P2902 in the hangar of Hawker Restorations Ltd in August 2014 awaits its newly-rebuilt wings. *(Gordon Riley)*

Following a successful forced-landing Mac was rescued by British soldiers from some French colonial troops, who had mistaken him for a German. He walked along the beach into Dunkirk and managed to board a Thames paddle steamer *The Golden Eagle.* After an eventful crossing, he landed late at night at Margate and was taken by squadron transport back to Hawkinge. Mac served with No. 245 Sqdn throughout the Battle of Britain and continued to serve with the RAF post-war, attaining the rank of squadron leader and being awarded the Air Force Cross in 1950.

Meanwhile P2902 lay on the beach at Leffrinckoucke, being pillaged by German souvenir hunters, until it eventually disappeared from view under the sand. It lay undisturbed until 1989 when the sand shifted sufficiently to reveal its substantially intact remains and members of the local aero club and others took it upon themselves to attempt to recover the wreck. This they achieved, with the help of some earth-moving equipment and slings, the wreck being left in the care of the local police station overnight – only to have the wings stolen that very night. The fuselage, wing centre-section and engine – complete with the remains of a Rotol three-bladed propeller – were displayed in the Memorial du Souvenir in Dunkirk as part of their Operation Dynamo display.

With the upsurge in interest in restoring World War 2 aircraft the museum was approached many times with offers for the aircraft, none were successful until 1994 when Craig Charleston secured a deal to acquire both P2902 and the remains of P3311 (qv), both aircraft arriving at Craig's workshop in Essex on 29 April 1994. Craig contacted Tony Ditheridge of Hawker Restorations Ltd and within days the aircraft had changed hands, being sold on to its current owner, Ricky Roberts, with an understanding that it would be restored to fly by Hawker Restorations Ltd. In June 1994 Craig received a letter from S/Ldr Kenneth McGlashan, AFC, RAF (Retd) from his home in New South Wales, Australia, in which he commented that if he "… hadn't put it down on the beach so gently there would be nothing to restore!" Mac had been to Dunkirk to see his old Hurricane in the museum during the Battle of Britain 50th Anniversary events of 1990 and took a keen interest in the restoration work but died in 2005; his wife Doreen died in August 2014.

P2902 was registered G-ROBT on 19 September 1994 to Ricky A Roberts and restoration to flight, powered by a Rolls-Royce Merlin 35 in place of the original Merlin III, continues at the Milden premises of Hawker Restorations Ltd.

P3173
Hawker Hurricane Mk I

Paul Cole, W Sussex, UK

P3173 was built at Brockworth by the Gloster Aircraft Company Ltd (a subsidiary of Hawker Aircraft Ltd) as part of a batch of 500 Hurricanes ordered against Contract No. 962371/38. The aircraft bore serials between P2535-P3264, with P3173 forming part of the serial block P3140-3179. Powered by a 1,280 hp Merlin III and fitted with a Rotol three-bladed propeller it was allocated to No. 10 MU at Hullavington, Wilts, and taken on charge on 29 June 1940 – the same day as the RAF Museum's sister aircraft P3175.

Unlike P3175, which was not allocated to a squadron until 9 August, P3173 was transferred to No. 1 Sqdn at Tangmere on 11 July where it was coded JX-O. The squadron had been

The cockpit section of P3173 in Paul Cole's workshop in the spring of 2015. (*Paul Cole*)

based in France as part of 67 Wing of the Advanced Air Striking Force but as Luftwaffe attacks intensified during May and June 1940 it found itself retreating, finally returning to Tangmere on 23 June where it began to regroup, P3175 being one of its replacement Hurricanes. The squadron opened its account in the Battle of Britain by shooting down two Bf 110s on 1 August and later in the month moved from Tangmere to Northolt, with detachments operating from Manston, North Weald and Heathrow.

Nineteen-year-old P/O J F D 'Tim' Elkington had been granted a permanent commission on 14 July 1940 and was posted to No. 1 Sqdn at Northolt, shooting down a Bf 109 on 15 August, but was himself shot down and wounded the next day whilst flying P3173. Tim was flying as 'top weaver', flying back and forth over the rest of the squadron to provide an early warning of enemy fighters, when they encountered 100 German aircraft in the vicinity of Portsmouth Harbour. In the ensuing mêlée, Tim never saw the aircraft that riddled his Hurricane with cannon shells – although, amazingly, his mother did. From nearby Hayling Island and quite unaware that her son was involved, she watched the lone Hurricane pursued by three Bf 109s. A fuel tank exploded, peppering Tim with shrapnel; as he bailed out he forgot to disconnect his oxygen supply and the mask was subsequently ripped from his face – leaving a scar which he bears to this day. Tim lost consciousness and would have drifted out to sea and certain death if it had not been for the actions of his flight commander, F/Sgt Fred Berry, who followed him down and used the slipstream of his own Hurricane to blow Tim's parachute back towards land. Despite being fired on by the Home Guard, after landing at West Wittering Tim was taken to the Royal West Sussex Hospital at Chichester, from where he was put on sick leave and was sent to convalesce. Fred Berry was killed on 1 September, before Tim had a chance to thank him.

P3173 had turned inland crashing in flames at Manor Farm, Chidham, between Chichester and Portsmouth, from where in 1975 the Wealden Aviation Archaeological Group excavated the Merlin engine, armour plate and cockpit controls. These parts, together with components from other digs, have been assembled by Paul Cole who is restoring the fuselage to static display condition. In the long term Paul plans to reconstruct a pair of wings and to have the Hurricane able to taxy under its own power once again.

P3175
Hawker Hurricane Mk I

RAF Museum, Hendon, UK

P3175 was built at Brockworth by the Gloster Aircraft Company Ltd (a subsidiary of Hawker Aircraft Ltd) as part of a batch of 500 Hurricanes ordered against Contract No. 962371/38. The aircraft bore serials between P2535-P3264, with P3175 forming part of the serial block P3140-3179. Powered by a 1,280 hp Merlin III and fitted with a Rotol three-bladed propeller, it was allocated to No. 10 MU at Hullavington, Wilts, and taken on charge on 29 June 1940.

Following preparation for service – which seems to have taken a surprisingly long time – it was eventually allocated to No. 257 Sqdn at Northolt on 9 August and took up the code DT-S. The squadron had been reformed at Hendon on 17 May and was initially equipped with Spitfires but these were soon replaced by Hurricanes and the squadron moved to Northolt on 4 July. Its first combat was on 9 July when a section of three Hurricanes was scrambled and Sgt Forward fired at a Dornier Do 17 with inconclusive results.

The squadron lost three pilots and aircraft in a battle fought over the Isle of Wight on 8 August. P3175 was a replacement for one of the three Hurricanes lost that day and took up the code DT-S. Whilst at Northolt the squadron's operational area was the English Channel, in particular protecting coastal convoys. On 15 August it relocated to Debden and for the remainder of the month operated from there or its satellite base at Martlesham Heath. During its brief life P3175 flew from Northolt, Tangmere, North Weald, Debden and Martlesham Heath.

Its first recorded operational sortie was a recce of the Northolt Sector between 1020 and 1050 hours on 12 August with Sgt Hulbert at the controls; later that afternoon F/O Mitchell flew it to Tangmere from where he took part in a convoy patrol and combat over Portsmouth, landing at 1640. The return to Northolt took 25 minutes that evening, from 2000 to 2025. The following day F/O Mitchell scrambled from Northolt at 0620 and engaged enemy aircraft south of

Tangmere – claiming a Ju 88 probable on landing at 0735. A few days later, on 18 August, P/O Gerard Maffett scrambled P3175 from its new base at Debden at 1700 hours and the squadron engaged a mixed formation of 50 Heinkels and Dorniers over the Thames Estuary, Maffett claiming a Do 215 damaged. The following day the same pilot flew it to Martlesham Heath and it operated from this base until 22 August when it was flown back to Debden where it was under maintenance between 23-24 August, returning to Martlesham Heath in the hands of P/O Gundry on 25th.

Maffett must have taken a liking to P3175 as he was the only pilot to fly it for the remainder of the month and was at the controls for its last flight when nine Hurricanes were scrambled from Martlesham Heath at 0825 hours on Saturday 31 August to patrol the base at 10,000 feet. New orders were given to patrol Debden at 15,000 feet but as they climbed through 14,000 feet they encountered what they reported to be two large formations of Ju 88s escorted by Bf 110s. Unable to catch the bombers the Hurricanes attacked the escorts over Clacton at around 14,000 feet – six were destroyed for a loss of two Hurricanes, P3175 crashing on the foreshore at Walton-on-the-Naze at 0850 hours. Gerard Maffett had bailed out at about 400 feet and, although eye-witnesses saw his parachute deploy, he was too low to save himself and was killed, being buried at Bray, Berks, on 4 September. His grave, at his late mother's request, is still marked by the simple wooden cross which was placed as a temporary marker by the (then) Imperial War Graves Commission, and as such it is unique amongst Battle of Britain pilots.

Although ammunition and other parts were recovered from the crash site by the Home Guard the site was located in a military area and was simply abandoned, P3175 being struck off charge on 21 September 1940. By the time that the beach was re-opened after the war the soft mud and sand

The conserved wreckage of P3175 displayed in the Battle of Britain Hall, RAF Museum, Hendon, January 2015. *(Gordon Riley)*

had enveloped the remains although it was known to locals – including Geoff Rayner who recalls first visiting the site around 1961. By the late 1960s some three-four feet of the starboard wing front spar were visible above the mud and Geoff's digging revealed part of the fuel tank.

By August 1971 coastal erosion had exposed more of the airframe and as a consequence souvenir hunters started to appear on site. In an effort to retrieve and preserve the wreck Geoff surveyed the site in December 1972 and established that the wreck was lying inverted at a depth of about four feet under the mud at an approximate angle of 30 degrees. Despite damage due to impact and fire the structure was remarkably well preserved owing to the characteristics of the muddy environment.

Additional manpower, and access to heavy recovery equipment, was provided by cadets and helpers from No. 308 Sqdn Air Training Corps (Clacton and Colchester), so that the bulk of the remains were recovered during the first week of April 1973; the Merlin III (No. 22637) being recovered the following month. The group stripped and cleaned the remains with the engine being displayed at Coltishall in August 1973 and at a cinema in Clacton the following December. With the RAF Museum having just opened to the public Geoff Rayner contacted Jack Bruce, the curator, and it was agreed that the remains should be displayed at the museum, the airframe parts being collected on 31 July 1977 with the engine following in June 1978.

The parts were vacu-blasted after their arrival at Hendon and carefully reassembled to create the dramatic – and remarkably complete – crash-site display which was initially

located as the first item in the Battle of Britain Hall when it was opened to the public on 28 November 1978. With the redevelopment of the hall over the years the exhibit is perhaps not as dramatically positioned today but still serves as a poignant reminder of the sacrifice made by Gerard Maffett and his fellow pilots.

Digging in progress, 21 April 1973, engine bearers bottom left, rear fuselage top right, port wing top middle, stub of starboard wing bottom middle. (*Geoff Rayner*)

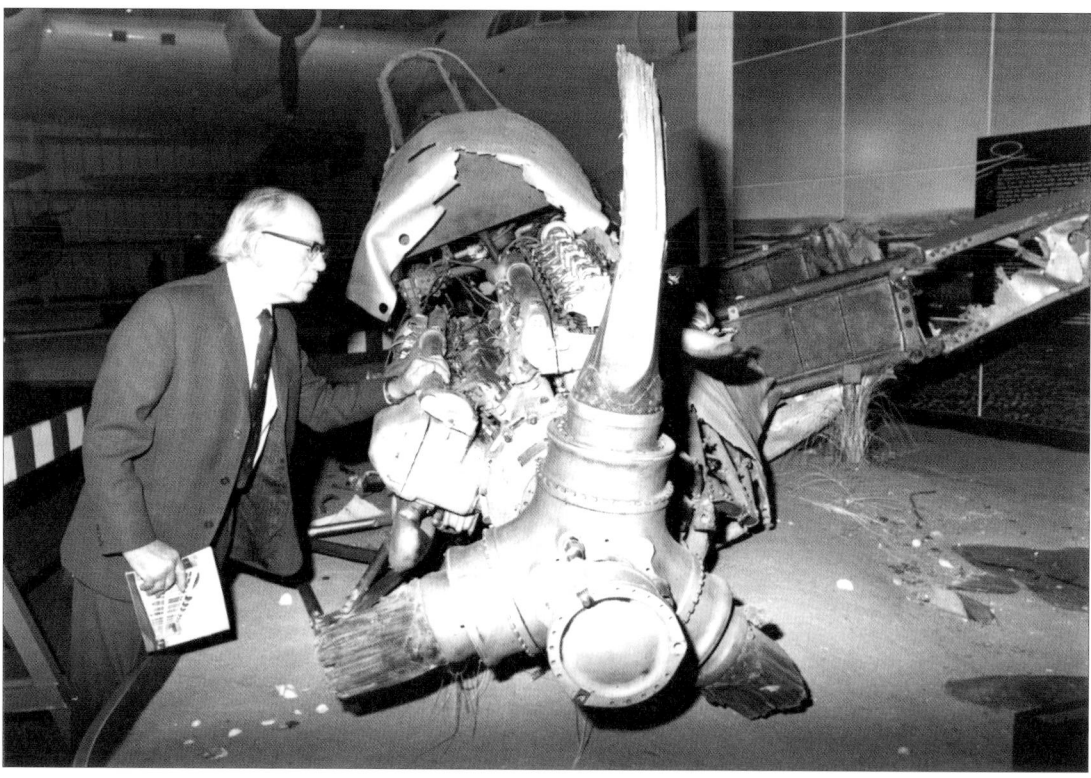

A poignant moment as Alan Maffett, brother of Gerard, touches the aircraft shortly after it was unveiled in the museum. Alan died in 2010. (*W G Ramsey/After The Battle*)

P3179
Hawker Hurricane Mk I

Tangmere Military Aviation Museum, Tangmere, W Sussex, UK

P3179 was built at Brockworth by the Gloster Aircraft Company Ltd (a subsidiary of Hawker Aircraft Ltd) as part of a batch of 500 Hurricanes ordered against Contract No. 962371/38. The aircraft bore serials between P2535-P3264, with P3179 being the last aircraft of the serial block (P3140-3179). Powered by a 1,280 hp Merlin III and fitted with a Rotol three-bladed propeller it was allocated to No. 15 MU at Wroughton, Wilts, on 22 June 1940 and taken on charge on 2 July.

Following preparation for service, P3179 was issued to No. 43 Sqdn – 'The Fighting Cocks' – based at Tangmere, Sussex, on 9 August, the squadron having returned to its pre-war home after a short spell of operational training at Northolt. Its first flight was a 15-minute air test by Flt/Lt Morgan at 1835 hours on Sunday 11 August and the following day, having been allocated to B Flight, it was flown on two sorties against 'X-plots' by F/O Du Vivier. (All radar plots were received in the Filter Room at Fighter Command HQ, Bentley Priory; if

The reconstructed cockpit section and engine of P3179 on display at Tangmere in February 2015.
(*Pete Pitman/Tangmere Military Aviation Museum*)

they could not be identified immediately they were labelled 'X' until a filter officer had assessed them. If they were an enemy formation they were given a plot number and passed to the Command Operations Room in the bunker next door to the Filter Room.) On Tuesday 13 August, it made one sortie in the hands of P/O Ven den Hove, again against an 'X-plot' target, which resulted in a patrol over Southampton in which the squadron dispatched one Ju 88 and one Do 17 with another Ju 88 damaged. The following day, Wednesday 14 August, it made three separate sorties, one flown by Ven den Hove and the other two by Du Vivier; during an afternoon patrol near the Needles B Flight dispatched another Ju 88.

Its next sortie, in the afternoon of Friday 16 August, was in the hands of the squadron CO, S/Ldr J V C Badger who had just 10 minutes on the ground between landing P3971 at 1310 hours and taking off again at 1320 hours in P3179, not landing again until 1505 hours. During this action twelve Hurricanes of No. 43 Sqdn attacked a large formation of enemy aircraft which had attacked Tangmere at 1300 hours, setting the squadron's hangar ablaze and destroying four Hurricanes on the ground. The Luftwaffe force took a pounding from the Hurricanes with no less than 17 Stukas claimed as destroyed with another four probables and a further six damaged. (In hindsight these figures may seem somewhat inflated but in the heat of battle they were accepted.)

P3179 did not fly on Saturday 17 August – suggesting that it may have been receiving maintenance or repairs – but on 18 August it was taken up three times by 20-year-old Sgt Dennis Noble, who had joined the squadron from No. 6 OTU at Sutton Bridge on 3 August. Noble's sorties were at 0930 hours, 1255 hours and 1410 hours – indicating the ferocity of the fighting that day – and it was flown again by the CO, S/Ldr Badger, at 1445 hours – Noble taking Badger's regular mount P3903. During this attack on Tangmere the squadron dispatched another eight Stukas and a Bf 109 with a ninth Stuka claimed as a probable.

Noble seems to have settled on P3179 as he flew it on 19, 20, 21, 23, 24, 25, 27, 29 and 30 August the last date being his final and fatal flight. He took off from Tangmere at 1125 hours on Friday 30 August as the squadron intercepted an enemy raid on S Kent, Sussex and Surrey. An eye witness report states that it was a beautiful sunny morning and as the Hurricanes were engaged in combat with Bf 109s in the blue sky over Hove, W Sussex, one of them was seen to fall out of the sky and dive into the ground nearly vertically, creating a large crater at the top of Woodhouse Road at 1150 hours. Photographs taken at the time show a water-filled hole and the LDV cordoned off the area, later reporting that the wreckage and the pilot's body had been recovered. Dennis Noble was given a funeral in his home town of Retford, Notts, but there were lingering doubts in the Hove area about the story of his recovery.

After several years of campaigning, local aviation enthusiast Keith Arnold was eventually granted a licence for the recovery of the Hurricane by the MoD, as it was thought that Dennis's body had already been recovered. The dig was carried out over three days in November 1996. Some parts of the aircraft were discovered up to 15 feet below ground and it was calculated that the impact speed was around 400 mph. On the second day of the dig, Saturday 9 November 1996, the body of Dennis Noble was found. The excavation at this stage was around 12 feet deep. The very next day was Remembrance Sunday, and it had been agreed to hold a service at the site. The service was conducted by the Revd Anthony Martlew, who as a 12-year-old schoolboy had witnessed the crash.

Following a formal inquest, Dennis Noble's body was buried with full military honours in the grave bearing his name in Retford, Notts, on 22 January 1997 and the wreckage of P3179 now forms a fitting tribute to him in the Tangmere Military Aviation Museum.

P3311
Hawker Hurricane Mk I

Privately owned, Denver, Colorado, USA

P3311 was built at Brooklands by Hawker Aircraft Ltd as part of a batch of 500 Hurricanes ordered against Contract No. 962371/38. The aircraft bore serials between P3265-P3984, with P3311 falling into the second serial block (P3300-3324). Powered by a 1,280 hp Merlin III (No. 143738) and fitted with a de Havilland three-bladed propeller it was allocated to No. 20 MU at Aston Down, Glos, on 27 January 1940 and taken on charge on 15 March, being designated as a reserve aircraft.

With the Battle of France in full swing and the BEF in retreat, P3311 was allocated to No. 56 Sqdn, based at North Weald, Essex, on 18 May. B Flight was dispatched to Vitry-en-Artois, France, where it spent four very hectic days defending its own airfield before withdrawing to North Weald; A Flight in the meantime operated from Lille during daylight hours, returning to North Weald each evening. Detachments also operated from Manston and Biggin Hill.

P3311 was allocated to B Flight as US-R and its first sortie seems to have been on 23 May when it took part in a patrol lasting for 4 hours and 20 minutes in the hands of Sgt Whitehead. Although no details of individual patrols were recorded it would appear that seven Hurricanes flew to Manston – where they presumably landed to refuel – before patrolling over St Omer and Calais, after which they landed at Manston and then returned to base. Two of the aircraft dropped messages at Merville aerodrome whilst others acted

The corroded centre section of P3311 in store in Dunkirk in April 1994.
(*Craig Charleston*)

as bomber escorts – being attacked by three Bf 109s – three other Hurricanes chased a Henschel 126 but lost it in cloud before a dogfight broke out with 12 Bf 110s in which F/Lt R H A 'Dickie' Lee's aircraft was badly shot up.

The following day, 24 May, Lee took over P3311 and flew it from North Weald to Manston, the squadron (alongside No. 151 Sqdn) taking part in patrols over St Omer, Dunkirk and Calais and later in the afternoon in offensive sweeps escorting bombers over a wood to the east of Calais and the area around Courtrai. No enemy aircraft were encountered and the squadron returned to North Weald via Manston that evening. Lee flew it again the next day, noting that Dunkirk and other towns in the area were in flames. At 1630 hours they took off again from Manston escorting 24 Blenheims which were bombing St Omer, fires were started and AA fire was encountered before the Hurricanes returned to North Weald via Hawkinge, arriving back at base at around 1930 hours.

This pattern was repeated on 26 May when the squadron flew from North Weald to Manston, departing at 1730 hours to escort bombers attacking a target in the Dunkirk area. Lee flew P3311 again, returning to Manston at 1930 hours before arriving back at North Weald at 2130 hours – there was no combat or casualties that day which was rainy with a light southerly wind.

Monday 27 May started out just like the previous few days had done with B Flight's Hurricanes departing North Weald at 1320 hours and arriving at Manston 25 minutes later. Lee was again flying P3311 and at 1533 hours they took off on an offensive patrol to St Omer and Ostend. This time they encountered 10 He 111s near Dunkirk and S/Ldr Knowles (N2667) shot one down whilst sharing another probable with Sgt Baker. Another was shared by three pilots and F/Sgt Cooney claimed another probable. Unfortunately P/O Maxwell in P3478 was shot down by Belgian AA fire and 'Dickie' Lee in P3311 was hit by return fire from one of the Heinkels or possibly a Bf 110 escort. Both pilots bailed out and Lee landed in the sea from where he was rescued by a Royal Navy destroyer.

Lee was 23 years old and Lord Trenchard's godson, had been awarded the DFC on 8 March 1940 and was awarded the DSO on 31 May, the citation reading: 'This officer has displayed great ability as a leader and intense desire to engage the enemy. On one occasion he continued to attack an enemy aircraft after his companion had been shot down, and his own machine hit in many places. His section shot down a Dornier 215 in flames one evening in May, and another in the course of an engagement the next day. In his last engagement he was seen at 200 feet on the tail of a Junkers 88, being subjected to intense fire from the ground over enemy occupied territory. This officer escaped from behind the German lines after being arrested and upheld the highest traditions of the Service.' In June 1940 he was promoted to flight commander with No. 85 Sqdn but did not return from a patrol on Sunday 18 August, being last seen at 1750 hours in pursuit of an enemy formation some 30 miles off the east coast. No trace of Lee or his Hurricane, P2923/VY-R, was ever found.

The wreck of P3311, however, was discovered in 1989, excavated from the beach like P2902 (qv) and taken to the Memorial du Souvenir in Dunkirk where its remains were found to be far more badly damaged, both by fire and the subsequent impact. Craig Charleston negotiated the purchase of P2902 and secured the remains of P3311 at the same time – although the Merlin III and the de Havilland propeller were retained by the museum and are still displayed there. The centre-section and other parts were brought back to the UK on 29 April 1994 and, following the sale of P2902, the remains of P3311 were sold to Gordon Page operating as Air Assets International/Warbirds Recovery of Colorado, USA, the plan being that they would be restored in Fort Collins by Ray Middleton with Hawker Restorations Ltd and Craig Charleston supplying parts as required.

The remains of P3311 were crated up by Craig Charleston and shipped directly to Ray Middleton's hangar in Fort Collins where they arrived in early 1995. The restoration plans fell through and Page sold the package to a private owner in the Denver area in 2005. Since that time work has been carried out on acquiring, rebuilding or manufacturing parts and sub-assemblies. All of the woodwork is done, the fuel tanks are constructed structurally, but not moulded to complete the bladder, and many of the sub components are complete. All work is being completed in accordance with AC-4313, which is the US standard for certificated aircraft, with the intention that P3311 will emerge as a flyable aircraft in due course.

P3351/DR393
Hawker Hurricane Mk I

Jan Frisco Roozen, Cannes–Mandelieu, France

P3351 was built as a Mk I at Brooklands by Hawker Aircraft Ltd as part of a batch of 500 Hurricanes ordered against Contract No. 962371/38. The aircraft bore serials between P3265-P3984, with P3351 falling into the second serial block (P3345-3364). Powered by a 1,280 hp Merlin III (No. 148156) it was allocated to No. 5 MU at Kemble, Wilts, on 28 March 1940 and taken on charge on 6 April, being designated as a reserve aircraft.

According to its AM Form 78 Movements Card, P3351 was allocated to RAF Tangmere on 13 June 1940 and issued to No. 73 Sqdn five days later on 18 June. This was probably paperwork trying to keep up with events on the ground as it had actually be issued directly to No. 73 Sqdn as a replacement aircraft at the end of May. At the outbreak of World War 2, No. 73 Sqdn had been one of the two Hurricane squadrons (the other being No. 1 Sqdn)

P3351, now registered F-AZXR, formates with the camera ship near Duxford on 15 July 2013.
(Darren Harbar Photography)

attached to the Advanced Air Striking Force dispatched to France, its first base being at Le Havre/ Octeville. After the German attack in May 1940, No. 73 helped to cover Allied airfields and bases, falling back as its airfields were overrun by enemy columns. At the start of June 1940 the squadron was based at a temporary aerodrome on farmland at Gaye, south of Reims in the Champagne region, and P3351 was noted flying a defensive patrol to Hautmont in the hands of P/O Peter Carter (Red section of A Flight) between 1010 hours and 1120 hours on 1 June 1940. The squadron did not carry unit codes (TP) on most of its aircraft, they simply carried individual aircraft letters – P3351 being coded 'K'. Carter had crash-landed his previous Hurricane after he was attacked by a Bf 109, the aircraft sustaining significant damage from cannon and machine-gun rounds; he was lucky to escape as that aircraft had turned over on its back after landing in soft ground.

The squadron was awaiting orders to move to a new base at Raudin, east of Le Mans, and the CO, S/Ldr J W C 'Hank' More, visited it on 1 June although the signal to move out was not received until 2 June with confirmation that the move would take place on 3 June. Doubts were expressed that the ground component of the Advanced Air Striking Force would be able to cover the 300-odd kilometre distance without enemy interference but the Hurricanes would provide air support from a temporary base at Echimenes. The first aircraft left for Echimenes at 0430 hours on 3 June with two spare aircraft being flown direct to Le Mans. The day proved to be remarkably sunny and hot and the convoy made excellent progress, arriving at the village of Raudin at 1800 hours – although one lorry was lost due to a fire caused by a dropped match!

P3351 was one of the aircraft which operated from Echimenes and was ferried there by P/O Carter, landing at 1815 hours on 3 June, although he also seems to have flown it from Gaye on a 2hr 20min defensive patrol over Reims four days later on 7 June. The squadron ORB (Operations Record Book) indicates that the aircraft moved between bases as operational requirements dictated and were to be found flying from Gaye, Echimenes, Le Mans (Raudin), Saumur, Bagneux and Nantes throughout the remainder of the month. It has been suggested that P3351 was used by S/Ldr More to fly from Le Mans to attend the funeral of F/Lt E J 'Cobber' Kain at Troyes on 8 June following his death in a flying accident at Echimenes the previous day.

No. 73 Squadron's final base in France was Nantes, which they reached on 15 June in order to cover the retreating members of the AASF – Operation Ariel. P3351 was flown by Sgt Scott as part of a defensive patrol over the port of St Nazaire on the morning of 17 June and the squadron's final patrols were flown on 18 June, Peter Carter flying P3351 three times during the day; the first patrol was between 0440–0550 hours, the next between 1105–1155 hours and the last time was the dash home. Carter and P3351 left Nantes at 1415 hours in a group led by F/Lt Nicholls, landing to refuel at Boscombe Down before proceeding to Tangmere where they received orders to go to Church Fenton, N Yorks – finally arriving there that evening. Most of the ground personnel had already left for St Nazaire to embark on the troop ship RMS *Lancastria*, together with the headquarters of British Air Forces in France and hundreds of other RAF personnel. Thirty-eight members of the squadron were killed when the *Lancastria* was sunk by three bombs from a Ju 88 during the afternoon of 17 June. The remaining ground crew, under the command of F/Lt Brown of 67 Wing, set fire to the unserviceable machines left on the ground and escaped in a Bristol Bombay and Avro Anson – making No. 73 Sqdn the last RAF unit to leave France.

Following their arrival at Church Fenton the squadron was given a brief respite and personnel were given home leave. The aircraft were thoroughly overhauled; P3351 was repainted with its full squadron codes of TP-K and by 7 July No. 73 had resumed operations. On 19 July, A Flight flew to Prestwick, Scotland, for night-flying experience. All went well until, in the early hours of Sunday, 21 July, Alf Scott undershot the runway in P3351, causing the undercarriage to collapse and tipping the aircraft onto its nose. That night saw three Hurricanes damaged (including another by Scott) and all were set aside for repair.

As the Battle of Britain developed in the south P3351 underwent repairs at No. 4 MU from 27 July – although the note 'Rolls-Royce' is made on its Movements Card so it is quite possible that the work was carried out at Hucknall, Rolls-Royce being part of the Hurricane Repair Organisation. By 27 August P3351 was ready for dispatch to No. 22 MU at Silloth and on 6 September, complete with a replacement Merlin, it was allocated to No. 32 Sqdn at Acklington, Northumberland. Having had a torrid time 'down south' No. 32 had been allocated to 13 Group on 27 August and tasked with convoy patrols and fighter cover.

Having been retrieved from its crash site on the Kola Peninsula, P3351 was exhibited in Archangel in September 1991 as part of the 'Dervish 91' commemorations. (*Peter R Arnold Collection*)

For three months, P3351 was flown extensively by P/O Jack Rose over north-eastern England until 16 December when No. 32 Sqdn moved south to Middle Wallop, Hants, as part of 10 Group. Within five days P3351 was reassigned to the American volunteers of No. 71 'Eagle' Squadron based at Kirton-in-Lindsey under the command of S/Ldr W M Churchill, DSO, DFC, probably flying directly from its old base at Acklington the few miles south to Yorkshire. It would have been coded XR- but records are incomplete for this period and although P3351 arrived on 21 December 1940, its first recorded flight was not until 16 February 1941. On 10 March two of the Hurricanes undertook a patrol over the Humber estuary but on returning in the early evening, P/O Sampson-Taylor crashed and damaged P3351 on landing.

After a month undergoing repairs, the Hurricane re-joined the same squadron on 18 April 1941, by then based at Martlesham Heath, near Ipswich, Suffolk, ready for further operational flying but by the beginning of May new Hurricane IIAs began to arrive as replacement aircraft and P3351 was transferred to No. 55 Operational Training Unit at Usworth, near Sunderland where it would have taken up a unit code commencing PA-.

No sooner had it arrived than on 13 May 1941 a Polish flying instructor, Sgt Stanislaw Karubin, flew it into some high-tension power lines, fortunately managing to land safely at Ouston, Northumberland, where the damaged wing leading edge was repaired on-site. P3351 also received a new engine

– presumably the propeller or reduction gear had been affected by impact with the power cables. It is interesting to note that when the wreck was recovered from Russia it was found to carry Polish red and white chequerboard markings on both the port and starboard cowlings – probably added when being flown by Karubin or other Polish pilots at Usworth.

Upon her return to Usworth two remarkable coincidences occurred. Trainee P/O William Miller, from Invercargill, New Zealand, flew the aircraft twice. 'Dusty' Miller was to retire to Wanaka, New Zealand, where decades later he would be reunited with P3351, acting until his death as a guide at the New Zealand Fighter Pilots Museum, where he was especially proud to show visitors 'his' Hurricane. Meanwhile, on 9 September 1941, another Invercargill pilot, Sergeant Ness Polson was flying P3351 on an evening training mission when – officially – the Merlin engine overheated and seized. Polson bellied her into a field near Headingley, Leeds. Unofficially, it seems that Polson was competing with his wingman to see how low each could fly. Polson won – flying low enough to hit a hedge which precipitated the forced-landing.

This ended P3351's RAF flying career. It was allocated to Rolls-Royce at Hucknall on 16 September 1941 for a repair in works (RIW) and upgraded to Mark IIA Series 2 specification with a Merlin XX engine as part of a batch of 40 aircraft being prepared for shipping to Russia under the Lend-Lease programme, and during the upgrade it was given a new serial, DR393. Whether all of the work took place at Rolls-Royce is not clear as it seems to have passed from one facility to another with notes on its Form 78 as 'Repaired Aircraft Awaiting Allocation' (RAAA) on 8 November, allocated to No. 51 MU (Lichfield) a storage/packing unit on 20 November, then further modifications at works (location not specified) on 23 January 1942, another RAAA comment on 14 February, allocated to No. 29 MU (High Ercall, Shropshire) on 20 February and then on to the Packing Unit at No. 52 MU, Cardiff on 9/10 March before finally being taken by road to the Port of Glasgow.

On 3 May 1942, accompanied by 23 other Hurricanes, it sailed on the SS *Ocean Voice*, in Convoy PQ16. Routed via Iceland, PQ16 was subjected to incessant attack as it approached the northern Russian coast. The *Ocean Voice* took a serious hit which opened a 20-foot hole barely two feet above her waterline and set her on fire. Miraculously she managed to berth safely at Murmansk, Convoy PQ16 having

P3351 being assembled by Air New Zealand Engineering Services, Christchurch, NZ, in April 1998. *(Tony Clarke)*

lost 'only' some 770 vehicles, 147 tanks and 77 aircraft – a success by Arctic Convoy standards…

In Russian hands, DR393 was quickly unloaded and re-assembled. It then flew in Soviet service – cannon-armed – for the following year. No operational details have been located but it would undoubtedly have resumed combat against the Luftwaffe. It is believed it ultimately crashed in the winter of 1943. During the subsequent rebuild process, a 7.9mm copper-jacketed projectile was found lodged in the oil-cooler, having passed through the radiator from the lower face. Possibly ground fire, it is certain that this was the bullet which brought her down.

The Hurricane's very substantial remains were recovered in 1991 and, following temporary display at Archangel in September that year as part of the 'Dervish 91' celebrations to mark the 50th anniversary of the arrival of PQ16, they were brought to the UK by Sussex-based Jim Pearce before being purchased by Wanaka-based aviation enthusiast, Sir Tim Wallis, in 1992. Sir Tim formed a joint venture between his Alpine Fighter Collection and Tony Ditheridge of AJD Engineering to be called Hawker Restorations Ltd (HRL) which undertook the rebuilding of the fuselage while the wings were sub-contracted to Airframe Assemblies at Sandown on the Isle of Wight.

Air New Zealand Engineering Services (ANZES) reached agreement with Sir Tim Wallis to participate in the restorations project from their base in Christchurch NZ and the rebuild programme progressed under their stringent ANZES Quality Management System. The original Hurricane Type Data had been located and agreement was made to not deviate from these design specifications and full engineering design support was provided by Air New Zealand Engineering's Technical Services.

The Hawker Hurricane's Warren girder form of tube-framed fuselage construction is – though essentially simple – quite sophisticated and demands special tooling. Every mechanical joint requires special equipment to roll the 50 tonnes tensile steel. Tony Ditheridge gained access to the original equipment needed to form the 12-sided steel tube stock used in the wing centre section, fin and tailplane spars. ANZES salvaged many parts from the original airframe which were then shipped to HRL for restoration and inclusion in the rebuilt structure. Having thoroughly researched the history of this particular airframe it was decided to restore it as P3351 – making it the only airworthy Hurricane which had fought in the Battle of France, although the airframe still retains its Mk IIA configuration and is powered by a post-war Merlin 35 (as fitted to the Boulton Paul Balliol) which is also the engine of choice of the RAF's Battle of Britain Memorial Flight.

Late in 1995 HRL returned the restored fuselage and empennage, centre section and wings to New Zealand for completion by ANZES. Many enthusiastic individuals and organisations contributed to P3351's completion. The radiator core was made by Replicore in Whangarei NZ and the casing and assembly by Auto Restorations in Christchurch NZ. The propeller hub was secured by the Alpine Fighter Collection, the complex wooden propeller blades were made by Hoffman of Germany, and Dowty Rotol approved Skycraft Ltd in the United Kingdom to make the remainder of the parts and to overhaul and test the completed propeller. The Croydon Aircraft Company in Mandeville NZ applied the fabric fuselage covering at ANZES. The outer wings were re-attached in early 1998 and by December 1998 P3351 was ready for painting. In late 1999 the freshly restored Merlin 35 was started up at Christchurch Airport and in early January 2000, P3351 was ready to fly, the civil registration ZK-TPL bearing testimony to its codes when serving with No. 73 Sqdn – although the paint scheme chosen only replicated the single 'K' individual aircraft letter and large red/white/blue rudder markings which were applied in France to counter attack by French forces. The under-surfaces were finished with one wing black and the other silver as worn during the first part of 1940.

The first post-restoration flight took place on 12 January 2000 with P3351 taking pride of place in Sir Tim Wallis's collection at Wanaka, flying at the prestigious 'Warbirds Over Wanaka' displays, but following Sir Tim's decision to close down his collection the Hurricane was advertised for sale, finally finding a fitting new home in France and leaving New Zealand by ship on 10 February 2013. It was assembled at Dijon-Darois by Bruno Ducreux's Aero Restauration Service for new owner Jan Frisco Roozen who bases it, now registered as F-AZXR, at Cannes-Mandelieu, France, and it has made appearances in the UK at the 'Flying Legends' air displays at Duxford in both July 2013 and 2014.

Stop press: P3351 suffered a landing accident on Sunday 24 May 2015 and will be out of action for at least the whole of 2015.

P3554
Hawker Hurricane Mk I

Tony Dyer/Air Defence Collection, Andover Hants, UK

P3554 was built as a Mk I at Langley by Hawker Aircraft Ltd as part of a batch of 500 Hurricanes ordered against Contract No. 962371/38. The aircraft bore serials between P3265-P3984, with P3554 falling into the serial block (P3515-3554). Powered by a 1,280 hp Merlin III (No.151637) it was allocated to No. 20 MU at Aston Down, Glos, on 11 May 1940 and following preparation for service use it then went to Manston on 20 May 1940 before being issued to No. 32 Sqdn at Biggin Hill two days later on 22 May. On 29 May P3554 was involved in a landing accident at Wittering which resulted in damage to the engine and airframe. A replacement engine was supplied by Rolls-Royce at Hucknall and was fitted by No. 4 MU (based at Hanworth). The aircraft re-flew after repairs on 1 July 1940 and later the same day it was flown to No. 5 MU at Kemble.

The Air Ministry Movement Card (Form 78) for P3554 states that it joined No. 56 Sqdn at North Weald on 11 July 1940, but this is believed to be an error (the first of a few, hardly surprising given the tumultuous times and often paperwork would catch up slowly and incorrectly). In fact P3554 had been shot down on 10 July 1940 (the first of two occasions in which it would be downed during the Battle of Britain) when it was hit in the engine during combat with a group of Bf 110s over a convoy off Dungeness, Kent. One Bf 110 was shot down near Folkestone by its pilot, Flt/Lt E J 'Jumbo' Gracie, and was almost certainly an aircraft from 8./ZG 26. The Merlin III seized and P3554 was damaged in the ensuing crash-landing at Manston but it was deemed repairable.

Whilst being flown by pilots from No. 56 Sqdn, P3554 claimed a number of German aircraft:

10 July 1940 – as above. The Bf 110 in question was almost certainly an aircraft of 8./ZG 26.

20 July 1940 – One Junkers Ju 88 shot down at Cockett Wick Farm, Burnham, Essex, by F/O P S Weaver (shared with E J Gracie and A G Page of No. 56 Sqn) with all four crew captured.

25 July 1940 – One Junkers Ju 87 'Stuka' shot down off Folkestone by P/O A G Page. This was an aircraft of 6./StG1 with Uffz Viktor Schroeder and Gefr Herbert Lipsius both killed.

29 July 1940 – One Messerschmitt Bf 109 shot down ten miles east of Dover by F/O P S Weaver.

12 August 1940 – One Dornier Do 17 shot down by F/O P S Weaver ten miles north of Margate.

P3554's Form 78 suggests that it went to No. 13 MU at Henlow, Beds, on 13 August followed by No. 27 MU at Shawbury, Salop, on 21 August 1940. It is not certain if these were repairs or mods carried out by each MU on-site rather than at their home base. Given the known number of 'kills' it would suggest that the aircraft was probably dispatched to Henlow (a major Hurricane repair centre) for essential work to be carried out and then on to Shawbury (a storage facility). The aircraft was re-allocated to No. 213 Sqdn in September 1940, probably joining the squadron at Tangmere as it moved up from Exeter.

Although the Form 78 card does not mention No. 607 Sqdn, it is possible that the Tangmere-based squadrons did mix aircraft, especially since it was eventually lost when flying with No. 607 Sqdn. On 5 October 1940, whilst flying with No. 607 (County of Durham) Squadron, P3554 was shot down (for the second and final time) during combat over Swanage, Dorset, by a Messerschmitt Bf 109E of 1/JG2. The pilot, P/O D Evans, bailed out safely and the Hurricane crashed at Woodhorn Farm, Aldingbourne, at 1400 hours.

The crash site was fully excavated by the Wealden Aviation Archaeological Group in September 1979 and the intact Merlin III was recovered together with the control column and the instrument panel. Parts from P3554, including the brass constructor's plate, were obtained by Tony Dyer

The cockpit section of P3554 in Tony Dyer's workshop in February 2010. (*Tony Dyer*)

and have been incorporated into a static restoration which has been assembled from parts of well over 65 different Hurricanes. The project started in 1980 when Tony acquired a Hurricane tailwheel from a blanket trolley used at Witney, Oxfordshire, and which had originated from the disused aerodrome nearby. This led to archaeological digs at CRU dumps – which yielded many stainless steel parts – and the acquisition of several Hurricane canopies which had been used as cloches for strawberry plants near North Weald!

As the project grew Tony exchanged potentially airworthy parts and obtained scrap components from the original rebuilds of RCAF 5589 (G-HURR), Z7015, LF363 and PZ865 – including the original wooden 'Dog House'

cockpit structure from PZ865 which still shows traces of its blue and gold civilian colour scheme as G-AMAU. Countless parts came from aircraft shot down in the Battle of Britain – all of which are documented. The ultimate aim is to have a complete taxyable Hurricane which, although not airworthy, will consist of 85% or more original Hurricane parts, making it as much a memorial as a 'phoenix survivor'. In 2004, P3554 was named after Tony's daughters 'Jessamy'.

P3708
Hawker Hurricane Mk I

Norfolk and Suffolk Aviation Museum, Flixton, Suffolk, UK

P3708 was built as a Mk I at Langley by Hawker Aircraft Ltd as part of a batch of 500 Hurricanes ordered against Contract No. 962371/38. The aircraft bore serials between P3265-P3984, with P3708 falling into the serial block (P3700-3709). Powered by a 1,280 hp Merlin III (No. 144612) it was allocated to No. 15 MU at Wroughton, Wilts, on 22 May 1940 and taken on charge on 31 May, being designated as a reserve aircraft.

It was allocated to No. 257 Sqdn on 11 June; the squadron had been reformed at Hendon on 17 May and was initially equipped with Spitfires but these were soon replaced by Hurricanes and the squadron moved to Northolt on 4 July. Its first combat was on 9 July when a section of three Hurricanes was scrambled and Sgt Forward fired at a Dornier Do 17 with inconclusive results.

P3708 was coded DT-E with No. 257 Sqdn and ranged over the English Channel from its base at Northolt, being involved in a particularly big battle over the Isle of Wight on 8 August in which they lost three aircraft and their pilots but P/O Gundry in P3708 claimed one Bf 109 destroyed and one damaged. P3708 survived until Sunday 18 August – when the Luftwaffe carried out raids on many Fighter Command bases. By this time No. 257 Sqdn had been transferred to Debden in Essex, from where it was mainly engaged in

The rear fuselage frame of P3708, partially assembled with some wooden components, at the Norfolk and Suffolk Aviation Museum seen here in April 2013; the canopy in the foreground is from LF363 after its accident at RAF Wittering. *(Geoff Rayner)*

convoy patrols but also got tangled up with fighting over the Thames Estuary. On that particular day it was flown no less than six times by the same pilot – Sgt Alex Girdwood. Starting in the early morning at 0520 hours with a 30-minute transfer flight from Debden to Martlesham Heath, it was followed by three stints of convoy patrol, totalling four hours. At 1500 hours, after a 45-minute rest, they were scrambled, but without contact with the Luftwaffe, which lasted 30 minutes. Finally the last flight of the day lasted about an hour, from 1700 hours until the time when Sgt Girdwood parachuted gently down on to Foulness Island, off the coast of Essex, whilst P3708 dived into the ground nearby at Nazewick Farm, to be totally buried in the soft ground by the force of the impact.

The following account is taken from Sgt Girdwood's combat report:

'I was Red 3. While following Red Leader at a height of about 12,000ft, we came upon a section of He 111s flying in a big bomber formation. Red 1 (Flt/Lt Beresford) made an astern attack on one of the He 111s. When he broke off firing, I closed in and fired until it started to smoke and go down. As I broke away bullets entered my cockpit which exploded and caught fire. After a struggle I managed to bail out and as I fell I succeeded in pulling the ripcord and untwisting the lines which wound round my legs. A toe of my right foot was fractured by a bolt, which was forced into it by a bullet. I received some burns and bruises. Subsequently I found that the He 111 had crashed near Foulness just beside my own plane. Two of the wounded German airmen were brought to the same hospital at Foulness as myself.'

The remains of P3708 lay buried where it had crashed until the site was investigated by members of the East Anglian Aircraft Research Group in 1990. Local eyewitnesses suggested that the Hurricane had disappeared into the ground leaving just a crater. This was never filled in, just ploughed around until over the years it faded to level ground. Once the impact point was established, the first signs showed the wreckage to be badly corroded, having been subjected to intense heat as it burnt underground. The wing remains and one undercarriage leg were amongst this. At about five feet below the surface it was obvious that the burning hadn't reached any further down. Wooden formers, stringers and pieces of the fabric covering were seen to be poking out of the soil.

Partial wing section from LF363 which will be utilised in the restoration of P3708. *(Geoff Rayner)*

What was left to find was basically most of the aircraft, albeit totally smashed. The tail fin, with fin flash; large amounts of fabric; tailwheel leg, tyre, and inner tube; oxygen and compressed air bottles; the other main undercarriage leg, both mainwheel tyres and inner tubes; hydraulic cylinder for the undercarriage and flaps; many feet of the steel tube fuselage, joints, spars and frames; the radio; seat armour, and seat with the Sutton seat harness still wrapped around it all came to light as they delved into the mud. From the cockpit, the flap, undercarriage and throttle levers; control column; rudder pedals and adjustment slide; instrument panel, the blind-flying panel folded around the spade grip, the firing button set to 'fire'; Ki-gas primer pump; and cockpit breakout door were all recovered. One of the stranger items discovered was the gunsight which had one of the pilot's gloves wrapped around it. Did Girdwood, when injured, take off his glove to feel his foot? More cockpit items included the Form 700 (signed by Flt/Lt Beresford), four bullet-holed maps of southern England, the first aid kit, and Girdwood's gas mask.

A significant amount of fuselage structure has been transferred to the Norfolk and Suffolk Aviation Museum at Flixton, Suffolk, where it is being cleaned, straightened and slowly reassembled under the guidance of Geoff Rayner who was present at the 1990 recovery and who was also instrumental in the recovery of the RAF Museum's P3175 (qv) in the early 1970s.

P3717/DR348
Hawker Hurricane Mk I/IIA

Hugh Taylor/Hawker Hurricane Ltd, Turweston, Northants, UK

P3717 was built as a Mk I at Brooklands by Hawker Aircraft Ltd as part of a batch of 500 Hurricanes ordered against Contract No. 962371/38. The aircraft bore serials between P3265-P3984, with P3717 falling into the serial block (P3710-3739). Powered by a 1,280 hp Merlin III (No. 144660) it was allocated to No. 19 MU at St Athan, South Wales, on 13 May 1940 and taken on charge on 3 June, being designated as a reserve aircraft.

Its first unit was No. 238 Sqdn, to which it was assigned on 18 June, and which was based at Middle Wallop as part of 10 Group. It had re-formed at Tangmere on 12 May, initially equipped with Spitfires, and was operational under the command of S/Ldr C E J Baines by 2 July. Whether it ever reached this unit is doubtful as two days later it was returned to No. 19 MU and then re-issued to No. 253 Sqdn in early July. During May this squadron had been based at Kenley in Surrey for ferrying duties. The squadron pilots delivered replacement Hurricanes to the squadrons fighting in France and for a three-week period A Flight were detached to Poix, where despite claiming 11 e/a destroyed, they were themselves decimated. Following this severe pounding No. 253 had withdrawn to Kirton-in-Lindsey on 24 May to regroup, with detachments at Ringway and Coleby Grange.

By the end of July the Battle of Britain was in full swing and in anticipation of the inevitable requirement 'down south', No. 253 were brought up to operational status, moving from Kirton-in-Lindsey to Turnhouse on 21 July, then to Prestwick on 23 August and finally back into the thick of things on 29 August when the squadron returned to Kenley, one of the main 11 Group sector stations. Replacing an exhausted No. 615 Sqdn, the 18 Hurricanes (the full complement should have been 26) of No. 253 landed at Kenley shortly after lunch on 29 August. Commanded by S/Ldr Harold Starr, No. 253 was unusual in that the flying personnel included another senior pilot of the same rank, 32-year-old S/Ldr Tom Gleave.

The two men were close friends with Gleave commanding A Flight and effectively sharing command of the squadron.

Their introduction to the Battle of Britain came very quickly when at 1600 hours with the Hurricanes barely refuelled, Gleave and his flight were scrambled to patrol the airfield, the standing patrol proving uneventful. It would appear that P3717 had been allocated to B Flight and it was being flown by P/O W M C Samolinski, when on the following morning (Friday 30 August), it was one of 13 aircraft participating in a squadron scramble at 1050 hours when the squadron was ordered to patrol over Maidstone, ready to face any threat to its Kenley base.

Luftwaffe raids had started shortly after dawn with a series of probing attacks that never reached their targets, the RAF airfields in the southeast. However from 1000 hours Albert Kesselring's Luftflotte 2, based in Holland, Belgium and northeastern France, launched three main attacks each a half hour apart, which by 1130 hours had been fragmented all over Kent and Surrey, with no fewer than 48 Observer Corps posts reporting air activity overhead.

When no attack on Kenley materialised, No. 253 were vectored towards Brighton where they joined Hurricanes of No. 43 Sqdn from Tangmere and Spitfires from No. 222 Sqdn based at Hornchurch. As they headed southwest, one of the A Flight sections led by Tom Gleave and accompanied by F/Lt George Brown and P/O C D Francis lost touch with the main formation. They ran into a large formation of Bf 109s and although Gleave shot down three and damaged another, in what proved to be a short but spectacular career at Kenley (he was himself shot down and badly burned the following day), both Brown and Francis (L1965) were shot down, Brown being wounded but Francis killed. (A major recovery of L1965 was undertaken by Steve Vizard in 1981 and P/O Francis was subsequently buried at Brookwood Military Cemetery on 29 September that year.)

Seen here at Milden in August 2014, P3717 left by road in February 2015 for final checks and flight tests to be performed at Turweston, Northamptonshire. (*Gordon Riley*)

The rest of the squadron, led by Starr in P2960, ran into the scattered formations of He 111s of KG 1, briefed to attack Farnborough, and Bf 110s of ZG 2. Most of the squadron appear to have joined other Hurricanes from Nos 85 and 79 Sqdns in attacking the bombers, P/O Greenwood shooting down one of the KG 1 Heinkels. A dogfight between elements of No. 253 and aircraft of ZG 2 broke out over Redhill in Surrey and P3717, flown by Samolinski, was involved in this with Samolinski claiming and subsequently credited with the destruction of a Bf 110 in this action. F/Lt W P Cambridge dispatched a Bf 110 (Wk Nr 3315) of 5/ZG 2, which is the only German aircraft whose loss in this action can be positively attributed to No. 253 Sqdn, so it seems that Samolinski's 'kill' may have made it home after all.

P3717 made it back to Kenley but not before one of the Bf 110s had damaged it to such an extent that it had to be sent to No. 13 MU at Henlow, Beds, a major Hurricane repair facility, for significant repairs the following day. The repairs were quickly carried out – No. 13 MU holding the record for changing a pair of Hurricane wings – and it was allocated to No. 48 MU at Hawarden near Chester on 3 September, arriving on the 10th before being allocated to No. 257 Sqdn two days later on 12 September, the same day on which F/Lt 'Bob' Stanford Tuck took over command of the unit. Although based at Debden the squadron was also operating from Castle Camps and Martlesham Heath at this time with aircraft being ferried from base to base as the need arose. P3717 made its first 'op' with the unit, a patrol from Martlesham Heath over Chelmsford in the hands of P/O North, at 1550 hours on Wednesday 18 September. The following day the squadron carried out a convoy patrol and P3717 was flown by P/O Capon, taking off at 1320 hours and returning at 1440 hours, the same pilot flying it on another convoy patrol later that afternoon. Friday 20 September saw P/O Chelmecki take part in an X-raid patrol in the morning and flying to Debden with other aircraft that afternoon before returning to Martlesham Heath in the early evening. The Saturday morning saw Chelmecki and P3717 take off for an X-raid patrol which was swiftly cancelled, the squadron continuing on to Debden where they remained for the day, returning to Martlesham Heath after another X-raid patrol between 1800 hours and 1915 hours.

There was no flying on Sunday 22 September due to bad weather but precisely what happened to P3717 on 23 September is not clear. P/O Chelmecki was posted away to No. 17 Sqdn at North Weald that day and 12 Hurricanes under the command of F/Lt Stanford Tuck flew to Castle Camps at 0705 hours, arriving 25 minutes later. Unfortunately the squadron ORB does not list all of their serials and P3717 is not amongst those identified. At 0920 hours the aircraft scrambled to join others from Nos 17 and 73 Sqdns over Debden and were then ordered to patrol over Southend and Gravesend at 20,000 feet. Having been warned of approaching enemy aircraft coming in from the east at 5,000 feet the aircraft lost height but when passing through 13,000 feet they were ordered to climb back up to 'Angels 20'. At that very moment they were attacked by a large group of single-engined fighters – probably all Bf 109s although it was reported at the time that they were both Bf 109s and He 113s (which was a propaganda type based on the He 100D-1 and which never actually existed). Tuck ordered the squadron to break up and engage, managing to shoot down a Bf 109 himself, all pilots returning safely apart from Sgt Aslin who bailed out and landed near Detling.

P3717 is not mentioned but may well have taken part in this action – according to its Form 78 it suffered FBO(2) damage (Flying Battle – Operations) on that date but the squadron ORB shows that the Martlesham Heath CO, Wg/Cdr A D Farquhar, DFC, flew it on a non-operational local flight lasting 45 minutes in the afternoon of 26 September. Whatever happened to it resulted in it needing repairs and it was dispatched to de Havilland – part of the Hurricane Repair Organisation – on 28 September suffering from Cat B damage (beyond repair on site). Exactly one month later, on 28 October, it arrived at the storage unit at No. 22 MU, Silloth in Cumbria, having been allocated there on 21 October.

It remained stored until 20 January 1941 when it was assigned to No. 43 Sqdn, 'The Fighting Cocks', who were being rested and based at Drem, Scotland, with a detachment at Crail, the CO being S/Ldr T F D Morgan. There was little activity to report and P3717 led a relatively uneventful life before being transferred into the hands of the trainee fighter pilots of No. 55 OTU at Aston Down, Gloucestershire, on 24 April – although a note on its Movements Card that it was allocated to Air Service Training Ltd, a major repair and overhaul contractor, on the very same day is somewhat puzzling. Wherever it went to, it was posted to No. 8 Service Flying Training School (SFTS), Montrose, Scotland on 12 June 1941 but almost immediately dispatched to Rolls-Royce at Hucknall on 28 June where it was converted to Mk IIA standard by the installation of a Merlin XX and other modifications to become DR348. As with P3351/DR393, the venerable Mk I had been selected as one of the batch of 40 Hurricanes being upgraded for dispatch to Russia and it took a similar route. It was sent to No. 22 MU at Silloth on 4 October and was probably flown south to Cardiff to arrive at the Packing Unit of No. 52 MU on 10 October, being allocated to 'Russia' the next day.

Details of its actual dispatch to and arrival in Russia are not known but it seems as though it was one of the first to arrive in the winter of 1941-42. Service details are also not known at present but its crashed remains were recovered and brought back to the UK by Jim Pearce around 1991 and acquired by Steve Milnthorpe who started a static rebuild to a very high standard at his home in Hinckley, Leicestershire. The fuselage structure was very nearly complete when Steve sold the project to Tony Ditheridge of Hawker Restorations Ltd who decided to bring it up to full airworthy condition.

The project was subsequently sold to Hugh Taylor, trading under the name of Hawker Hurricane Ltd, and was registered as G-HITT on 19 December 2008. Although structurally restored to Mk II configuration the aircraft has been rebuilt in its original markings as P3717/SW-P and restoration to flying condition was completed at Milden, Suffolk, before it was taken by road to Turweston, Northants, on 10 February 2015 for final preparation and flight testing. At the time of writing (July 2015) this aircraft was available for sale.

This photo from June 2013 gives an idea of the complex structure of the Hurricane. *(Darren Harbar Photography)*

R4118
Hawker Hurricane Mk I

Peter & Polly Vacher, Kidlington, Oxfordshire, UK

Peter Vacher first set eyes on R4118 in March 1982 when he and a friend, John Fasal, were travelling through India searching for historic Rolls-Royce motor cars. During a visit to Banaras Hindu University the pair stumbled across two derelict aircraft, one of which Peter assumed to be a Spitfire. Eleven years later Peter showed a photograph of the aircraft to his wife's flying instructor – Pete Thorn, once a pilot with

the RAF Battle of Britain Memorial Flight – who immediately pointed out that the 'Spitfire' was in fact a Hurricane. Having personally restored ten vintage cars, including four Rolls-Royces, Peter eventually decided to attempt to acquire the mystery Hurricane and have it restored to fly and to that end arrived in Banaras – now known as Varanasi – on 5 January 1996. The story of how Peter managed to buy the Hurricane

Newly-restored R4118 banks towards the camera in October 2009. *(Darren Harbar Photography)*

and return it to England is a book in itself, *Hurricane R4118* written by Peter and published by Grub Street. Suffice it to say that the following account summarises the history of this Battle of Britain veteran but anyone seeking the full story can read it in Peter's own words.

R4118 was built as a Mk I at Brockworth by the Gloster Aircraft Company Ltd (a subsidiary of Hawker Aircraft Ltd) as part of a batch of 100 Hurricanes ordered against Contract No. 19773/39. The aircraft bore serials between R4074-R4232, with R4118 forming part of the first block (R4074-4123). Powered by a 1,280 hp Merlin III (engine number 24927…incredibly this engine was still installed in the airframe when found) it would have been flown from Brockworth to No. 22 MU at Silloth, Cumbria, between 18-23 July 1940. It joined its first unit, No. 605 (County of Warwick) Sqdn, RAuxAF, at Drem, Scotland, on 17 August, where the unit was 'resting' following a period of intense activity – including the loss of its CO, S/Ldr Perry – whilst covering the BEF withdrawal from France from a temporary base at Hawkinge during May. The squadron flew south to Croydon, re-joining 11 Group, on 7 September and R4118 was flown by P/O (later W/Cdr, DSO, DFC and Bar) C F 'Bunny' Currant – who dropped in to Abingdon to refuel en route. 'Bunny' was to provide many details and stories about R4118 to Peter Vacher during the restoration of 'his' old Hurricane; he died in March 2006 at the age of 95.

Once the squadron had arrived at Croydon it was thrown into the thick of the Battle of Britain, R4118 being flown by the CO, S/Ldr Walter Churchill, on 9 September when F/Lt Archie McKellar, leading B Flight, picked off three He 111s in a single attack. Churchill had earlier led his section in to draw off the fighter escort and had his knee grazed by a bullet – sending him spinning out of formation. Churchill was injured by a bullet in his arm two days later on 11 September and R4118 was then turned over to P/O Jock Muirhead, who on 24 September shared a Do 215 with P/O Glowacki – who did not return and was posted as missing. Muirhead himself was killed in action on 15 October, on which date R4118 was air-tested by P/O Alec Scott and, starting on 26 September, it became the regular mount of P/O J A 'Archie' Milne, a Scots Canadian who had volunteered for the RAF in May 1939 and joined No. 605 Sqdn in August 1940. The next day, 27 September, 'Archie' downed a Bf 110 in R4118. Other pilots who flew R4118 at

the time include P/O (later W/Cdr, DFC) Bob Foster who damaged a Ju 88 on 28 September and shared another on 1 October. Bob was another of the pilots who were reunited with their old Hurricane during the restoration process and wrote the foreword to Peter Vacher's book; he died on 30 July 2014 aged 94.

P/O (later W/Cdr, DFC) Alec Ingle flew R4118 just once but it was his logbook entry for that flight which confirmed the individual squadron code letter which it carried. Alex had written 'W' alongside R4118 – confirming the full code as UP-W – letters which now grace the restored Hurricane once more. Another ace to fly R4118 was none other than P/O (later Gp/Capt, DFC) Peter Thompson who – when serving as commanding officer of Biggin Hill in 1957 – managed to secure the RAF's last airworthy Hurricane, LF363 (qv) as the very first aircraft of what developed into the RAF Battle of Britain Memorial Flight.

R4118's luck ran out on 2 October when 12 Hurricanes took off from Croydon at 1411 hours to patrol Kenley and Biggin Hill at 20,000 feet (Angels 20), a dogfight with a group of Bf 109s breaking out to the east of Tonbridge at 22,000 feet. Derek Forde, flying R4118 as Yellow 1, sustained Cat 2 damage (beyond repair on site). In less than two months it had flown 49 sorties with 11 different pilots and had been directly or partially responsible for the destruction of five enemy aircraft.

It was dispatched to the Service Aircraft Section (SAS) of the Austin Motor Company at Longbridge, Birmingham, on 23 October, Austin being part of the Hurricane Repair Organisation and R4118 being one of 13 Hurricanes it repaired that year. Austin also built 300 Hurricane IIBs virtually all of which were shipped to Russia, one of which survives (AP740 qv). R4118 was completed by 17 December when it was allocated to No. 18 MU at Dumfries, Scotland, where it was stored until issued to No. 111 Sqdn on 18 January. The squadron was 'resting' at Aberdeen (Dyce) and R4118 was assigned to A Flight and ferried to the detached base at Montrose on 3 February by the squadron commander, S/Ldr A J Biggar. No. 111 was acting as a training unit at the time and no less than 11 pilots flew it over the next eight weeks – with the aircraft itself making up to seven sorties in a single day. In service with No. 111 the aircraft was coded JU-J and Peter Vacher tracked down the family of one of its pilots, another Canadian 'Skid' Hanes, who were able

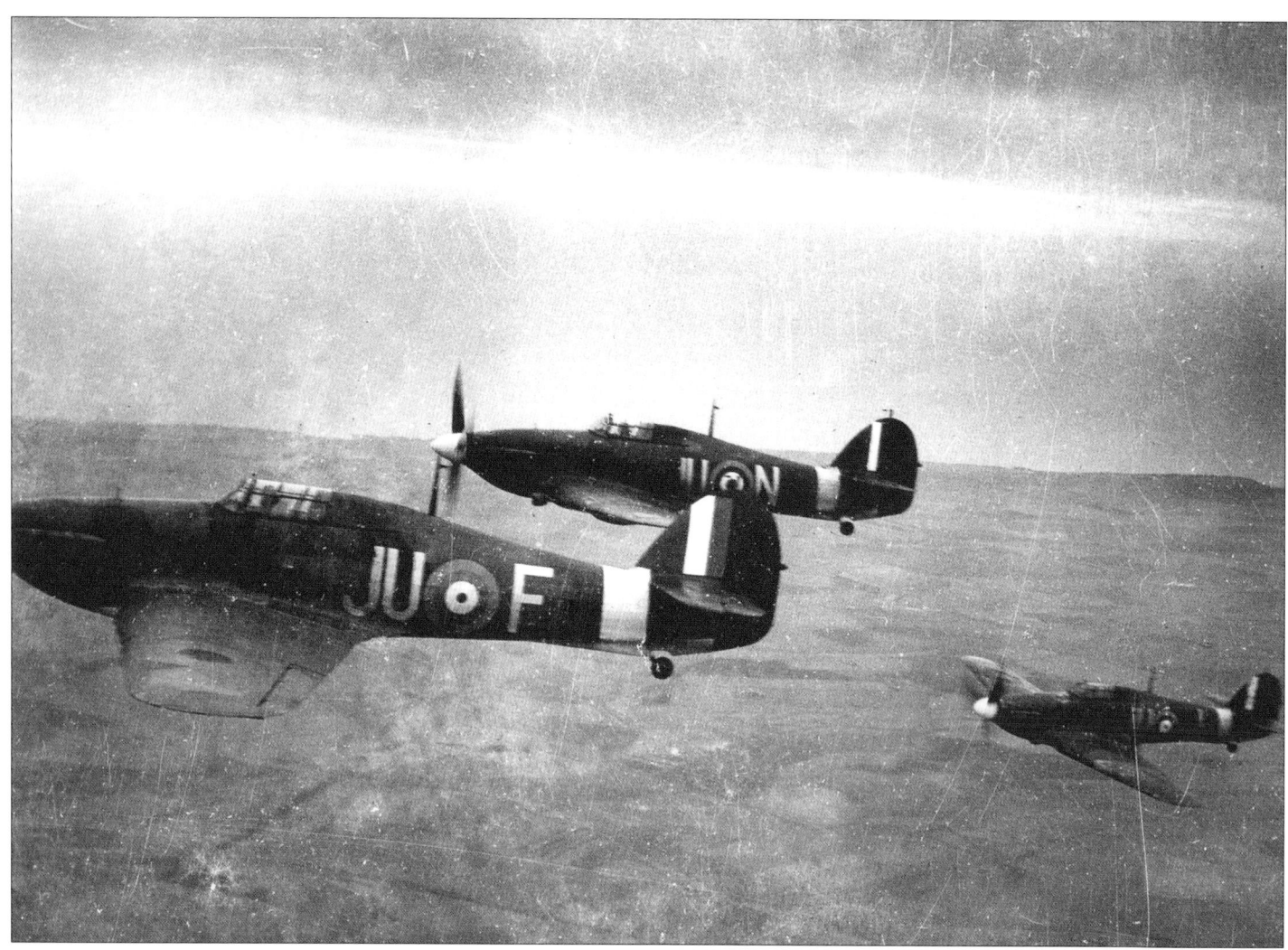

R4118 / JU-J at rear serving with A Flight of No. 111 Sqdn based at Montrose, Ayrshire, on 9 March 1941; Sgt John Stein is at the controls. (*F/Lt Peter Simpson DFC via Peter Vacher*)

to provide an air-to-air photograph of R4118 flying from Montrose on 9 March 1941. Alongside its training role the squadron took part in sorties against raids mounted from German bases in Norway, R4118 participating in one on 24 March 1941 flown by Sgt Seaman.

On 26 April 1941 R4118 was posted to join No. 59 OTU at Crosby-on-Eden, Cumbria, oddly enough under the command of Alec Ingle who had flown it twice during the Battle of Britain with No. 605 Sqdn. It survived the hazardous life of an advanced training aircraft unscathed until 7 October when a New Zealander, Sgt (later F/Lt) F J M Palmer hit a lorry at the end of his landing run at Longtown, Cumbria, which was a satellite airfield. Peter

Vacher contacted Palmer in Auckland and he recounted how the wind had changed direction causing the runway to be switched but that a contractor's vehicle somehow got onto the active runway.

The damage was sufficient for R4118 to be dispatched to Taylorcraft at Rearsby, Leicestershire, a major contractor within the Hurricane Repair Organisation which repaired 64 Hurricanes during 1941 alone, and when the airframe was being surveyed prior to restoration a Taylorcraft inspection stamp was found on the rudder. It was repaired and awaiting collection (RAAA) on 12 December and by 22 December had been allocated to No. 44 MU at Edzell, Angus, Scotland, where it was stored but during a test flight on 23 February

1942 it swung on landing and was damaged when it hit a snow bank. The accident was put down to insufficient brake pressure having built up in the pneumatic system but the damage was repaired on site (ROS) by a civilian contractor starting on 1 March and the Hurricane was back with the MU on 1 April 1942.

Its next unit was No. 56 OTU which was based at Tealing, north of Dundee, Scotland, to which it was allocated on 24 May and where it probably served mainly on air gunnery training – possibly even acting as a target tug as well as firing live ammunition at towed drogue targets. It survived unscathed for a further 11 months until it was allocated to David Rosenfield Ltd, part of the Hurricane Repair Organisation, which received it at Barton, Manchester, on 5 April 1943. During the overhaul / repair the company placed a stamped aluminium plate over the top of the original Hawker Aircraft Ltd brass constructors' plate and both were

still in place in the cockpit when the aircraft was recovered from India, confirming the identity beyond question as R4118. Oddly enough the plates on both wings indicate that they were manufactured by Canadian Car and Foundry (CCF) at Fort William and rebuilt or repaired in Derby in the workshops of the London, Midland & Scottish Railway Company; whether they were fitted by David Rosenfield or by Taylorcraft cannot be established. Other components came from a variety of subcontractors.

The repaired and rebuilt R4118 was awaiting collection from Barton on 28 May 1943 and despatched to No. 5 MU at Kemble, Wilts, on 16 June as one of a batch of 203 Hurricanes received that month which were to be overhauled and sent to Air Command, South East Asia (ACSEA) as training aircraft for Indian pilots. The Japanese army had invaded Burma and was advancing towards India so the plan was to boost pilot numbers in the region by sending Hurricanes as

R4118 under restoration at Hawker Restorations Ltd, Milden, Suffolk. *(Geoff Rayner)*

training aircraft. On 11 November it was sent to the Packing Unit of No. 52 MU at Cardiff where it was crated and by 12 December it was on board the cargo ship the SS *Singkep*, a 6,607-ton Dutch merchantman built in 1924. Following a perilous journey at just 12 knots R4118 was received by the Aircraft Erection Unit at Santa Cruz, Bombay (Mumbai), India, between 6–12 February 1944 and, being a relatively ancient Mk I, remained in its packing crate and, following an order of July 1944, was 'converted to ground instructional' on 4 October, being finally struck off charge on 1 January 1947.

How and when it was moved from Santa Cruz to Banaras Hindu University – a distance of approximately 1,500 km – to be utilised as an instructional aid is not recorded but move it certainly did. In the event the aircraft was simply emptied from its crate and left in the open until Peter Vacher was lucky enough to stumble upon it some 40-odd years later.

After tortuous negotiations the aircraft finally returned to the UK in July 2001 and having been removed from its shipping container it was reunited with several of its former pilots at the Oxfordshire home of Peter and Polly Vacher. The gathering also included the families of many pilots as well as test pilot, Duncan Simpson, who had flown PZ865 when owned by Hawker Siddeley, and the Strathallan Collection's example, G-AWLW (now sadly destroyed in a hangar fire. R4118 was registered with the civil registration G-HUPW on 21 August 2001. The subsequent stripping of the airframe was carried out in Peter's own workshop with new and repaired parts being provided by Hawker Restorations Ltd. Much preparation and bead-blasting was carried out in Oxfordshire and as many original components

and fittings as possible were renovated but – as with all airworthy Hurricane restorations – the steel tubing was remanufactured using modern equivalents. The wings were rebuilt in Bob Cunningham's specialist workshop in Bournemouth and the stripped fuselage was shipped to Hawker Restorations in Suffolk in January 2002 whilst the Merlin III was dispatched to Maurice Hammond, also in Suffolk. Many detail components and sub-assemblies were provided by Guy Black and a Griffon engine – purchased from the university at the same time as the Hurricane – was exchanged for a Rotol propeller hub with Stephen Grey of The Fighter Collection, the new blades being made by Hoffman in Germany and the whole propeller was assembled by Mike Barnett of Skycraft Services Ltd – Andrew Wood of P & A Wood coming up with a CSU.

The aircraft was assembled in the Suffolk workshops of Hawker Restorations Ltd, the paint scheme applied by Clive Denney of Vintage Fabrics and the aircraft finally taken by road to Cambridge Airport where Terry Holloway of Marshalls had offered hangarage and flight test facilities. The great day finally came on 23 December 2004 when, despite a wind gusting to 25 kts, Pete Kynsey lifted the Hurricane off the ground on her first flight since 1943. Restored in her original markings as carried in service with No. 605 Sqdn, R4118 is the only airworthy Hurricane which served in the Battle of Britain – let alone scored victories in it – and is probably the most authentic as it is still powered by its original Merlin III and carries its original (de-activated) Browning .303 machine guns, in addition to a host of internal fittings such as a TR9 radio and IFF equipment. It has now been put up for sale.

This is how R4118 looked at Banaras during 1996; it had deteriorated badly since Peter Vacher first saw it in 1982. *(Peter Vacher)*

V7350
Hawker Hurricane Mk I

Romney Marsh Wartime Collection, Brenzett, Kent, UK

V7350 was built by Hawker Aircraft Ltd as part of a batch of 691 Hurricanes ordered against Contract No. 62305/39 and which bore serials in the range V7200-V8127, of which V7350 fell into the serial block V7326-7360. Production was split between Hawker's factories at Kingston, Brooklands and Langley and V7350, powered by a Merlin III, was allocated to No. 48 MU on 25 July 1940, arriving at Hawarden, near Chester, on 1 August where it was prepared for service and issued to Peter Townsend's No. 85 Sqdn on 26 August.

The squadron had moved from its home at Debden in Essex to Croydon, south of London, to relieve No. 111 Sqdn on 19 August and on 29 August V7350 was amongst 12 Hurricanes which took off at 1520 hours with orders to patrol Hawkinge at 15,000 feet – 'Angels One Five'. It was being flown by one of the squadron's more experienced pilots, Sgt

The substantially complete cockpit section from V7350 on display at Brenzett in October 2010. *(Tony Dyer)*

Frank Walker-Smith. As the aircraft were climbing through 7,000 feet the pilots spotted 18 German bombers which were being escorted by about 30 fighters and as they attempted to intercept them more joined the party – something in the region of 300 aircraft of all types appearing in the sky above Beachy Head and Hastings.

Townsend was leading the squadron to a point from where they could attack out of the sun when at 1628 hours V7350 was struck by gunfire as Walker-Smith climbed through 14,000 feet over Hawkhurst. Walker-Smith was hit in his right foot and, as he dived away, he realised that the Hurricane had lost both throttle and rudder controls. He bailed out of the stricken Hurricane at around 1,600 feet and floated down to safety as V7350 crashed into soft ground near the River Dudwell at Underwood Farm near Etchingham, Kent.

Walker-Smith returned to flying duty but was killed, along with F/Lt 'Sammy' Allard and P/O 'Ace' Hodgson, in the crash of a Douglas Havoc, BJ500, at Wimbish, Essex, in March 1941. All three are buried in the cemetery at Saffron Walden, Essex. His great-nephew, S/Ldr Graham Duff, served for three years as 'Red 8' with the Red Arrows having joined the team in 2007.

As for V7350, the surface wreckage was rapidly cleared away and it was written off charge on 5 September 1940 but significant parts were recovered in 1980 by members of the Wealden Aviation Archaeological Group. A further dig by the Etchingham Aviation Society found more large parts and following display by the Robertsbridge Aviation Society the re-assembled forward fuselage is now displayed in the Romney Marsh Wartime Collection, Brenzett, Kent.

V7497
Hawker Hurricane Mk I

Hawker Restorations Ltd, Milden, Suffolk, UK

V7497 was built by Hawker Aircraft Ltd as part of a batch of 691 Hurricanes ordered against Contract No. 62305/39 and which bore serials in the range V7200-V8127, of which V7497 fell into the serial block V7461-7510. Production was split between Hawker's factories at Kingston, Brooklands and Langley and V7497, powered by a Merlin III, was allocated to No. 20 MU on 25 August 1940, arriving at Aston Down, Glos, on 17 September where it was prepared for service and issued to No. 501 (County of Gloucester) Sqdn, RAuxAF, at Kenley two days later on 19 September.

At 0955 hours on Saturday 28 September raids totalling 120+ aircraft approached the Kent coast, of which 70 penetrated inland in two waves. The first wave of 30 aircraft flew to Biggin Hill and about six of these reached Central

The fuselage of V7497 under reconstruction in the workshops of Hawker Restorations in March 2015. (Gordon Riley)

London. The second wave did not penetrate further west than Maidstone. No. 501 was one of several squadrons which were scrambled to intercept these raids which were finally dispersed at about 1040 hours. The number of enemy fighters employed appears to have greatly exceeded the number of bombers. Enemy aircraft were reported to have been stepped up to a great height and to have attacked the defending fighters from above and out of the sun. In some cases, slight haze hindered interception of the raids.

P/O E B Rogers took off from Kenley in V7497/SD-X but was attacked by Bf 109s over Deal in Kent and shot down at 1010 hours. Rogers bailed out safely but his Hurricane crashed and was burned out at Chartway Street, East Sutton,

Maidstone. One of 16 Fighter Command aircraft lost that day with nine pilots killed, Rogers had a Do 17 to his credit which he had downed over Ramsgate on 15 September; he returned to the squadron to resume flying and was eventually promoted to flight lieutenant and awarded the DFC after pressing home an attack in a damaged aircraft while serving with No. 615 Sqdn.

The surface wreckage of V7497 was cleared from the site but an archaeological dig recovered artefacts from the aircraft and the identity plate and other parts were eventually acquired by Tony Ditheridge of Hawker Restorations. The aircraft is now being completely rebuilt at Milden, Suffolk, and will fly again in due course.

Z2330
Hawker Hurricane Mk IIA Srs 1

Brian Davis, Hamilton, Ontario, Canada

Z2330 was built by Hawker Aircraft Ltd as part of a mixed batch of 1,000 Hurricanes ordered against Contract No. 62305/39 and which were delivered as Mks IIA, IIB and IIC. Production was split between the three sites at Brooklands, Kingston and Langley and Z2330 was built in September 1940 as part of the first block of 50 aircraft with serials from Z2308-Z2357. Powered by a 1,480 hp Merlin XX and fitted with a Rotol three-bladed propeller it was taken on charge on 7 September 1940 and delivered to No. 27 MU at Shawbury, Shropshire, on 20 September where it was placed in store until allocated to Rolls-Royce (Service Aircraft Section) on 19 December for unspecified work (possibly engine-related but not necessarily as Rolls-Royce were part of the Hurricane Repair Organisation). It was returned to Shawbury on 15 January 1941.

Following preparation for service use it was allocated to No. 258 Sqdn on 5 March 1941, which at the time was based at Jurby on the Isle of Man, but just three days later it was reallocated to No. 238 Sqdn based at Chilbolton in Hampshire as part of 10 Group. The similarity of the two squadron numbers may simply indicate a mix-up in the paperwork. The latter squadron moved to Pembrey, Carmarthenshire, with a detachment at Carew Cheriton, Pembrokeshire, for a short time in April before returning to Chilbolton in preparation for transfer to Egypt and the Suez Canal Zone, becoming non-operational on 1 May 1941.

No. 238's aircraft were then re-allocated to other units, Z2330 finding itself assigned to No. 401 'Ram' Sqdn, RCAF on 2 May. This squadron had previously served as No. 1 Sqdn, RCAF, bringing its own Hurricanes over from Canada

The centre section and cockpit of Z2330 seen in John Norman's workshop in October 2004. *(John and Heather Norman)*

in June 1940, but was renumbered on 1 March 1941 whilst based at Digby, Lincolnshire. No. 2 (Canadian) Sqdn was renumbered as No. 402 Sqdn RAF at the same time; both squadrons were equipped with Hurricanes. The Canadian Digby Wing was formed on 24 April 1941 when the station received three further squadrons, No. 409 Sqdn, flying Boulton Paul Defiants, together with Nos. 411 and 412 Sqdns flying Supermarine Spitfires.

Occasional scrambles took place throughout May and June with little to report and it was not until early July, when the squadron began operating offensive sweeps over France from West Malling, Kent, that any real action took place. On 8 July Z2330 found itself posted away from the Canadians but its record card is unintelligible and its new unit is not readable; wherever it was it remained with that unit until 14 September 1941 when it was allocated to No. 242 Sqdn. The unit was being withdrawn from its base at Manston, Kent, from where it had been flying 'Roadstead' offensive sweeps throughout August – attacking shipping, mainly flak ships, R-boats and E-boats along the occupied coastline. Due to the amount of losses No. 242 was withdrawn to Valley on Anglesey, North Wales, and presumably Z2330 was assigned to that base whilst the squadron prepared for transfer to the Far East the following December. It is interesting to note that the mystery squadron to which Z2330 was allocated on 8 July may have been No. 615 Sqdn – which was based at Valley in July 1941 but which was posted south to Manston that September as No. 242 was posted in the opposite direction. The entry on the record card is smudged but could indeed read '615' in which case the aircraft probably stayed at Valley with the units exchanging their aircraft – a not uncommon practice.

In the event Z2330 did not last long with this famous Hurricane unit as on 27 September it was allocated to an unknown civilian repair organisation (CRO) for repairs in works (RIW) which were not completed until 5 December when it was marked for dispatch to Russia under the Lend-Lease agreement. There is no record of an accident having befallen the aircraft so it is reasonable to assume that the 'repairs' may well have been a complete overhaul and upgrade in preparation for transfer to Russia. Just when it was dispatched is not known but the first available convoy after 5 December was PQ6, which left Hvalfjord, Iceland on 8 December 1941 and arrived at Murmansk on 20 December 1941.

Nothing is known of its Russian service but it is reasonable to assume that it was pressed into service in the Kola Peninsula and shot down in combat sometime in early 1942. The wreckage is thought to have been recovered around 1990 and stored in the St Petersburg area, along with several other wrecks, before eventually being offered for sale as part of a package of three ex-Russian Hurricanes by Ben Kolotilin of Kolair Inc based in Roswell, near Atlanta, Georgia, USA. The three aircraft (subsequently found to be Z2330, AM274 and one other unidentified Mk I) were sold to Ed and Rose Zalesky of the Airplane Supply Centre of White Rock, BC, Canada, in August 1995 who had them stored at Blaine, Washington, USA, before advertising them for sale as a package of three.

John Norman, of JNE Aircraft LLC, inspected them in June 2003 and bought them on the spot, taking them back to his workshop at Burlington, WA, USA, where work began on figuring out exactly what he had bought. Of the three Z2330 had the best wing centre section and this was used to build a jig in which John would reconstruct the centre section from AM274 (qv). Other parts were taken from Z2330 and incorporated into AM274 until John felt that it was time to dispose of his substantial spares holdings – consisting of major components from two Hurricanes.

Z2330 and the anonymous aircraft were sold to Brian Davis of Hamilton, Ontario, who also acquired a CCF-built Hurricane, BW862 (qv) from The Canadian Museum of Flight of Langley, BC. Brian is now concentrating his efforts on finding and manufacturing components for these two aircraft, which will be rebuilt to flying condition in due course, whilst the anonymous example has been passed on to Darrell Brown of Oshawa, Ontario, who will be building up a static Hurricane Mk I for museum display.

Z2389
Hawker Hurricane Mk IIA Srs 1

Brooklands Museum, Weybridge, Surrey, UK

Z2389 was built by Hawker Aircraft Ltd as part of a mixed batch of 1,000 Hurricanes ordered against Contract No. 62305/39 and which were delivered as Mks IIA, IIB and IIC. Production was split between the three sites at Brooklands, Kingston and Langley and Z2389 was built in October 1940 as part of the second block of aircraft with serials from Z2382-Z2426. Powered by a 1,480 hp Merlin XX and fitted with a Rotol three-bladed propeller it was allocated to No. 5 MU, Kemble, Wilts, on 14 October 1940 and delivered on 6 November where it was placed in store until allocated to Rolls-Royce (Service Aircraft Section) on 14 December for unspecified work (possibly engine-related but not necessarily as Rolls-Royce were part of the Hurricane Repair Organisation). It was returned to Kemble on 24 December and stored until 14 February 1941 when it was delivered to No. 249 (Gold Coast) Sqdn at North Weald, Essex. Allocated to B Flight, Z2389 wore the squadron code GN and probably had the individual code letter 'O'. Operations flown at the time included convoy patrols, and logbook entries record some of Z2389's pilots – including

Z2389 under restoration by the Brooklands Museum is seen here in November 2007. *(Gary Brown)*

'Cass' Cassidy, 'Tommy' Thompson, S/Ldr Pat Wells, F/Lt S F Cooper and W/Cdr Victor Beamish.

No. 249 became non-operational at the end of April and set off for Malta, where it arrived on 21 May, which probably explains why on 27 April 1941 Z2389 was re-assigned to No. 71 'Eagle' Sqdn, which was upgrading from the Hurricane Mk I and based at Martlesham Heath, Suffolk. Issued to A Flight of this American-manned squadron, Z2389 wore the unit's 'Boxing Eagle' emblem on the starboard engine cowling – remarkably the battered remains of this panel survive with the aircraft today! The squadron relocated to North Weald to start 'Rhubarbs', convoy patrols, sweeps and bomber escorts, in June but on the 13th the Hurricane was re-allocated to No. 247 Sqdn which was flying convoy patrols in the southwest peninsular based at Portreath in Cornwall, although it moved to Predannack (with a detachment at Exeter) on 18 June, remaining there for over a year.

Rather than staying in Cornwall Z2389 was re-allocated after just four months and on 17 October found itself on charge with No. 136 Sqdn which had been formed at Kirton-in-Lindsey, Yorkshire, on 20 August 1941 and became operational the following month. It carried out shipping patrols over the east coast for two months before preparing for overseas departure to Burma in November – although orders were received to divert to Alipore, India, whilst they were en route. Their aircraft remained in the UK and Z2389 was transferred to No. 253 (Hyderabad State) Sqdn, at Hibaldstow, Lincs, its final two flights with the squadron being on 12 December 1941 when it was flown by two different pilots, F/Lt Aas and F/Lt Christie. It was then declared Cat B (beyond repair on site) and allocated to Taylorcraft Ltd at Rearsby for repair/overhaul on 16 December, probably being transported by road by one of 43 Group's salvage units.

Just how long it took to repair is unclear as it was noted with Taylorcraft for 'repair in works' (RIW) on 9 February 1942 and awaiting collection following repair on 14 March, although records indicate that it was test flown on 24 February. Judging by its subsequent transfer to Russia it is very probable that the work involved a general overhaul and upgrade – including a tropical air filter and maybe a change from eight Brownings to 12 (see later).

It was allocated to the storage unit at No. 15 MU, Wroughton, Wilts, on 20 February and delivered by air on 26 March 1942 from where, on 24 April, it was dispatched to the Packing Unit at No. 52 MU, Pengham Moors, Cardiff, which was located in a group of Bellman hangars just off the airfield. Here it was broken down and crated for shipping to Russia by 29 April and taken by road to Middlesbrough Docks where on 4 May it was loaded – possibly as deck cargo – with 15 other Hurricanes onto the merchant ship SS *Empire Baffin* coded 'S85'.

The ship sailed from Middlesbrough to the Firth of Forth and then on to Iceland where, at 0100 hours on 21 May 1942 it set sail for north Russia as part of the convoy PQ16 comprising 35 ships (24 from the USA). This was the largest Russian convoy assembled up to that time and seven cargo ships were subsequently lost en route; *Empire Baffin* suffered bomb damage from a near miss but at 0400 hours on 30 May she (and 20 other ships) arrived at the Kola Inlet, Murmansk in Russia; they delivered 124 aircraft (77 others having been lost en route); Russian Hurricanes provided fighter escort for the final stage of the journey. On 1 June six ships (one British, five American) from PQ16 arrived at Arkhangelsk on the White Sea.

Z2389 had a very short life following its arrival on the Kola Peninsula as at 0920 hours on 20 June it was shot down by Bf 109Fs in the Murmansk area whilst in combat with four other Hurricanes of Red Air Force's 767 Regiment against two German Bf 109F and five Bf 110 aircraft. (NB. the Bf 110s claimed no victories that day and were flying on a fighter-bomber mission). The fate of its pilot, 1st Lieut Ivan Kalashnikov, after crash-landing Z2389 on rocky ground in a remote swampy area, is currently unknown – although he is believed to have survived WW2. Two other Hurricanes were shot down in the dogfight but the German aircraft survived unscathed. Another report suggests that the date of the crash was 23 June and that Kalashnikov, flying with 767 IAP, 122 IAD, PVO-Air Defence Forces, held the rank of Starshina – equivalent to a sergeant – and that he was killed in the dogfight with Bf 109s of JG 5.

What is definite is that the crash site of Z2389 was apparently discovered by Russian military personnel during 1992 and news reached Russian aviation historians active in the region who soon began to plan the aircraft's recovery. Inspection of Z2389's wartime crash site and its surviving remains on 5 July 1996 by a team from LOC International found evidence of an incomplete military serial number

'…38…' and subsequent research in Russia and the UK concluded that the aircraft was Z2389. The camshafts and engine rocker-covers bearing the Rolls-Royce name were missing when the aircraft was inspected. The wreckage was recovered by helicopter and tracked vehicle by LOC International during the summer of 1996 and some basic conservation work and repainting was carried out following the transfer of all parts to St Petersburg in preparation for onward sale.

The fuselage of Z2389 being inspected by Geoff Rodwell in St Petersburg in 1997. *(Julian Temple/Brooklands Museum)*

By 26 February 1997 reassembly of Z2389's main components had taken place in the St Petersburg workshop/store and a video was made by LOC International. The wings were laid out especially for this with one separate wing tip visible in the video. The following month the aircraft was examined by Jim Pearce, on behalf of Brooklands Museum; the airframe seemed relatively sound although virtually all wood and fabric had disappeared. The wings were identified as being from a Hurricane Mk IIB (with 12 Browning .303 machine guns) – these could have been fitted during either of its major 'repairs in works' at Rolls-Royce or Taylorcraft in the UK, at an RAF MU, or possibly during its Russian service – although this seems unlikely bearing in mind the fact that it only operated for a matter of days before it was shot down.

Following a meeting between Jim Pearce and Julian Temple, Curator of Aviation at the Brooklands Museum, on 19 March 1997, it was decided to go ahead with an attempt to purchase the Hurricane and on 7 April 1997 an application for funding was submitted by Brooklands Museum to the National Heritage Memorial Fund (NHMF) with letters of support from former Hurricane pilots Sir Peter Masefield, Roland Beamont and Ann Welch. Things then moved quickly and on 13 May 1997 the aircraft was inspected (with support from British Airways) in St Petersburg, via Dr Artak Meyroyan of LOC International, by Julian Temple, and consultant engineer, Geoff Rodwell, who found it to be suitable for restoration at Brooklands Museum. A National Heritage Memorial Fund grant towards the total purchase costs of Z2389 was offered on 27 June 1997, three days later an additional grant was offered by the PRISM Fund via the Science Museum and on 24 July an export licence was obtained in Russia by Dr Artak Meyroyan of LOC International.

18 September 1997 saw the Hurricane delivered to St Petersburg Docks (from its previous storage location at a nearby military airfield) packed inside a shipping container which arrived at Hull Docks, via Antwerp, on 10 October. From here it was collected on 14 October by Julian Temple and Geoff Rodwell with support from the National Rescue Group / Motor Trade Software; Z2389 arriving at Brooklands at 1820 hours, where it was unloaded by volunteers and placed in storage.

During the summer of 1998 the engine bearer was restored by several Brooklands Museum volunteers with help from Geoff Rodwell and Bob Coles; this proved that the new steel tubing could be 'squared' to the required accuracy using the museum's facilities. Later that year the decision was taken to start rebuilding the aircraft with a few volunteers led by Roy Lomax under the technical guidance of Bob Coles – albeit behind the scenes and with no publicity at this stage. As a result, in March 1999 new steel tubing was purchased and delivered for use in the rebuild of Z2389's fuselage and the first new tube was installed the following month.

Throughout 1999 further work took place including the Merlin XX being professionally surveyed by Andrew Wood, whilst the undercarriage legs were removed from the wing centre section which was then reunited with the fuselage centre section and engine bearers.

June 1999 saw an emotional reunion with the aircraft when one of No. 71 Sqdn's pilots, Roger Meier, and his wife Sandra paid a visit from their home in Dallas, Texas. The next major step was in December 2004 when a Rolls-Royce

By November 2014 much more progress had been made on the restoration. (*Peter Clarke*)

Merlin II engine was loaned by Mike Lodge and collected by Langley Vale Motors and museum volunteers from Suffolk. This was installed on a trial basis in January 2005 in order that new cowlings could be fabricated. The Merlin Mk II was successfully run again by rebuilder Peter Grieve in Leeds on 5 January 2015 – the first time since 1942.

Over the past ten years steady progress has been made in restoring Z2389 to taxyable condition in the markings of No. 71 'Eagle' Sqdn, the choice being made due to the fact that it is believed to be the only surviving squadron aircraft from World War 2.

Z2461
Hawker Hurricane Mk IIC (Prototype)

Museum of the Air Forces of the Northern Fleet, Safonovo Settlement, Murmansk, Russia

It was in January 2015 during background research on Z2461 that the author realised the true significance of this particular Hurricane, and the fact that over the years most books and articles on the type have misquoted its serial as 'V2461' (which was an Armstrong Whitworth Albemarle.) In fact Z2461 was built by Hawker Aircraft Ltd as part of a mixed batch of 1,000 Hurricanes ordered against Contract No. 62305/39, forming the fifth production block, and which were delivered as Mks IIA, IIB and IIC. Production was split between the three sites at Brooklands, Kingston and Langley with Z2461 being built at Langley in December 1940 as part of the third block of 20 aircraft with serials from Z2446-Z2465. Powered by a 1,480 hp Merlin XX (No. 25295) and fitted with a Rotol three-bladed constant-speed propeller (No. 17400) it was laid down as a Mk IIA Series 1 but then selected for conversion into one of several prototype Hurricane Mk IIC, armed with four Chatellerault belt-fed Oerlikon cannon.

Although a cannon-armed Hurricane (V7360) had flown in July 1940 with four drum-fed Oerlikons, using wings previously fitted to and flown on a Mk I, P2640, it had experienced problems when tested at Boscombe Down. Following six test flights and some adjustments it was delivered to North Weald on 3 September 1940 and issued to No. 151 Sqdn for evaluation under combat conditions. As the squadron had just been rested it was passed to F/Lt Alexander Rabagliati of No. 46 Sqdn at nearby Stapleford Tawney on 5 September – who proceeded to blast a Bf 109 of I./JG 54 to smithereens that same day. Following combat damage sustained when attacking a Do 17 two days later, V7360 was sent for repair but was to be found back with Hawkers on 5 December when Philip Lucas took it up for a gun-bay heating test, the first time it was referred to as a Mk IIC and was thus the first real prototype.

Hawker had been instructed to repair 30 sets of damaged metal wings, hand-tooling them to accommodate four cannon per set; 12 sets featured drum-fed Oerlikons, 12 sets featured Chatellerault belt-fed Oerlikons and six sets were fitted with Hispano Mk I 20mm cannon. The wings were fitted to 30 aircraft coming off the production lines at Langley and Brockworth (Glosters) and Z2461 was the first of these true prototypes, being allocated to the Director General of Research and Development (DGRD) at Langley on 14 December 1940 to test the Chatellerault belt-fed Oerlikons. By the end of February 1941, 11 had been built, three of them being delivered to Boscombe Down (DGRD) for performance trials. Z2461 was flown by Hawker test pilot K G Seth-Smith on 6 February and allocated to Boscombe Down on 9 February 1941. During the trials it was determined that the mean maximum speed recorded at 16,000 ft was 336 mph at an all-up weight of 8,100 lb, two were then fitted with Vokes filters and the speed dropped to 320 mph at 16,200 ft and an AUW of 8,260 lb. During its time at Boscombe Down Z2461 was also involved in hood jettison trials but 9 March 1941 saw it move on to the Air Fighting Development Unit (AFDU) at Duxford for further trials.

By the end of March some 40 Mk IIC Hurricanes were at MUs – but they were fitted with drum-fed Oerlikons due to icing issues encountered by Z2461. These were evidently overcome as it was issued to an operational squadron, No. 242, based at Martlesham Heath (with detachments at Stapleford Tawney) on 2 April 1941. The squadron was mainly engaged on convoy patrols and the ORB does not seem to show the cannon-armed Z2461 taking part in any operational sorties so perhaps it was purely used for operational trials. The squadron moved to North Weald in May 1941 remaining there until July when it went to

The prototype cannon-armed Hurricane Mk II, Z2461, on show in the Museum of the Air Forces of the Northern Fleet at Safonovo Settlement in August 2014. (*Oleg Alekseev/Museum of the Air Forces of the Northern Fleet*)

Manston and on 16 July Z2461 was transferred to No. 256 Sqdn at Squires Gate. This unit was a night-fighter squadron equipped mainly with the Boulton Paul Defiant, although it did also operate a small number of Hurricanes alongside them and it is assumed that the cannon-armed Hurricane was there on test as by 27 July it had been moved on again, this time to No. 247 (China-British) Sqdn which was based at Predannack, Cornwall. It is interesting to note that it was on the squadron at the same time as the Brooklands Museum Hurricane, Z2389 (qv). Z2461 was coded 'HP-O' with No. 247 Sqdn and was involved in an accident at Predannack on 18 August which necessitated repairs by 43 Group but it was back on strength by 27 August.

It remained at Predannack until 11 November when it was re-assigned to No. 79 Sqdn at Pembrey, Carmarthenshire, Wales, which was mainly engaged on convoy and sector

patrols with the odd sweep and scamble – the latter in defence of towns in South Wales or the Bristol Channel area. Once again its stay was brief and on 31 December it was posted back to No. 247 Sqdn at Predannack which was busy on night operations as well as 'Intruder' and 'Rhubarb' missions. Here it remained until 14 April 1942 when it was posted to No. 87 Sqdn, a night-fighter unit based at Charmey Down, Wilts, with a detachment at St Marys on the Scilly Isles. Shortly after its arrival it was involved in an accident, on 25 April, when being flown by F/Sgt K Gildner, the squadron losing four aircraft that day. The damage was categorised as Cat B – beyond repair on site – and the aircraft was allocated to Airtraining (Oxford) Ltd, part of the Hurricane Repair Organisation, for repairs in works (RIW) on 7 May. Z2461 was one of 130 Hurricanes repaired by this contractor during 1942 and was awaiting collection on 13

June, being allocated to No. 19 MU at St Athan on 27 June where it was stored until moved to Hawker Aircraft Ltd on 16 September. It is interesting to note that this was logged as a 'CRO' – civilian repair organisation – and, judging by its subsequent history, it is reasonable to assume that this was a thorough overhaul in preparation for its subsequent despatch to Russia.

The RAF serial was found stencilled on several detachable panels. *(Oleg Alekseev / Museum of the Air Forces of the Northern Fleet)*

The work was evidently extensive as it was not ready for despatch to No. 10 MU at Hullavington, Wilts, until 8 November, remaining there until 12 December when it moved on – probably by air – to No. 82 MU at Lichfield, Staffs, where it was crated for shipping to Russia. It arrived at Middlesbrough Docks on 28 December 1942 and remained there until loaded on board the ship 'S.131' (full name unknown) on 20 January 1943. Its arrival date in Russia is given as 27 February which suggests that it sailed as part of convoy PQ11, which departed Kirkness on 14 February and arrived at Murmansk on 22 February. All 13 ships arrived safely, there having been no German attacks whatsoever during the passage, thanks to the continuous darkness of the polar night.

Z2461 seems to have been officially transferred to the Russian forces on 10 March 1943 and was issued to the 78th IAP (Fighter Air Regiment) of the Northern Fleet Air Force. The period between March and June 1943 saw particularly fierce fighting over the Gulf of Motovsk with

Bf 109s and Fw 190s constantly on the prowl looking for Soviet shipping. This came to a head on 5 June when 50 Northern Fleet Air Force fighters were ordered to cover a tug towing a barge which was carrying ten new 122mm field guns and 60 artillerymen. The barge was accompanied by four Maritime Defence launches and air cover was essential. 78th IAP provided 20 Hurricanes whilst 16 more came from 27th IAP. Two major air battles took place that morning between 0445 and 0705 hours; the Hurricanes from No. 78 IAP attacked two formations of Bf 109s and Fw 190s and immediately lost four aircraft. Z2461 was being flown in the first action by Jnr Lt N A Kravchenko, who managed to pull off a wheels-up emergency landing on the Rybachiy Peninsular, only to be seriously injured when his aircraft was strafed and set on fire by a German fighter. Five more Hurricanes were lost in the second battle of the morning and two pilots were killed but the precious cargo got through to the defenders of Rybachiy and Sredniy.

The wreckage as discovered in 1980, following the crash which occurred as a result of combat on 5 June 1943. *(Oleg Alekseev / Museum of the Air Forces of the Northern Fleet)*

Kravchenko's Hurricane lay where it fell until it was found in 1980 by enthusiasts from the Museum of the Air Forces of the Northern Fleet and was taken to Safonovo Settlement, Murmansk, on the Kola Peninsula. Here it has been restored for static display along with several other aircraft found in similar circumstances, which include a Polikarpov I-15, I-153, Po-2 & I-16, Beriev MBR-2, Yakovlev Yak-7 & Yak-9, Ilyushin Il-2 & Il-4, Tupolev SB, Lisunov Li-2, Messerschmitt Bf 109 and a P-39 Airacobra.

Z2768
Hawker Hurricane Mk IIA Srs 1

Military Aviation Museum, Virginia Beach, VA, USA

Z2768 was built by Hawker Aircraft Ltd as part of a mixed batch of 1,000 Hurricanes ordered against Contract No. 62305/39 and which were delivered as Mks IIA, IIB and IIC. Production was split between the three sites at Brooklands, Kingston and Langley and Z2768 was built at Langley in February-March 1941 as part of the eighth block of 35 aircraft with serials from Z2741-Z2775. Powered by a 1,480 hp Merlin XX and fitted with a Rotol three-bladed propeller it was initially allocated to No. 20 MU at Aston Down, Glos, on 10 February but in the event it seems it was actually delivered to No. 5 MU at Kemble on 20 February, moving on to Aston Down three days later. Here it was prepared for service and issued to No. 310 (Czech) Sqdn on 8 March 1941.

The squadron had been formed at Duxford on 10 July 1940 and on arrival at the famous fighter base Z2768 was coded NN-H, making its first operation flight a few days later during an uneventful sortie over the Channel off Dover alongside Z2312, Z2400, Z2493, Z2661 and Z2671 in the early evening of 23 March, with Sgt Karel Seda at the controls. Four days later, on 27 March, it was one of 12 aircraft flown to Coltishall at 0605 hours and which flew convoy patrols in pairs all day. F/O Hybler in Z2768 was one of the second pair, which patrolled between 0805 hours and 0910 hours, and the same pilot flew another (uneventful) patrol between 1545 hours and 1645 hours.

The squadron seems to have carried out many patrols over the next few months with Z2768 being flown by F/O Hybler, F/Lt Bodie, Sgt Seda, Sgt Jiroudek, Sgt Mlejnecky, P/O Kimlicka and S/Ldr Weber at the controls at various times. Patrols were mainly flown over East Anglia and London with locations such as Duxford, Cambridge, Mildenhall and Norwich frequently mentioned but on 18 June S/Ldr Frantisek Weber flew it as part of a 'Big Wing' patrol at 8-12,000 feet between North Foreland and Dover with two squadrons operating from West Malling and on 26 June it was the turn of Sgt Mlejnecky (Yellow Section) who flew it between 1425 hours–1450 hours as one of seven coastal patrols flown by 14 Hurricanes of No. 310 Sqdn on the day the unit moved from Duxford to Martlesham Heath on the Suffolk coast.

Later that day P/O Karel Kasal of No. 313 Sqdn arrived from his base at Catterick, apparently to drop off a new Czech flag for the unit. It would seem that on his departure he decided to put on an impromptu display of Spitfire aerobatics but things went somewhat awry and he ended up crashing Spitfire R6709 on the airfield. The aircraft was a write-off and he was injured, suffering cuts and bruises to his head, as a result of which he was taken to Ipswich hospital. It appears that his aircraft made contact with Z2768 during the accident, causing it category B damage. The Hurricane was repaired by the Station Engineering Flight on site, but didn't fly again with No. 310. Kasal was able to put the incident behind him and later rose to the rank of squadron leader, becoming the CO of No. 313 Sqdn in the closing months of the war.

No. 310 Sqdn was re-equipping with the 12-gun Hurricane IIB; this, coupled with the damage suffered during the accident, probably precipitated the decision to dispatch Z2768 to Airtraining (Oxford) Ltd, part of the Hurricane Repair Organisation, at Kidlington, Oxon, on 1 July 1941. Here it was repaired and given a complete upgrade, including a tropical Vokes air filter, to prepare it for its new life in the Soviet Union. The work was completed in October and on the 10th it was allocated to No. 22 MU at Silloth, Cumbria, before being sent on to No. 82 MU at Lichfield, Staffs, where the Packing Unit would have broken it down and crated it ready for shipping to Russia.

The aircraft is officially listed as departing for Russia on 27 October 1941 but the actual date of departure has not been confirmed. It would have made the journey as part of the cargo of one of the early arctic convoys, possibly as part of Convoy PQ3, which departed Iceland on 9 November 1941, or as part of either PQ4 or PQ5. All of the convoys sailed from an assembly point off Iceland to Arkhangelsk (Archangel) on the Kola Inlet.

Once assembled the majority of the Hurricanes being received at this time were issued to units fighting on the Karelian Front during the spring and summer of 1942 and it is fairly certain that Z2768 would have been one of them. The 760th Fighter Regiment (IAP) of the Karelian Front Air Force (7th Air Army) was based at Beloe More between January and April 1941, moving to Boyarskaya in May 1941 where it remained until November 1943.

During the mid-morning of 21 February 1943, the regiment scrambled a mixed formation of two P-40s and five Hurricanes, of which Z2768 was one, to intercept an enemy formation of Ju 87 Stuka dive-bombers, with an escort of Bf 109s, which were operating in the area. A dogfight broke out during which Z2768 and its pilot, J/Lt

Boris Alexandrovich Lazarev, was shot down to the north of the town of Loukhi, Lazarev being subsequently listed as missing in action. The Luftwaffe pilot credited with shooting him down is thought to be Feldwebel Rudolf 'Rudi' Muller of JG5 'Eismeer', a holder of the Knights Cross. Muller was one of the aces of JG5 and had a final tally of over 90 victories, a total that included a large number of Soviet Hurricanes. He died in Soviet captivity, during the immediate post-war period.

The wreckage of Z2768 was located in a peat bog, some 40 kilometres to the north of Loukhi in August 1998 following extensive research by an aviation archaeology group, called 'Vysota'. The body of 22-year-old Lazarev was found in the cockpit in an amazing state of preservation due to the peat in which it had been immersed. His body was removed and he was given a military funeral and interred in a cemetery in nearby Chupa, on the White Sea coast. The wreckage was initially recovered to the Central War Museum at Poklonnoj near Moscow. The aircraft had been extensively used, it was fitted with tyres of Russian manufacture and its armament had been changed, the aircraft carrying two 20mm ShVAK cannon

Z2768, NN-H of No. 310 Sqdn, is seen here at Martlesham Heath on 26 June 1941. It was later in the day that it was damaged when hit by Spitfire R6709. *(Jaroslav Popelka / fcafa.wordpress.com)*

and two 12.77mm machine guns of Soviet manufacture. The majority of this modification work on Hurricanes was carried out at Factory 81 at Monino near Moscow, although some modifications were also undertaken at operational airfields such as Kubinka.

The wreckage of the aircraft was eventually purchased by Gerald 'Jerry' Yagen for his Military Aviation Museum at Virginia Beach, VA, and was transported to the USA where some initial restoration work was performed before the fuselage was placed in store. The wings for the project are being worked on in Russia. Owing to the fact that Jerry owns a flyable Hurricane, RCAF 5667 (qv), and with the significance of its Czech history well-known, he would be keen to see the aircraft move to a Czech museum or collection if a suitable exchange could be arranged.

Z3055
Hawker Hurricane Mk IIA Srs 1

Malta Aviation Museum, Ta'Qali, Malta

Z3055 was built by Hawker Aircraft Ltd as part of a mixed batch of 1,000 Hurricanes ordered against Contract No. 62305/39 and which were delivered as Mks IIA, IIB and IIC. Production was split between the three sites at Brooklands, Kingston and Langley and Z3055 was built at Langley in February-March 1941 as part of the 13th block of 50 aircraft with serials from Z3050-Z3099. Powered by a 1,480 hp Merlin XX and fitted with a Rotol three-bladed propeller it was allocated to No. 48 MU at Hawarden, Chester, on 27 February but in the event it seems it was actually delivered to the aerodrome at Abbotsinch near Glasgow on 17 March before moving to No. 5 MU at Kemble on 26 March. Here it was apparently stored until 18 March when it was flown back to Abbotsinch on 18 May, ready for dispatch to Malta the following month.

It was taken on charge in Malta by No. 126 Sqdn in July

Z3055 in the Malta Aviation Museum hangar at Ta'Qali in June 2013 – note the Hamilton Standard propeller. *(Phil Glover)*

This photo shows the Hamilton Standard propeller well in addition to the unfinished leading edge to the port outer wing. *(Phil Glover)*

1941. The squadron was made up from personnel taken from No. 46 Sqdn, which had been en route to the Middle East but they received orders to proceed to Malta where the new squadron was officially formed on 28 June at Ta'Qali with Hurricane Mk II aircraft. There was no time for the niceties of a 'working up' period and the pilots were thrown straight into the thick of the battle to defend the island, the first two enemy aircraft being destroyed just two days after the squadron was formed. Z3055 was one of the first aircraft to be taken on strength but had a tragically short life; taking off from Safi strip just before daybreak on 4 July 1941 it crashed into the sea off the island near the Blue Grotto at Zurrieq shortly afterwards. Its pilot, Sgt Thomas Hackston, was never found.

The aircraft was located by diver David Schembri, at a depth of 120 ft only a short distance from the coast in 1993,

known to be in the area as fishermen's nets often got caught in it. With help provided by Cassar Enterprises, who loaned an A-frame, the wreckage was raised from the seabed two years later, on 19 September 1995, for reconstruction by the Malta Historic Aircraft Preservation Group. The initial plan was to restore it for static museum display but as the restoration progressed it was decided to try to restore Z3055 to taxyable condition. The initial stages of the restoration were sponsored by Frank Salt Real Estate in memory of Frank's father, F/Lt J H Salt, and the ground crews which kept the Hurricanes running.

Considering the state of the structure, having been on the seabed since 1941, the basic fuselage steel tubes were reassembled by 1999 and the following year the woodwork, built by Lorry Borg, had been attached. The fabric covering was attached during 2001 by Clive Denney of specialist

UK company Vintage Fabrics Ltd and on 13 December the magnificently restored Rolls-Royce Merlin was started and run successfully. This is a composite which includes parts from two Merlin 224 engines. The engine was installed in January 2002.

Much exchange of parts and expertise has gone into the reconstruction project, a radiator and oil cooler came from the Cambridge Fighter and Bomber Society in exchange for a two-bladed Watts propeller to be fitted to their own Hurricane, L1639 (qv). The radiator was subsequently rebuilt by Replicore in New Zealand. The original Rotol propeller was too far gone for restoration but a de Havilland hub was located in the museum stores and this has been built up with Hamilton Standard blades (the DH unit was a Hamilton Standard design built under licence in the UK).

Final spraying in camouflage was carried out by Clive Denney and took place in July 2003, meantime many detail fittings and controls had been installed in the fuselage. Work on the wings started in 2004, using parts recovered from Russia as patterns, and by March 2005 one wing was very nearly complete with work starting on the other. Ten years later work continues on this magnificent restoration which is a credit to all who have worked on it for the past 20 years.

Z5207
Hawker Hurricane Mk IIB

Karl-Friedemann Grimminger, Munich, Germany

Z5207 was built by the Gloster Aircraft Company Ltd (a subsidiary of Hawker Aircraft Ltd) as part of a batch of 1,700 Hurricanes ordered against Contract No. 85730/40/23a. Production peaked at between four and five aircraft per day and Z5207 was built in July 1941 as part of the serial block Z5202-Z5236. Powered by a 1,480 hp Merlin XX and fitted with a Rotol three-bladed propeller it would have been flown from Brockworth to No. 5 MU at Kemble, Wilts, where it was taken on charge on 22 July 1941. Z5207 was flown to RAF Heathfield, Ayr, near Prestwick on 3 August bound for Russia on board the escort carrier HMS *Argus*. Two other survivors, Z5227 and Z5252 were also part of Force Benedict.

Operation Benedict was planned in July 1941 and as a consequence No. 81 Sqdn was re-formed from A Flight of No. 504 Sqdn on 29 July and established at Leconfield under S/Ldr Tony Rook. Likewise on 31 July 1941, No. 134 Sqdn, under S/Ldr Tony Miller, was formed at Leconfield from personnel taken from No. 17 Sqdn. These two squadrons constituted No. 151 Wing under the command of New Zealander Wg/Cdr (later Gp/Capt, DFC, Order of Lenin) Neville Ramsbottom-Isherwood. They were officially under the command of Admiral Nikolai Kuznetsov, head of the Soviet Navy and Naval Air Service, and their orders were to undertake 'the defence of the naval base of Murmansk and co-operation with the Soviet Forces in the Murmansk areas'. In practice, their job was to get the Hurricanes flying, train the Russians in their use, hand them over and return to Britain.

Fifteen crated Hurricanes were loaded on board the *Llanstephan Castle* at Liverpool and the ship left for Scapa Flow on 12 August, joining a convoy code-named 'Dervish', which departed for Arkhangelsk on 17 August and arrived on the night of 31 August / 1 September. The remaining 24 aircraft – complete with tropical air filters –

and their pilots were taken on board the aircraft carrier HMS *Argus* at Glasgow Docks and departed for Scapa Flow on 19 August 1941, arriving the following day. After 10 days at Scapa Flow they set sail for Arkhangelsk at 0700 hours on 30 August; Z5207 is believed to have been one of the 24 Hurricanes carried on board *Argus*.

Following a final briefing on 6 September the pilots on board HMS *Argus* were ready to fly their Hurricanes off the 400 ft flight deck the following morning, although the ramp at the end of the deck was a cause of some consternation. S/Ldr Miller of No. 134 Sqdn took off at 0700 hours, skipped over the ramp, dropped and flew clear. Next was F/Lt V Berg O/C A Flight in Z5206 who hit the ramp and damaged his undercarriage, which was unable to retract as a result. Sgt B Campbell, an Australian, was third away in BD823 and he also damaged his undercarriage. The remaining pilots of A Flight took off with no further problems. Following these six came the six Hurricanes of B Flight of No. 134 Sqdn, then six from A Flight of No. 81 and finally six from B Flight of No. 81 Sqdn. By 0815 hours all the Hurricanes were en route to Vaenga, 15 miles NW of Murmansk.

Following various technical issues No. 151 Wing was declared operational on 10 September and the first operational flights took place the following day although no German aircraft were encountered until 12 September. A Bf 110 was damaged by aircraft from No. 81 Sqdn that morning and in the afternoon five Hurricanes came upon an equal number of Messerschmitt Bf 109s of I./JG 77, which were flying fighter cover for a Henschel Hs 126 reconnaissance aircraft. In the subsequent skirmish, three Bf 109s were shot down for the loss of one Hurricane. F/Sgt N H Smith died in the crash and was thus the first member of No. 151 Wing to be killed in action.

It was at this time that the unusual markings were applied to the Hurricanes; the Russians used numbers rather than

The fuselage of Z5207 seen in Phoenix Aero's hangar at Thruxton in October 2014. *(Gordon Riley)*

letters to identify their aircraft so a compromise was made in which the two squadrons adopted a system of using two letters for RAF personnel and two digits for Russians, thus Z5207, which had been allocated to No. 81 Sqdn, became 'FO' instead of FL-O. The letters were carried ahead of the RAF fuselage roundel with its Russian number painted behind the roundel where the individual aircraft code letter 'O' would have been. Certain numbers seem to have been reserved for S/Ldr and flight commanders. A Flight of No. 134 Sqdn were given numbers in the 20s; B Flight were given numbers in the 30s; A Flight of No. 81 Sqdn were given numbers in the 40s and B Flight in the 50s. The Hurricanes at Vaenga were given the first numbers in the sequence and when the additional Hurricanes flew up from Keg Ostrov, Arkhangelsk, these were added onto the list using the next available number. The Russian number carried by Z5207 is thought to have been '52' so the full fuselage codes would have been 'FO*52' – the '*' representing the RAF roundel.

Z5207's first recorded flight was on 11 September when Sgt A Anson took it up for a gun-testing exercise lasting for 1hr 10 mins. The wing was plagued with armament issues with only a few Hurricanes mounting their full complement of 12 machine guns, some carrying as few as six. It flew again on 13 September, the pilot being Sgt B Rigby, as part of a patrol which took off between 1450 hours and 1455 hours. Sgt Anson was back at the controls on 15 September for a one hour local flight and in the evening of 17 September, taking off at 1835 hours for a defensive patrol of the airfield at Vaenga. Flying as 'Green 1' Anson had a share in a Bf 109 which had been initially attacked by S/Ldr Rook in BD792 who had succeeded in hitting it; the aircraft being finished off by Anson and Sgt Sims (Red 2) in Z5228 who saw it crash in flames. Following this Z5207 came under attack by four Russian fighters but Anson managed to shake them off by taking evasive action.

Z5207 was next flown by P/O Bush on a patrol which

Front view of Z5207 showing the firewall and the Rolls-Royce Merlin in its cradle. *(Gordon Riley)*

took off at 1700 hours on 20 September but no enemy contact was made and all eight Hurricanes landed safely at 1745 hours. Its next flight was on 24 September during No. 81 Sqdn's first mission to escort Russian bombers deep into German-held territory, Sgt Anson taking off at 1305 hours and returning to base at 1420 hours. A similar escort mission was undertaken on 26 September, Anson flying Z5207 as 'Black 2' taking off at 1805 hours; during this mission they encountered German fighter opposition in the form of several Bf 109s and a dogfight broke out during which Anson fired but did not hit any of the enemy aircraft. The Hurricanes were all safely back at base by 1855 hours with three Bf 109s claimed as shot down. Another escort mission was flown the next day but Sgt Anson returned to base early, landing at 1135 hours as Z5207 had developed a fault and he thus missed out on a dogfight in which two more Bf 109s were claimed. With repairs effected Z5207

was up again with Sgt Anson at the controls at 1710 hours on 28 September when several aircraft were scrambled to provide 'High Cover' to a group of Russian bombers, the aircraft landing back at Vaenga at 1820 hours.

The first six days of October featured particularly bad weather and no flying was possible until 6 October when some local flying took place in the morning before notice was received of an impending German attack on the airfield that afternoon. As a consequence eight Hurricanes from No. 81 Sqdn and six from No. 134 took off between 1600 hours and 1645 hours to carry out defensive patrols and managed to fend off the incoming 12 Ju 88s with considerable success. F/Lt Micky Rook (cousin of S/Ldr Tony Rook, the squadron CO) who was flying Z5207 as a weaver to the main group of Hurricanes, split off when the squadron went after the Ju 88s. After going for a Ju 88 he saw a group of six aircraft ahead of him, which he took to be Hurricanes of No. 134

Sqdn, and tried to join up with them. Waggling his wings in recognition he was rudely brought to his senses when one peeled off and, with its yellow nose coming towards him, opened fire. F/Lt Rook had actually tried to join up with six Bf 109Es of I/JG77 that were supposed to be escorting the Ju 88s, although they seem to have been late. F/Lt Rook, in Z5207, returned fire and destroyed the Bf 109 but was then chased at low level by the remaining five Bf 109s right up until he was nearly home. Later, having landed after one of the stiffest dogfights of his life, he sat sweating in his cockpit for a good five minutes before he could lever himself out. The Germans, he said, "must have thought I was either bloody brave or bloody foolish".

On 15 October the Hurricanes of A Flight, No. 81 Sqdn, were handed over to their Russian pilots with the remainder from B Flight joining them a week later on the 22nd, No. 81 Sqdn's pilots officially ending their operations that day although some personnel continued for a while with No. 1 Soviet Hurricane Squadron.

Z5207's subsequent history is not known until it was discovered wrecked on the Kola Peninsula in the late 1980s and brought to St Petersburg in the early 1990s. Allegedly acquired by a Swiss consortium (possibly Marcel Boschung AG) which had plans to have it restored in Hungary, it eventually found its way to Audley End, Essex, the original home of Historic Flying Limited, where it arrived in July 1994. Two years later it was acquired by warbird collector Ricky Roberts of Billingshurst and placed on the UK Civil Aircraft Register on 17 November 1998 as G-BYDL. It was re-registered on 11 December 2001 in the name of Retro Track and Air Ltd and is thought to have been moved to their premises at Dursley, Glos, where it was placed in store until bought by Phil Lawton and re-registered in his name on 13 September 2007.

At that point no restoration work had been carried out on the aircraft and it remained as recovered from the Kola Peninsula. Phil then commissioned Classic Aero Engineering Ltd at Thruxton, who were already working on another Hurricane (G-CBOE, qv) to restore the aircraft and Z5207 was moved to Thruxton where restoration was started by chief engineer Bruce Ellis. Phil had bought a Canadian Hurricane XII (RCAF 5385 / G-RLEF, qv) from Maurice Bayliss during 2006 and this provided the dog-house and fuselage woodwork, together with a pair of Canadian wings and a further set of wing components – manufactured on the Isle of Wight in the 1990s. The Merlin engine was dispatched to Retro Track and Air for overhaul. When Classic Aero Engineering ceased trading in 2011 Phil purchased their Hurricane project, G-CBOE, and some workshop machinery, setting up Phoenix Aero Services Ltd in order to complete both aircraft. As G-CBOE was much more advanced it was decided to concentrate all effort into getting it flying and as a consequence work on Z5207 ceased in March 2011.

It had always been Phil Lawton's intention to sell his airworthy Hurricane (G-CBOE) to fund the completion of Z5207 but in the event both aircraft, together with the assets of Phoenix Aero, were sold to Munich-based collector Karl-Friedemann Grimminger in December 2014 and restoration will continue at Kaelin Aero Technologies near Stuttgart Germany.

Z5227
Hawker Hurricane Mk IIB
Ken McBride, San Martin, CA, USA

Z5227 was built by the Gloster Aircraft Company Ltd (a subsidiary of Hawker Aircraft Ltd) as part of a batch of 1,700 Hurricanes ordered against Contract No. 85730/40/23a. Production peaked at between four and five aircraft per day and Z5227 was built in July 1941 as part of the serial block Z5202-Z5236. Powered by a 1,480 hp Merlin XX and fitted with a Rotol three-bladed propeller it would have been flown from Brockworth to No. 20 MU at Aston Down, Glos, where it was taken on charge on 21 July 1941. Z5227 was flown to RAF Heathfield, Ayr, near Prestwick on 2 August bound for Russia on board the escort carrier HMS *Argus*. Two other survivors, Z5207 and Z5252 were also part of

Force Benedict. Details of the transfer of the aircraft to Russia are given in the entry for Z5207 (page 80) so they have not been repeated here.

Z5227 was allocated to B Flight of No. 81 Sqdn and its first recorded mission was on 14 September when P/O S 'Scottie' Edmiston took it up alongside F/Lt 'Micky' Rook and P/O Bush for a flight lasting for 1hr 5mins. It carried the Wing's combined markings of 'FE*53' and was one of the most photographed of the Vaenga Hurricanes. Sgt Reed flew it on a local flight the following day for 1hr 10mins. This was possibly a gun-firing exercise as the wing was plagued with armament issues at the time with only a few

A container full of the components from Z5227 with the serial number clearly showing on the wing root. *(Ken McBride)*

Hurricanes mounting their full complement of 12 machine guns, some carrying as few as six. The aircraft's first combat experience came in the evening of 17 September when eight Hurricanes, four from each flight, took off at 1830 hours to cover the withdrawal of Russian bombers and got tangled up with eight Bf 109s which were preparing to attack them. P/O Edmiston was flying Z5227 during this action in which three Bf 109s were shot down – together with a Bf 110 which was probably hit by Russian fighters but which, nevertheless, was credited to No. 81 Sqdn.

The following ten days saw sporadic flying in which no enemy aircraft were encountered by Z5227 or its pilots but on 27 September it was one of 12 Hurricanes, six drawn from each flight, which took off late that morning to escort four Russian bombers. Z5227 was flown, once again by P/O Edmiston, who was 'Blue 3' of B Flight on this occasion. They encountered a group of Bf 109s at 1200 hours; Edmiston attacked one of the 109s from astern and, after firing 40 rounds from each gun, he saw its hood fly off and the aircraft span into the ground. The following day, 28 September, Z5227 was one of six Hurricanes which took off at 1710 to provide 'High Cover' for six other Hurricanes escorting Russian bombers. On this flight the pilot was Sgt Crewe and he landed back at Vaenga at 1820 hours.

Z5227 was not involved in the dogfight which broke out on 6 October when Vaenga came under attack by Norwegian-based Ju 88s but 'Scottie' Edmiston took it up one last time two days later, taking off at 1200 hours on 8 October and landing after a short 20-minute flight in the company of BD818 and Z4006. These were the final three sorties made by No. 81 Sqdn pilots in their own aircraft before they were handed over to the Russians – although they did fly again using No. 134 Sqdn's Hurricanes.

On 15 October the Hurricanes of A Flight, No. 81 Sqdn, were handed over to their Russian pilots with the remainder from B Flight joining them a week later on the 22nd, No. 81 Sqdn's pilots officially ending their operations that day although some personnel continued for a while with No. 1 Soviet Hurricane Squadron.

Z5227's subsequent history is not known until it was discovered wrecked on the Kola Peninsula in the late 1980s and brought to St Petersburg in the early 1990s. It was sold to American collector Greg Herrick in 1995 and stored at Anoka County, Minnesota, for a time before being sold to Ken McBride, who has the project stored at San Martin, California, where he hopes to restore it to flying condition in due course.

Z5227 on the airfield at Vaenga with another Hurricane of 151 Wing flying overhead. (© *IWM*)

Z5252
Hawker Hurricane Mk IIB

Central Museum of the Air Forces, Moscow, Russia (Unconfirmed)

Z5252 was built by the Gloster Aircraft Company Ltd (a subsidiary of Hawker Aircraft Ltd) as part of a batch of 1,700 Hurricanes ordered against Contract No. 85730/40/23a. Production peaked at between four and five aircraft per day and Z5252 was built in July 1941 as the first of the serial block Z5252-Z5271 (35 aircraft). Powered by a 1,480 hp Merlin XX and fitted with a Rotol three-bladed propeller and a Vokes tropical filter (due to dust being foreseen as

a hazard in its operational area) it would have been flown from Brockworth to No. 5 MU at Kemble, Wilts, where it was taken on charge on 24 July 1941. Z5252 was flown to RAF Heathfield, Ayr, near Prestwick on 3 August bound for Russia on board the escort carrier HMS *Argus*. Two other survivors, Z5207 and Z5227 were also part of Force Benedict. Details of the transfer of the aircraft to Russia are given in the entry for Z5207 (page 80) so they have

The forward fuselage and wings from Z5252 resting on the lake shore on 15 October 2004 following its recovery the previous day. *(Boris Osetinskiy)*

Z5252 painted as '01' at Vaenga in September 1941 following its presentation to Major General A. A. Kuznetsov.
(BAE SYSTEMS)

not been repeated here save to say that Z5252 was carried on board the steamer SS *Llanstephan Castle* which sailed with Convoy 'Dervish' and arrived in Arkhangelsk on 31 August with 16 Hurricanes in crates, which were assembled at the Russian base in Keg-Ostrov from where the aircraft departed to Vaenga between 12 and 16 September. Z5252 was air-tested by P/O Woolaston on 11 September and five days later, on 16 September Sgt J Mulroy of No. 81 Sqn flew Z5252 to Vaenga and on arrival it was kept as a reserve aircraft.

On 25 September Major General A. A. Kuznetsov, CO, Naval Air Forces, Soviet Northern Fleet (VVS SF), arrived to test-fly a Hurricane. He was an expert pilot with many thousands of hours to his credit and nobody doubted his ability to fly the Hurricane for the first time. Kuznetsov was presented with his own Hurricane so the roundels and fin flash of Z5252 were painted over with Russian stars and the number '01' was added to the fuselage sides. The press photos taken at the time clearly show the Russian star painted over the RAF roundel beneath the wings. No. 78 IAP was

formed on 28 October 1941 as the first Russian Hurricane wing and, once 151 Wing had left Russia, began to carry out major operations. Kuznetsov, as the highest ranking officer in the region, would not have undertaken operations himself but it is assumed that he would have flown Z5252 between bases within his area of command.

On 1 November Capt Boris Safonov HSU (Hero of the Soviet Union) became the commanding officer of No. 78 IAP, having previously been squadron leader of 4./72 SAP flying Polikarpov I-16s. In early 1942 it was Safonov who asked chief engineer Sobolevsky to look at altering the standard Hurricane armament and on 24 February Maj Kukharenko, squadron leader of 3./78 IAP flew a re-armed Hurricane fitted with two 20mm ShVAK cannon and two Berezin UBT 12.7mm heavy machine guns. By March, most Hurricanes were also fitted with two RS-82 unguided rockets rails on the underside of each wing.

A promoted Lt Col Safonov took command of 2gvSAP on 20 March and on 29 March Z5252 was transferred from 78 IAP to 2gvSAP (the same re-designated unit). Two weeks

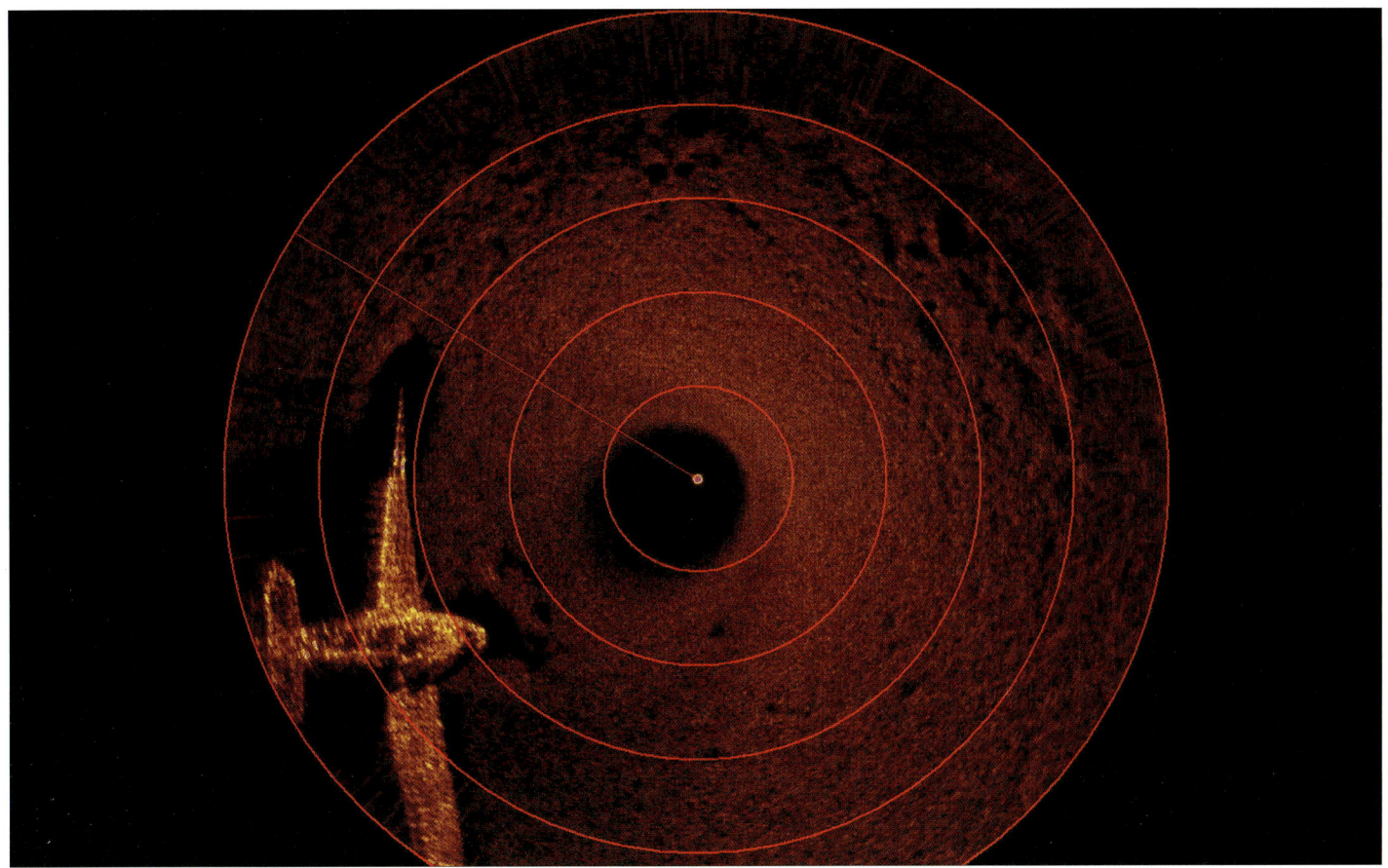

The side-scan sonar image which proved that the Hurricane was intact and resting on the lake bed. *(Boris Osetinskiy)*

later Z5252 was taken on charge with the staff flight of 2gvSAP and was probably flown by Safonov on a number of occasions. Z5252 soldiered on until 2 June when between 1410 and 1450 hours (Moscow time), seven Hurricanes of 2gvSAP were involved in a dogfight near Lake Njal-Javr, west of Murmansk with 12 Bf 109Es belonging to 8./JG5, during which three Hurricanes of 3./2gvSAP were shot down. Sgt V A Vanjukhim was killed and SSgt P D Klimov had to force land two and a half miles west of Murmansk. The third loss was Lt Pavel Markov who was flying Z5252 which suffered hits to the fuel tank and electrical panel (which caused the circuits to fail and is the reason why the RS-82 rockets had not been fired); moreover, an explosive round hit the port wing and one bullet passed through the top engine cowling but missed the engine. With no electrical power, Lt Markov was forced to put down on a small frozen lake four miles west of Murmansk. Even though it was early June, the winter of 1941 was one of the coldest on record

and the lakes were still partially frozen. Markov completed a perfect belly landing on the ice, exited Z5252 and headed for the settlement of Mishukovo. He was later brought back to his unit at Vaenga by motorboat. By the time a salvage team got to the lake the ice had given way and Z5252 had sunk to the bottom. Deemed too difficult to salvage, it was written off and forgotten. Lt Markov claimed a Bf 109F shot down some eight miles west of Murmansk but according to Luftwaffe records, no Bf 109s from JG 5 were recorded as lost that day. Markov did not survive the Great Patriotic War, as on 16 January 1943 he was killed in a flying accident when his Hurricane, HL555 '72' of 1./78 IAP, flew into a hill near Vaenga in fog.

With the upsurge in interest in relics of the Great Patriotic War (the Soviet name for World War 2) a research group called the 'Federation of Aviarestoration' found a wartime report whilst going through naval archives in 2001 and decided to try to find Z5252.

The tail section detached during the lift but was recovered safely. *(Boris Osetinskiy)*

After two years searching various potential lakes the wreck was finally located on 17 August 2003, coincidentally 'Russian Air Force Day'. The team returned in February 2004 with a side-scan sonar and the images showed the Hurricane was there, complete and apparently in very good condition. One of the team members dived through the ice and found the Hurricane at a depth of 18m and at an angle of 60 degrees nose down. It was covered in silt and sat in a 1.5m bed of arctic moss, a common aquatic plant found at the bottom of tundra lakes. Video footage showed the rear fuselage and tail still covered in wood and fabric after 60 years! Subsequent video analysis showed the serial Z5252 stencilled below the tailplane and the decision was made to raise this historic aircraft.

On 13 October 2004 the recovery commenced in less than ideal conditions, with a temperature of only 3-4 degrees above freezing, driving wind, snow flurries and a choppy lake surface. At the bottom of the lake in poor visibility, a lifting line was connected to the centre section. The initial lift fractured the fragile fuselage structure and the tail with all the wooden structure and fabric fell away. The recovery was not going as planned and the conditions were not improving. After the initial lift, the team decided to calm the spirit of the lake by offering her a bottle of whisky! Less than three hours later they were presented with perfect diving conditions with the clouds gone, the sun out and the wind dropped to zero. The Hurricane was raised to the surface and pulled to the shoreline; just as it was about to be lifted clear of the water, the team discovered that she was still fully armed with four RS-82 rockets located on rails attached to the underside of the wings. The rails and rockets were quickly detached and left at the water's edge. Once the tail was recovered the team could finally relax.

On 14 October the team returned to dismantle the

The Gloster constructor's plate showing the RAF serial and the c/n, G5/120840. (*Boris Osetinskiy*)

Hurricane. All of the metalwork was in exceptionally good condition and many panels had been stencilled with Z5252. She was still fully armed with the original twelve 0.303 inch Browning machine guns, indicating that she was not one of those Hurricanes to have been re-armed with Soviet cannon and heavy machine guns. The only visible combat damage was a hole in the upper cowling and one in the port wing leading edge. The Rolls-Royce Merlin XX seemed to be in excellent condition, having been protected by the silt and moss of the lake bottom. Once the wings were off and the cowlings removed, Z5252 was loaded onto a wooden sledge and pulled back to base camp, four miles away, by Snowcat. A few days later she was loaded onto a lorry and transported to Moscow where she remains stored to this day, the hope being that funding will eventually be secured to have her restored to flying condition and kept in Russia as a memorial to the Hurricane pilots of the Great Patriotic War.

Note: In 1996 a Hurricane which had been statically restored and displayed in Russia as 'Z5252' was brought to the UK and purchased by Hugh Taylor. On stripping down it was discovered that its true identity was Z5053 (qv). Although some restoration work had been performed it was reduced to spares by Hawker Restorations Ltd. The restored components are thought to have been incorporated into P2902 / G-ROBT (qv) and only parts from Z5053 remain today.

Z5663
Hawker Hurricane Mk IIB

Ross McNeill, Bewdley, Worcs, UK

Z5663 was built by the Gloster Aircraft Company Ltd (a subsidiary of Hawker Aircraft Ltd) as part of a batch of 600 Hurricanes ordered against Contract No. 85730/40/23a. Production peaked at between four and five aircraft per day and Z5663 was built in November 1941 as the first of the final block Z5649-Z5693. Powered by a 1,480 hp Merlin XX and fitted with a Rotol three-bladed propeller it had a tragically short life.

Having been allocated to No. 48 MU at Hawarden near Chester, it was picked up from the factory airfield at Brockworth by an American pilot of No. 2 Ferry Pilot Pool Unit, Air Transport Auxiliary, F/O (First Officer) Ernest Edward Gasser, on 7 December 1941. Gasser flew into a snowstorm at Button Oak in the Wyre Forest near Bewdley, Worcs, and was killed when the Hurricane ploughed into the ground and burst into flames. It was a dreadful day with seven other aircraft lost during the same snowstorm. Gasser's body was recovered from the wreckage and he was buried in Wribbenhall (All Saints) Churchyard, Bewdley. He was 31 years old and was from Chevy Chase, Maryland.

Although the bulk of the wreckage was cleared at the time by a team from one of 43 Group's salvage units, further pieces of wreckage were found on the surface by aviation enthusiasts belonging to Midland Aircraft Recovery Group during the 1980s. Some of these parts were dispersed amongst members of the group but others have been collected together by Ross McNeill who is incorporating them into a composite Hurricane restoration project which is being built for static display.

Ross McNeill's Hurricane project, Z5663, laid out at the Newark Air Museum's 'Cockpitfest' on 20 June 2010. *(Howard Heeley)*

AP740
Hawker Hurricane Mk IIB

Vadim Zadorozhny Technical Museum, Arkhangelskoye,
Moscow, Russia

The Austin Motor Company, of Longbridge, Birmingham, was heavily involved in aircraft production during World War 2, building the Fairey Battle, Hawker Hurricane, Miles Master, Airspeed Horsa, Short Stirling and Avro Lancaster at the Austin Aero shadow factory at Cofton Hackett. The single-engined aircraft were transferred from the Flight Shed in Cofton Lane to the adjacent aerodrome on an ingenious motorised sled which took the aircraft up a significant height. The company received an order for 105 Hurricane Mk IIBs (AP516-AP648) in 1940, followed by a further order for another 295 (AP670-AR207), and the first Austin-built Hurricane, AP516, flew on 8 October 1940.

Virtually all of the Hurricanes built by Austin were

destined to be shipped to Russia and AP740 was no exception. Built in 1942 against Contract No. 124304/40 it was allocated for dispatch to No. 51 MU at Lichfield, Staffs, on 29 March 1942, this unit's role being to receive aircraft from the manufacturers and carry out any modifications before delivery to the squadrons. The next day AP740 followed the well-trodden route to Russia, being re-allocated to No. 82 MU (also at Lichfield) which was under the command of 53 Wing at Andover and had been formed on 4 April 1941 as a packing depot to crate aircraft for dispatch to overseas units. Whether it was actually crated at Lichfield is unclear as on 4 April it was allocated to No. 52 MU at Pengham Moors, Cardiff – which also operated a packing depot – but

Although painted as 'BN323' with the tactical code 'White 77' this Hurricane, seen here in August 2012, is actually an Austin Motors - built example, AP740. *(Alan Wilson)*

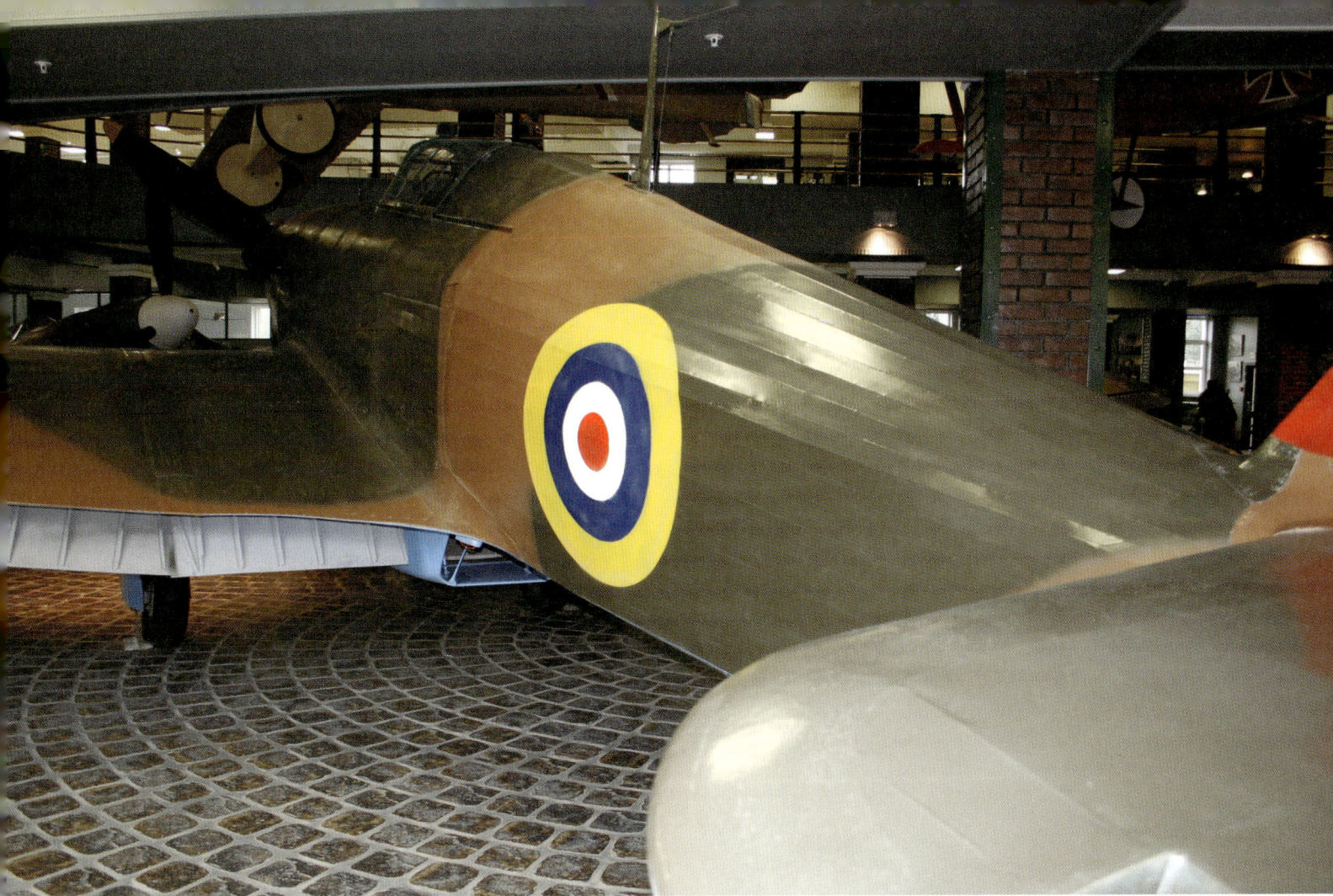

When first displayed AP740 was in RAF camouflage and markings but without a serial, as seen in August 2009. *(Ken Duffey)*

by 9 April its paperwork indicated its final destination was Russia and on 14 April it was at Sunderland Docks ready to join an Arctic convoy to Arkhangelsk.

Judging by the dates it very probably sailed on convoy PQ16, which assembled at Reykjavik, Iceland, from where it departed on 21 May, arriving at Murmansk on 30 May 1942. At this time of the year the convoy was sailing in the perpetual daylight of the Arctic summer; this lessened the effectiveness of U-boat attack, but made round-the-clock air attack more likely. It also increased the chance of early detection by German reconnaissance aircraft.

On 25 May PQ16 met its cruiser escort, but on the same day was spotted by a Fw 200 Condor reconnaissance aircraft, which commenced shadowing it. That evening the Luftwaffe began a series of attacks which continued for the next five days, until the convoy was in range of Soviet fighter cover. On 25 May one ship was damaged

and forced to return under escort; on 26 May all air attacks were repulsed, but one ship, the *Syros*, was torpedoed by *U-703*. By 27 May the air attacks began to break through; three ships were sunk and another damaged around mid-day; another sunk and one damaged in mid-afternoon. That evening two more ships were sunk, and another damaged. On 28 May the convoy was joined by the Eastern Local escort; three Soviet destroyers and four minesweepers. Their extra firepower enabled all further air attacks to be beaten off. On 29 May the convoy divided, six ships making for Arkhangelsk (which they reached on 1 June), while the remainder docked at Murmansk. Eight merchant ships were lost: six by air attack, one by submarine *U-703* and one by a mine. Two U-boats were damaged during attacks by escorts, and an unknown number of attacking aircraft were shot down.

AP740 would have been uncrated and assembled soon

after arrival and issued to the 3rd Guards Aviation Regiment of the 61st Fighter Air Brigade of the Air Force of the Baltic Fleet. Precise details of its Russian service are not known but the plaque in front of the restored aircraft gives the following account:

'This particular aircraft was found in the area of so-called 'Neva Patch'. Piloted by Guard Captain Aleksandr Fedorovich Myasnikov who had fought on the Leningrad Front and was killed in air combat on 11 September 1942. During his Air Force service Myasnikov flew 315 combat missions and shot down 18 enemy aircraft. He was awarded the Order of Lenin and two Orders of the Red Banner.'

Myasnikov was the assistant commander of the 3rd Guards Aviation Regiment of the 61st Fighter Air Brigade of the Air Force of the Baltic Fleet. For the first nine months of the Great Patriotic War of the Soviet Union, the squadron shot down 64 confirmed enemy aircraft. 11 September 1942 was Myasnikov's 315th combat sortie during which he led a group of three Hurricanes in support of Pe-2 bombers in the Mustolovo area.

Following its recovery the Hurricane was restored by the Voenno-Patrioticheskoe Obshestvo 'Vysota' (the Military-Patriotic Association 'Height') in Kolpino, St Petersburg, which was founded in 1994 by former Russian North Fleet Navy pilots with the goal to commemorate the Heroes of the Great Patriotic War (WW2). It is said to have a runnable Merlin XX fitted and when initially put on display it was in RAF camouflage and markings with no serial. These markings were subsequently changed and it now carries Soviet camouflage and markings with the tactical No. '77' in white on either side of the fuselage – the Soviet stars under the wing are painted over the RAF roundels previously carried which is how it would have appeared during its Soviet service. For some reason the RAF serial 'BN233', which was a Hawker-built Hurricane IIB, has been applied to the aircraft rather than its real identity of AP740.

BD731
Hawker Hurricane Mk IIB

Wings Museum, Balcombe, W Sussex, UK

The centre section, rear fuselage, tail section, Merlin engine and other components from BD731 are displayed in a diorama setting in the Wings Museum as part of the 'Ghosts of the Tundra' exhibition which aims to display relics as they were found in Russia. Other fuselage components were sold to the Cambridge Fighter and Bomber Society and have been utilised in the reconstruction of their Hurricane Mk I, L1639 (qv), at Little Gransden.

BD731 was built at Brooklands in the summer of 1941 as one of the first serial block, BD696-BD745 (50 aircraft), of a batch of 600 Hurricanes which had been ordered as the sixth production batch from Hawker Aircraft Ltd and which carried serials in the range BD696-BE716. It was allocated to No. 27 MU at Shawbury, Salop, on 10 August and following preparation for service it was issued to No. 135 Sqdn on 21 August. The unit had been formed at Baginton,

The crashed remains of BD731 are part of the 'Ghosts of the Tundra' exhibition at the Wings Museum in Balcombe. Most of the rear fuselage was used in the restoration of L1639. *(Peter Clarke)*

Coventry, on 15 August under the command of S/Ldr F C Carey DFC & Bar, DFM, moving to Honiley – between Coventry and Birmingham – the following month and becoming operational on 3 October, flying its first defensive scramble that same day.

No. 135 had been formed with the intention of being posted to Burma and BD731 did not stay long – just two days in fact (which suggests that the first allocation may have been in error). On 23 August it was re-assigned to No. 605 (County of Warwick) Sqdn, RAuxAF, which by coincidence also happened to be based at Baginton. The squadron had been serving in the Midlands for most of the summer of 1941 but that September it moved south to Kenley, re-joining 11 Group, and started a month of bomber escorts and fighter sweeps before it moved to Sealand in October in advance of orders to sail for Singapore, embarking on HMS *Indomitable* in December 1941.

As the squadron moved to Sealand to prepare for its overseas posting its Hurricanes were withdrawn and BD731 was dispatched to No. 13 MU at Henlow, Beds, the Hurricane specialist MU, on the 13th of that month for 'repairs in works' – although the note 'CRO' (civilian repair organisation) is appended to the entry – indicating that the work could have been performed elsewhere within the Hurricane Repair Organisation. Judging by its subsequent movements it is very likely that this work was a thorough overhaul and fitting of a Vokes filter in preparation for dispatch to Russia as it was not awaiting collection until 13 December and did not

arrive at No. 18 MU until 28 December. This was a storage MU which was mainly based at Tinwald Downs, Dumfries, although it also operated from local satellite airfields at Low Eldrig near Stranraer, Lennoxlove near Haddington, Wath Head in Cumbria and Hornby Hall, Cumbria. Here it was stored, although there was a packing depot on site and it may have been crated here, before being transferred to No. 47 MU at Sealand, near Chester, on 12 February 1942 then finally allocated to Russia four days later on 16 February.

Sealand was convenient for the docks at both Birkenhead and Liverpool so BD731 probably left on board a ship from one of those ports which would have joined an Arctic Convoy heading for the White Sea, possibly PQ12 which departed Reykjavik on 1 March and arrived in Murmansk on 12 March 1942.

BD731 served with the 3rd Fighter Squadron, 2nd Fighter Regiment in the Murmansk area and was shot down by Bf 109s of JG 5 in October 1942, crashing in Karelia near the border with Finland. It was recovered in 1997 and initially acquired by Martin Cobb of Bournemouth who offered it for sale together with parts from another Hurricane, BD736, and it was passed on to the East Surrey Aviation Group at Redhill aerodrome. This group developed into the Wings Museum, under the leadership of brothers Daniel and Kevin Hunt who have considerable experience in recovering WW2 wrecks from Russia. The museum has now moved to new premises at Balcombe, W Sussex.

BE146*
Hawker Hurricane Mk IIB

Imperial War Museum, Duxford, Cambs, UK

The identity associated with this Hurricane is speculative and based on a serial found stamped on some of the parts which were used during its restoration. The aircraft is a composite, constructed with parts from at least two airframes which were recovered from Russia and subsequently acquired by Stephen Grey of The Fighter Collection.

BE146 was built in the summer of 1941 as one of the serial block BE130-BE149, which was part of a batch of 600 Hurricanes which had been ordered as the sixth production batch from Hawker Aircraft Ltd and which carried serials in the range BD696-BE716. Production was split between Brooklands and Langley and this aircraft was built at Brooklands. BE146 was allocated to No. 51 MU at Lichfield, Staffs, on 11 September, this unit's role being to receive aircraft from the manufacturers and carry out any

modifications before delivery to squadrons. It may have been passed directly to the packing depot at Lichfield, No. 82 MU, for crating, but if so this was not mentioned on its Movements Card, the next recorded allocation being to No. 47 MU at Sealand on 30 September. Sealand was convenient for the docks at both Birkenhead and Liverpool so BE146 probably left on board a ship from one of those ports which would have joined an Arctic Convoy heading for the White Sea, possibly PQ2 which departed Liverpool on 13 October 1941, arriving at Arkhangelsk on 30 October 1941.

Details of the Russian career of this aircraft are unknown, all that can be said is that two crashed Hurricanes were acquired by Stephen Grey in the early 1990s and these were transported to the Imperial War Museum's airfield at Duxford, Cambridgeshire. Negotiations took place which

Finished as 'Z2315', the Imperial War Museum's composite Hurricane is thought to contain parts from BE146. It is seen here in a rare external photo after it was completed on 13 June 2000. *(Andy Robinson)*

Only a week before the external photo was taken the Hurricane still had a long way to go as seen here on 6 June 2000. *(Andy Robinson)*

The aircraft as it is today, familiar to visitors to Duxford. *(Gordon Riley)*

resulted in the museum getting sufficient parts to build a static Hurricane and Stephen Grey acquiring the Mosquito T.III, TV959, which had been displayed at Lambeth for many years. Between 1992 and 2000 the best components from the two Hurricanes were selected and, together with many new and other sourced parts, used to build the composite airframe now displayed in the markings of 'Z2315', 'JU-E'

of No. 111 Sqdn – the first Hurricane squadron. The leftover Hurricane parts are still stored at Duxford by The Fighter Collection (see Other Projects). The Mosquito was traded with Paul Allen to join his Flying Heritage Collection and is now in New Zealand where it is to be restored to flying condition.

BH238
Hawker Hurricane Mk IIB

Peter Monk and Partners, Sandown, IoW, UK

BH238 was one of 450 Hurricanes ordered from the Gloster Aircraft Company Ltd (a subsidiary of Hawker Aircraft Ltd) and was built at Brockworth in early 1942. The serials ranged from BG674-BH723, broken up into serial blocks and BH238 fell into a block of 50 aircraft with serials between BH215-BH264. Destined for delivery to Russia, it was dispatched from the factory to No. 52 MU at Pengham Moors, Cardiff, where it was broken down at the packing

The mortal remains of BH238 are stored in a secure area at Sandown on the Isle of Wight. *(Chris Michell)*

The skeletal fuselage and centre section was displayed in the Frontline Aviation Museum at Sandown until it closed. *(Chris Michell)*

unit and noted as shipped to Russia on 26 January 1942. Details of which port it left from are not known but the date suggests that it may have been carried as cargo on either of the Arctic Convoys PQ9 or PQ11, both of which arrived in Murmansk during February 1942.

Details of the Russian career of this aircraft are unknown, all that can be said is that the badly damaged fuselage and centre section arrived at Sandown on the Isle of Wight around 2000. Displayed for a time at the now closed Frontline Aviation Museum the wreck is stored by Airframe Assemblies Ltd on behalf of its owners, Peter Monk and Partners.

KX829
Hawker Hurricane Mk IV

Thinktank, Millennium Point Discovery Centre, Birmingham, UK

KX829 was ordered from Hawker Aircraft Ltd as one of the eighth production block (Contract No. 62305/39) and was built at Langley in early 1943. The aircraft in this block of 1,200 were a mixture of Mks IIB, IIC, IID and IV with serials in the range KW696-KZ612, although 60 aircraft were delivered as Sea Hurricanes and given new serials between NF668-NF703 (36) and NF716-NF739 (24). KX829 fell into the serial batch KX796-KX838 (43 aircraft) and was allocated to No. 22 MU at Silloth, Cumbria, on 22 February 1943, arriving there on 28 February. It is one of only two surviving Hurricanes that have still got the Form 700 (Servicing Log) still with the aircraft (the other is LF363

KX829, masquerading as Arthur Clowes' Mk I, P3395, during the Battle of Britain, is displayed in the Thinktank at Millennium Point, Birmingham. (*Gordon Riley*)

qv) and some of the dates in that are slightly at odds with those on its Form 78 (Aircraft Movements Card), which is not unusual as paperwork often took a few days to catch up with the facts. It is also the most original and complete of the four surviving Mk IVs, retaining features such as the fixing strips for the radiator armour and the mounting blocks for the rocket rail blast plates, so it is a great pity that this historic aircraft, with a proven combat record, masquerades as a Battle of Britain-era Hurricane Mk I.

The aircraft was stored at Silloth until August 1943 when it was prepared for service and assigned to No. 137 Sqdn, then based at Manston, Kent, having been located at Rochford (Southend) for a short time during the summer while it was re-equipped with rocket-armed Hurricanes in place of its twin-engined Westland Whirlwinds. The squadron was busy on 'Rhubarbs' and anti-shipping strikes – for which both cannon and rockets were used – and KX829's first known sortie was on the 28th of the month when, flown by P/O A G Brunet, DFC, it was one of eight aircraft which took off to destroy lock gates near Walcheren Island, in the company of Hurricanes from Nos. 164 and 184 Sqdns. They were escorted by Typhoons of Nos. 3 and 198 Sqdns. In the event the operation was abandoned off the Belgian coast owing to insufficient cloud cover. At this point in its career KX829 is believed to have been armed with a pair of 40mm Vickers 'S' cannon mounted below the wings.

This set the scene for the next four months, No. 137 carrying out attacks on targets across the Channel from its base at Manston. During these sorties it was flown by P/O Brunet together with P/O R W Clarke, F/O G S Chalmers, F/Sgt J Gates and F/Sgt A Witham. A typical sortie was carried out in the early morning of 27 September when, flown by F/O G S Chalmers, KX829 (coded SF-C) was one of eight aircraft which took off at 0635 hours to 'finish off' a 3,000-ton ship reported as disabled by the navy during the night and which was drifting five miles off Berck-Sur-Mer. Escorted by Typhoons from Nos. 609 and 1 Sqdns, they returned empty-handed as nothing was found. Towards the end of its time with the squadron they found themselves increasingly attacking ground targets in France – such as on

The college repainted all of its training airframes in overall silver, obliterating all previous markings and identities. (*Author's Collection*)

Following its presentation to the Birmingham Science Museum in 1961 KX829 was repainted in the desert camouflage worn by No. 6 Sqdn's Mk IIDs in 1942. (*Gordon Riley*)

5 December when, flown again by Chalmers, KX829 took part in an attack on enemy construction work east of Berck-Sur-Mer alongside aircraft from Nos. 164 and 184 Sqdns. Due to the Hurricane's lack of defensive armament they were given a Spitfire escort over the target. No. 184 failed to locate the target, No. 164 turned back due to technical trouble but No. 137 fired 60 rocket projectiles (RP) in a 70 degree dive from 10,000 to 6,000 feet, observing palls of smoke from the objective. A similar attack took place on a construction site near Mesdin on 17 December, Chalmers flying KX829 yet again.

January 1944 saw No. 137 Sqdn giving up its Hurricanes for Typhoons (which it operated for the remainder of World War 2) and KX829 was assigned to No. 286 Sqdn, which flew a variety of aircraft to provide targets for anti-aircraft gun practice in the West Country from its base at Weston

Zoyland. The unit had originally been formed at Filton, Bristol, on 17 November 1941 from No. 10 Group AAC Flight and operated from Weston Zoyland, Culmhead, Colerne and Zeals before being disbanded on 16 May 1945. KX829 served in this important but second-line role of a gun-laying practice target for the rest of the war, moving on to No. 631 Sqdn at Towyn, mid-Wales, and No. 1606 (Anti-Aircraft Co-operation) Flight being finally retired on 31 July 1945 and sent back to No. 22 MU at Silloth on 2 August.

Although most of the stored Hurricanes at Silloth were scrapped, KX829 was selected for transfer to the Department of Aeronautical Engineering at Loughborough College, Leics, to which it was issued as a training airframe on 8 March 1946, arriving there the following day which suggests it may have been flown into the small aerodrome at the college. On arrival it was seen to be in full camouflage but lacking

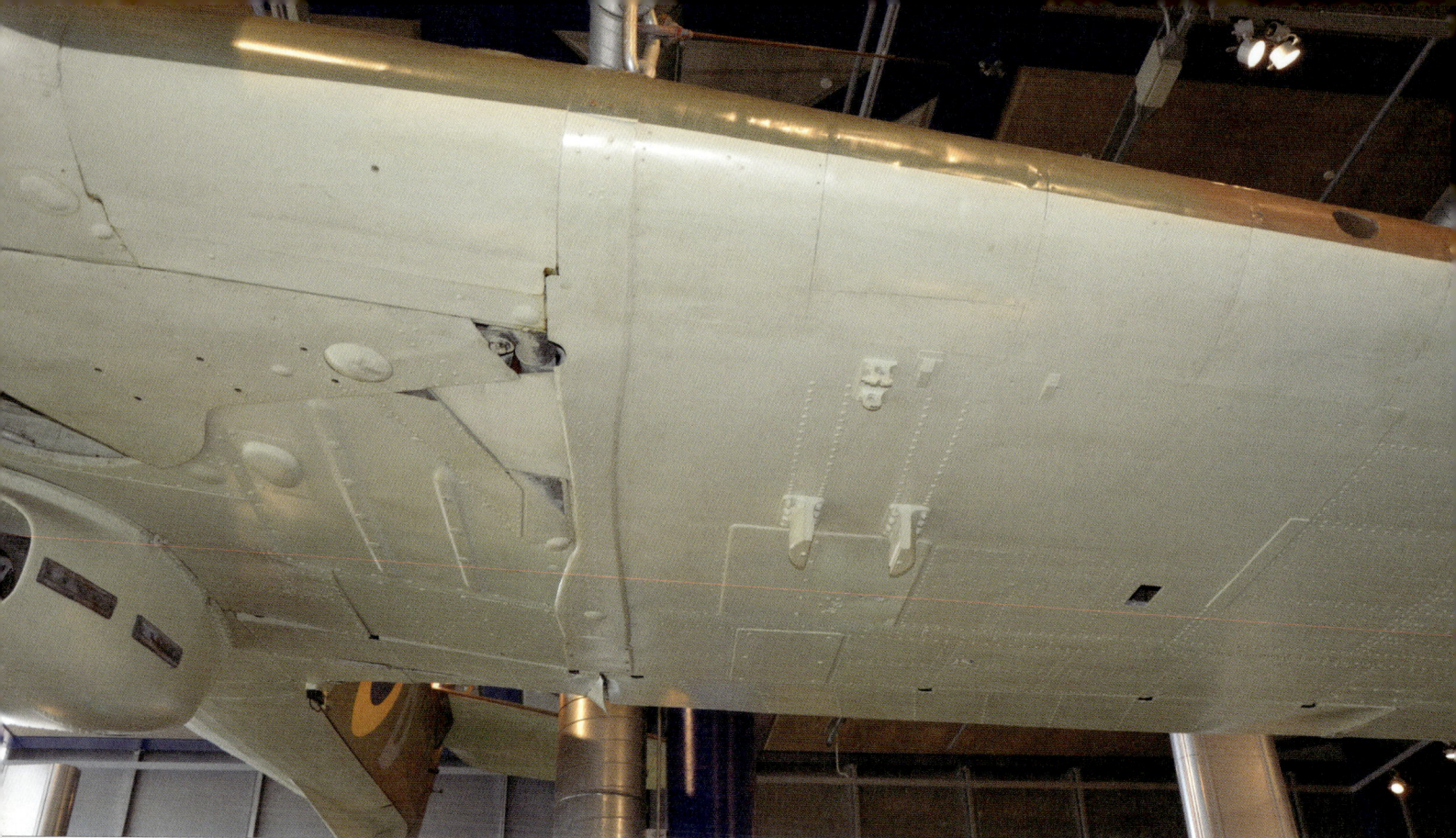

The attachment strips for the radiator armour are still clearly visible on the outside of the radiator 'bath', as are the mounting brackets for the Vickers S-type 40mm guns. (*Gordon Riley*)

any unit codes. The camouflage was soon covered over with a fresh coat of silver dope and the anonymous Hurricane served to train new engineers for the next fifteen years – alongside an interesting selection of other World War 2 types including the Shuttleworth Collection's Sea Hurricane IB, Z7015. The story that when the two Hurricanes were donated to their respective new homes in 1961 that the outer wings were swapped is completely untrue. KX829 retains its Mk IV outer wings complete with a single gun port in each wing and the underwing points for mounting Vickers 'S' guns plus the mounting blocks for the rocket rail blast plates.

By 1961 a Hurricane was of little value as a training airframe but the college had the presence of mind to present all of its aircraft to suitable homes when they were replaced by a Hawker Hunter and a Hunting Jet Provost, KX829 being gifted to the Museum of Science and Industry in Newhall Street, Birmingham, where it was repainted in the desert camouflage and squadron markings as 'JV-I' of No. 6 Sqdn – although those marks were actually carried by the

tank-busting Hurricane IIDs that the squadron operated in the Western Desert during 1942. The Hurricane took up its place in the cramped Aviation Gallery alongside a Spitfire IX, ML427, and remained on show until 1997 when the museum was closed by Birmingham City Council. The Spitfire was subsequently restored by Skysport Engineering Ltd in the correct camouflage and markings which it had carried when serving with the RAF Fighter Leaders School at Milfield in 1944.

KX829 was loaned to the RAF and moved to St Athan where the decision was taken to repaint it in the markings of the Mk I flown by Flt/Lt Arthur Clowes, DFM, during the Battle of Britain. This was done for the 60th anniversary of the Battle of Britain in 2000 and the aircraft was displayed as such during that year. Unfortunately it still carried these markings when it was returned for display in the new Thinktank at Millennium Point, Birmingham, which opened in 2002, and there are no plans for them to be changed.

KZ191
Hawker Hurricane Mk IV

Robs Lamplough, East Garston, Berks, UK

KZ191 was ordered from Hawker Aircraft Ltd as one of the eighth production block (Contract No. 62305/39) and was built at Langley in early 1943. The aircraft in this block of 1,200 were a mixture of Mks IIB, IIC, IID and IV with serials in the range KW696-KZ612, although 60 aircraft were diverted as Sea Hurricanes and given new serials between NF668-NF703 (36) and NF716-NF739 (24). KZ191 fell into the serial batch KZ185-KZ192 and made its first flight on 9 March 1943, being allocated to No. 22 MU at Silloth, Cumbria, the next day, arriving there three days later on 13 March.

It remained in store at Silloth until 21 August 1943 when it was allocated to the Air Fighting Development Unit at Wittering, near Peterborough, remaining there until 4 March

KZ191 remains stored at Robs Lamplough's private airfield in Berkshire. This photo is interesting as the radiator armour can clearly be seen in front of the radiator 'bath'. *(Stuart Lewis Photography)*

1944 when it moved on to No. 1695 BDF (Bomber Defence Flight) based at Dalton, Yorks. These units were employed on fighter affiliation duties, usually in conjunction with a conversion unit or operational training unit, and flew various types of fighters including Tomahawks, Hurricanes, Spitfires and Beaufighters. With the AFDU it may have carried the unit's code of 'AF-', which had been inherited from No. 607 Sqdn, whilst with No. 1695 BDF it would have been coded '3K-'. After a few months training air gunners how to fend off marauding fighters KZ191 was selected for active duty and on 28 July 1944 it was flown to Morrison Engineering Ltd at Peterborough, part of the Hurricane Repair Organisation, for a 'repair in works' (RIW), which involved giving it a complete overhaul and tropicalisation – including a Vokes filter – in preparation for dispatch to Casablanca.

The work was finished by 18 August and KZ191 was flown to the holding unit of No. 22 MU, Silloth, on 4 September where it was stored until 3 November when it was moved to No. 215 MU at Dumfries where the packing depot broke it down and crated it, delivering it by road to Manchester Docks. It was loaded onto the 5,205-ton steamer SS *Guinean*, coded 'L.S.2216', on 22 December; it is interesting to note that the *Guinean* had rescued 3,600 men – including many RAF servicemen – from France during Operation Ariel in May 1940 and that it was owned by the United Africa Company, whose chairman was none other than Lord Trenchard, 'The Father of the Royal Air Force'.

Although the Form 78 states that the ship was docked at Manchester, she actually left from Liverpool on 27 December bound for Belfast Lough and subsequently joined Convoy OS102/ KMS 76 which left Liverpool on 2 January, arriving in Gibraltar on 10 January 1945. The ship was carrying stores and general cargo (which included aircraft) plus 12 passengers. On Saturday 13 January the ship joined five other vessels in Convoy GC108 for the short crossing to Casablanca, where it docked the next day, KZ191 being officially logged as arriving on Monday 15 January 1945.

The next significant date on its Movements Card is 25 January 1945 when it was allotted to 'NAAF' (North African Air Force) and it was very probably assembled and tested by No. 145 MU at Cazes; from then on the Movements Card is very sketchy with a simple comment that it had been received by 'ME' (Middle East Air Force) on 2 August and finally struck off charge on 26 September 1946, however

research carried out by Richard Edgeler and others paints a very different picture.

It seems that KZ191 joined No. 351 Sqdn at Canne or Vis, in February 1945 or possibly at Prkos, the move from Canne, on the eastern coast of the 'heel' of Italy to Prkos in Yugoslavia (now the site of Zadar Airport, Croatia) taking place that month. Its first mission, recorded in No. 351's Operational Record Book, was on 14 March when P/O J Klokocovnik carried out an attack on a German dining hall NW of Lussingrande. The sortie lasted from 1200-1255 hours and he logged his time over the target as 1225 noting 'Carried out attack with 32 R.P. Four near misses, others overshot.' On the morning of 27 March it was in action again when P/O F Jez attacked a bridge near Primislje village. When over the target he observed the bridge was destroyed and some of the structure was under water.

This type of sortie was typical as the squadron attacked the retreating German forces over the next few weeks, targeting German positions, garrisons and enemy shipping to devastating effect. With the European war over in early May all Allied forces were withdrawn from the Balkans and No. 351 (and its sister squadron No. 352) were formally handed over to the Yugoslav Air Force on 15 June 1945. It was at this time that an exchange of aircraft was carried out between Nos. 351 and 6 Sqdns, both of which were based at Prkos. No. 6 had been based in Palestine throughout the inter-war period and it was scheduled to return there in August 1945. During the Balkan campaign its Hurricanes had flown with four RP's under the port wing and a long-range drop tank under the starboard; they were now required to carry the full eight RPs and, despite an extensive search, not enough blast plates and RP rails could be traced, hence the swap with No. 351's fully-armed Hurricanes.

No. 6 flew to Campomarino, Italy, in May, bringing KZ191 with it and they moved to Canne and then Megiddo before flying across the Mediterranean via Araxos (Greece), Hassani, Maleme (Crete), El Adem and Mersa Matruh to land at Petah Tiqva (Palestine) in August, eventually moving on to Ramat David where they remained based until June 1946. F/Lt B A Newman of No. 6 Sqdn flew KZ191 on several occasions between 20 September and 8 October 1945 and its last known flight was on 29 April 1946 when Sgt J H Jenkins put in 55 minutes of low flying practice. The squadron was now facing problems on two fronts; the

Hurricanes were getting more difficult to maintain (they were the last operational Hurricane squadron in the Royal Air Force) and there was increasing amounts of disturbance due to efforts to establish the State of Israel. The first problem was overcome by the supply of a few Spitfire IXs with 'zero-length' RP rails and gyro gunsights adapted for RP work which arrived in February 1946 – and the promise of new Hawker Tempests – the second was more difficult and on 13 September 1946 the squadron received orders to pack up and leave its base at Ein Shemer, to which it had moved in June 1946, and leave Palestine for Nicosia, Cyprus. The ground equipment was to be crated by the 16th and shipped from Haifa on the 18th whilst it was planned that the aircraft would fly out on the 21st.

In the event eight Hurricanes took off for Nicosia on 25 September and, escorted by a Halifax of 283 Wing, made landfall without incident – although one was smoking badly due to an oil leak. Two more Hurricanes were air-tested at Ein Shemer on the 26th, the adjutant being the only pilot available, and one of them was declared serviceable. By 30 September three Hurricanes were serviceable and they flew to Nicosia in the company of a Dakota provided by 283 Wing. Any unserviceable Hurricanes had already been stripped of parts and disabled (by smashing the reduction gear on the Merlin XX with a sledgehammer) so that they would be of little military value in the forthcoming War of Independence.

At least two of them, KZ191 and another so-far unidentified example (see 'KZ321') were abandoned and found their way into a scrapyard on the outskirts of Jaffa, along with sundry other hardware including a Mosquito wing. It was from here that Robs Lamplough retrieved the fuselage, complete with centre section, undercarriage and Merlin, in 1983 and brought it back to the UK where it was stored initially at Fowlmere near Duxford, Cambs. In 1985 it was moved to Robs' hangar at North Weald where it remained until 2002 when it was taken to his private airfield at East Garston, Berks, where it remains stored. No wings were found at Jaffa and it is assumed that as these were all metal they were 'recycled'. It is fascinating to see that the aircraft still retains the radiator armour that was installed – very probably – by Morrisons of Peterborough when it was being prepared for dispatch to Casablanca in the summer of 1944.

Some conservation and restoration work has been done in the cockpit area but all further work has been suspended. (*Stuart Lewis Photography*)

Robs has no plans for any restoration of KZ191. If a restoration to flying condition were performed it would necessitate replacing all of the fuselage steel tubing and the construction of new wings; the 'time capsule' that is KZ191 would then be lost forever.

KZ321*
Hawker Hurricane Mk IV

Vintage Wings of Canada, Gatineau, Ottawa, Ontario, Canada

The true identity of this aircraft is unknown, all manufacturer's plates and its original Merlin engine having disappeared in the years between its discovery alongside KZ191 (qv) in a Jaffa scrapyard in 1983 and its acquisition by Stephen Grey of The Fighter Collection some ten years later. It is reasonable to assume that it was ordered from Hawker Aircraft Ltd as one of the eighth production block (Contract No. 62305/39) and was built at Langley but that is all. The aircraft in this block of 1,200 were a mixture of Mks IIB, IIC, IID and IV with serials in the range KW696-KZ612,

'KZ321' flies in formation with Michael Potter's Spitfire LF XVIE on 21 September 2008. The colour scheme is based on that carried by No. 6 Sqdn in 1942 although the real KZ321 did not join the squadron until 1944 and would have been finished in 'temperate' grey/green camouflage. *(Eric Dumigan)*

although 60 aircraft were delivered as Sea Hurricanes and given new serials between NF668-NF703 (36) and NF716-NF739 (24). Most of the aircraft in the batch found their way to No. 22 MU at Silloth, Cumbria, where they were stored until prepared for issue to either operational or second-line units.

As this Hurricane was found with KZ191 it is obvious that it too must have served with No. 6 Sqdn in Palestine and may well have seen previous service at Prkos, Yugoslavia, either with No. 6 itself or with the Yugoslavian Hurricane unit, No. 351 Sqdn. No. 6 flew to Campomarino, Italy, in May 1945, and they moved to Canne and then Megiddo before flying across the Mediterranean via Araxos (Greece), Hassani, Maleme (Crete), El Adem and Mersa Matruh to land at Petah Tiqva (Palestine) in August, eventually moving on to Ramat David, where they remained based until June 1946 when they moved to Ein Shemer. On 13 September 1946 the squadron received orders to pack up and leave Palestine for Nicosia, Cyprus. The ground equipment was to be crated by the 16th and shipped from Haifa on the 18th whilst it was planned that the aircraft would fly out on the 21st. Details of the actual departure flights are given in the entry for KZ191 (page 109).

Any unserviceable Hurricanes were stripped of parts and disabled (by smashing the reduction gear on the Merlin XX with a sledgehammer) so that they would be of little military value in the forthcoming War of Independence. With absolutely no physical evidence to show on the airframe it

is a matter of conjecture as to which Hurricane this really is. KZ191 was officially struck off charge (SOC) on 26 September 1946, the same date as two of the squadron's other Hurricanes, KZ916 and LE292, so they may be considered as possible candidates, as might LE659 (SOC, 25 July 1946) or KZ726 (SOC, 28 August 1946).

All that is known for certain is that two wingless Hurricane fuselage frames, still with their centre sections and main undercarriage units, were found abandoned in a scrapyard in Jaffa in 1983. Robs Lamplough brought KZ191 home and alerted the late Doug Arnold about the other one. Arnold repatriated the other Hurricane a few months later and it was soon to be found in one of his hangars at Blackbushe, Hants, where some preliminary work was carried out on it.

Arnold had purchased a pair of Hurricane wings from The Doon School, Dehra Dun, India, during a visit in February 1976. The same school also possessed the reduction gear, propeller and spinner from the Hurricane which were acquired at the same time and these were combined with the anonymous fuselage to create a reasonable Hurricane project.

The aircraft was moved from Blackbushe to Arnold's new base at Biggin Hill and it was from here that it was obtained by Stephen Grey of The Fighter Collection during 1991 and moved to his base at Duxford. Some work was carried out at Duxford but in the end the decision was made to transfer the project to Hawker Restorations Ltd at Milden, Suffolk, where a full restoration to flying condition was carried out

One of the two
Hurricane wings
found in the Doon
School, Dehra Dun,
India, during a visit
in February 1976.
(Peter R Arnold)

The project laid out in one of Doug Arnold's hangars at Blackbushe. *(Philippe Denis via Ben Gilbert)*

between 2001 and 2003. During the work all of the steel tubing was replaced, although the stainless steel plates and attachments brackets, and items such as forgings which could be NDT-tested, were restored for use in the rebuilt aircraft. The Indian wings were rebuilt and fitted with four dummy Hispano cannon barrels, the gun bays being used for overload fuel tanks, and a civilian Merlin 500 driving a Rotol RS5/13 propeller was installed.

The final configuration chosen was representative of a cannon-armed Hurricane Mk IID, without a tropical Vokes filter, but the colour scheme represents a Mk IV, KZ321, which served with No. 6 Sqdn as 'JV-N' until it was lost on 24 May 1944 when being flown by P/O Grey. It may have been hit by ground fire or possibly crashed as a result of damage caused by its own exploding RPs. Grey bailed out at about 1,000 feet and was seen floating in the sea, apparently lifeless. His body was never recovered and he has no known grave.

The project had been registered by Doug Arnold as G-HURY on 31 March 1989 and this registration was retained when it was re-registered to Stephen Grey, operating as Patina Ltd, on 25 April 1991. It made its first flight from Earls Colne, Essex, on 8 July 2003 and was flown to Duxford the following day where it appeared in the 'Flying Legends' air display. It remained based at Duxford for three more years but was sold to Michael Potter's Vintage Wings of Canada and the UK civil registration was cancelled on 20 February 2006. It arrived at its new home at Gatineau Executive Airport, Ottawa, Ontario, on 18 May and made its first flight from Canadian soil on 15 June 2006. It is now registered in Canada as C-FTPM and retains the markings of No. 6 Sqdn.

LD619
Hawker Hurricane Mk IIC

Ditsong National Museum of Military History, Saxonwold, Johannesburg, South Africa

LD619 was ordered from Hawker Aircraft Ltd as one of the ninth production block (Contract No. 62305/39) and was built at Langley in the summer of 1943 as a tropicalised Mk IIC. The aircraft in this block of 1,961 were a mixture of Mks IIB, IIC and IV with serials in the range LB542-LF956. LD619 fell into the serial batch LD594-LD632 (39 aircraft).

Like most of the batch, it was allocated to No. 22 MU at Silloth, Cumbria, on 27 August, probably arriving there on the 30th, and was almost immediately flown to No. 215 MU at Dumfries, to which it was delivered between 8-10 September. Here it would have been crated for overseas dispatch and taken by road or rail to Glasgow Docks where

Hurricanes of B Flight, No. 11 OTU, St Albans, Port Elizabeth, in the immediate post-war period. *(SAAF archives)*

LD619, wearing its SAAF serial 5285, on show at the Ditsong National Museum of Military History in September 2014. *(Alan Wilson)*

it was loaded on board the SS *Empire Marlowe* for shipment to Casablanca.

The ship had docked in the Clyde on 22 September and remained there until early October when she sailed for Liverpool to join Convoy OS86 which left Liverpool on 8 October bound for Casablanca and Freetown. Her cargo consisted of coal and aircraft! She docked in Casablanca on 19 October and LD619 was officially taken on charge by North African Air Forces (NAAF) on 31 October, probably being assembled and test-flown by No. 145 MU at Cazes, Casablanca.

What happened to it during the next six months is not recorded but it was allocated to the South African Air Force on 30 April 1944 and noted as still on charge in the Census of Aircraft which was held on 1 October 1945. It is believed that it was not issued to an operational squadron but flown to

South Africa, probably via the eastern route, where it joined No. 11 OTU at Waterkloof. No. 11 OTU had been formed at Zwartkop on 1 July 1943 and operated three flights; A Flight aircraft were coded 'AX', B Flight were 'GL' and C Flight carried 'DB'. Hurricanes started replacing P-40 Kittyhawks from May 1944 and post-war they continued to be operated by No. 7 Wing at Waterkloof until they started to be retired from October 1946 onwards. SAAF Hurricanes were given serials in the range 5201-5355; LD619 was allocated the SAAF serial 5285 and may have been coded 'AX-E' of A Flight.

The National Museum of Military History had been established during World War 2 and was opened on 29 August 1947 and Hurricane 5285 joined the collection in May 1950. Initially displayed parked on its undercarriage it is now preserved in an elevated location within the aircraft collection.

LD975
Hawker Hurricane Mk IV

Museum of Aviation, Nikola Tesla Airport, Belgrade, Serbia

LD975 was ordered from Hawker Aircraft Ltd as one of the ninth production block (Contract No. 62305/39) and was built at Langley in the autumn of 1943 as a rocket-armed Mk IV. The aircraft in this block of 1,961 were a mixture of Mks IIB, IIC and IV with serials in the range LB542-LF956, LD975 falling into the serial batch LD931-LD979 (49 aircraft). Like most of the batch, it was allocated to No. 22 MU at Silloth, Cumbria, on 26 September, probably arriving there on the 28th, and was stored until early 1944 when it was prepared for service and allocated to No. 438 Sqdn on 5 February, probably joining the unit two days later. The squadron had been formed on 15 November 1943 by

renumbering No. 118 (BR) Sqdn RCAF which had been serving in Nova Scotia and Alaska, initially as a coastal reconnaissance squadron but later as a P-40 Kittyhawk fighter unit. Following the move to the UK it received its first Hurricane Mk IVs at its new home of Digby on 22 November and began working up, initially with rockets but changing to fighter-bombing in January 1944 as it became part of the Ayr-based 143 Wing. Although the squadron was intended as a Typhoon unit it was still receiving Hurricanes in February 1944 and was mainly equipped with them when it moved to Hurn, Dorset, to commence operations in March 1944.

LD975, painted as 'O' of No. 351 Sqdn as based at Prkos in the spring and early summer of 1945. *(Phil Glover)*

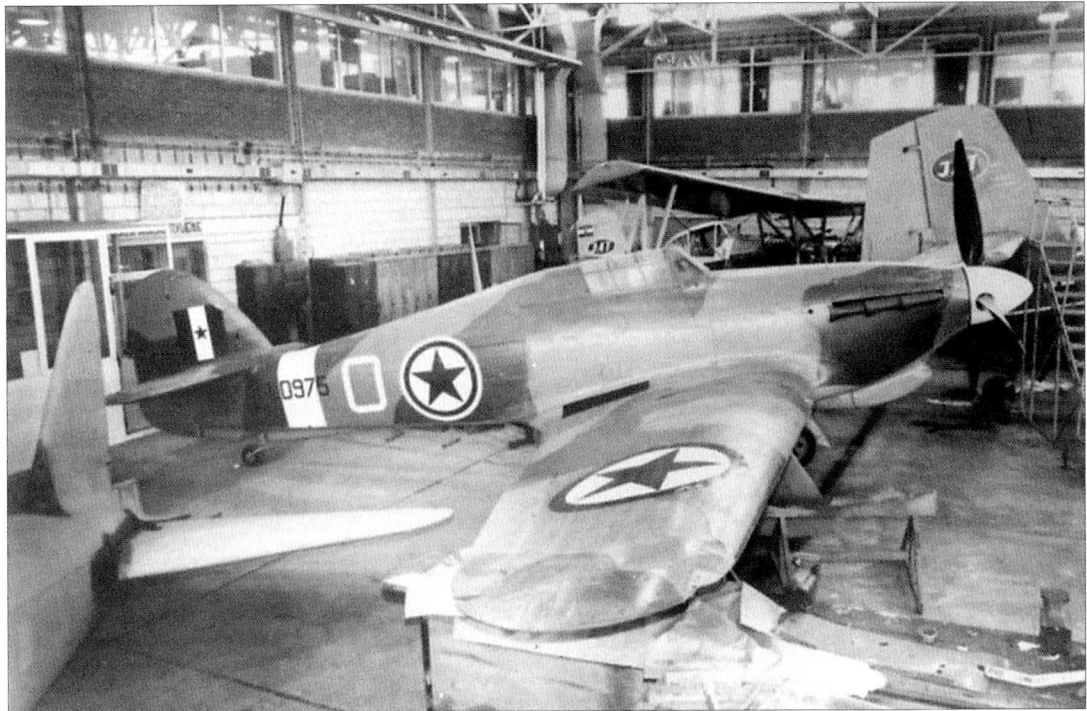

As the Typhoons started to arrive the squadron performed its first fighter sweep with them on 20 March and by the end of April it was fully engaged on hitting 'Noball' targets and radar installations in the run-up to D-Day. This meant that the Hurricanes could be moved on and LD975 was assigned to No. 1 Tactical Exercise Unit (TEU) at Tealing, Angus, Scotland, on 21 April, probably arriving on the 26th of the month. This unit had previously been known as No. 1 Combat Training Wing and prior to that No. 56 OTU; it specialised in air firing and evasive action training.

By January 1944 No. 1 TEU was operating with up to 110 aircraft and during February 1944, it exchanged 40 Hurricanes for 38 Spitfires from Grangemouth. Just prior to D-Day the TEU was put on operational readiness in the unlikely event of a counter-attack from Norway but was stood down on 15 June and disbanded on 31 July 1944. In light of the winding-down of Hurricane operations at Tealing, LD975 was sent to No. 22 MU at Silloth, Cumbria, on 9 June 1944, probably arriving two days later, and was very probably overhauled and brought up to tropical standard, complete with a Vokes air filter, before being sent to the Packed Aircraft Transit Pool (PATP) at No. 215 MU, Dumfries, where it was crated for overseas dispatch by sea. It arrived at Dumfries on 27 October and was crated by 3

November before being sent by road or rail to the docks at Liverpool where it was loaded aboard the SS *Silverlarch*.

The vessel sailed from Liverpool on 13 November 1944 as part of Convoy OS95 and docked at Casablanca on 23 November where LD975 would have been unloaded and probably transported to No. 145 MU at nearby Cazes for assembly and test flying. It was officially issued to the Yugoslav Air Force on 14 June 1945 but for the previous few months it had been on charge with No. 351 (Yugoslav) Sqdn of the RAF which had operated from Canne, Italy – with a detachment on the island of Vis – until moving to Prkos (present-day Zadar Airport, Croatia) in mid-February 1945. As such it was a contemporary of Robs Lamplough's KZ191 (qv). The squadron was heavily involved in attacking the retreating German forces over the next few weeks, targeting German positions, garrisons and enemy shipping with its RP-equipped Hurricanes to devastating effect. With the European war over in early May all Allied forces were withdrawn from the Balkans and No. 351 (and its sister squadron No. 352) were formally handed over to the Yugoslav Air Force on 15 June 1945.

Unlike KZ191, LD975 was not exchanged with No. 6 Sqdn but remained on charge with the newly-created Yugoslav Air Force. Hurricanes were no strangers to the

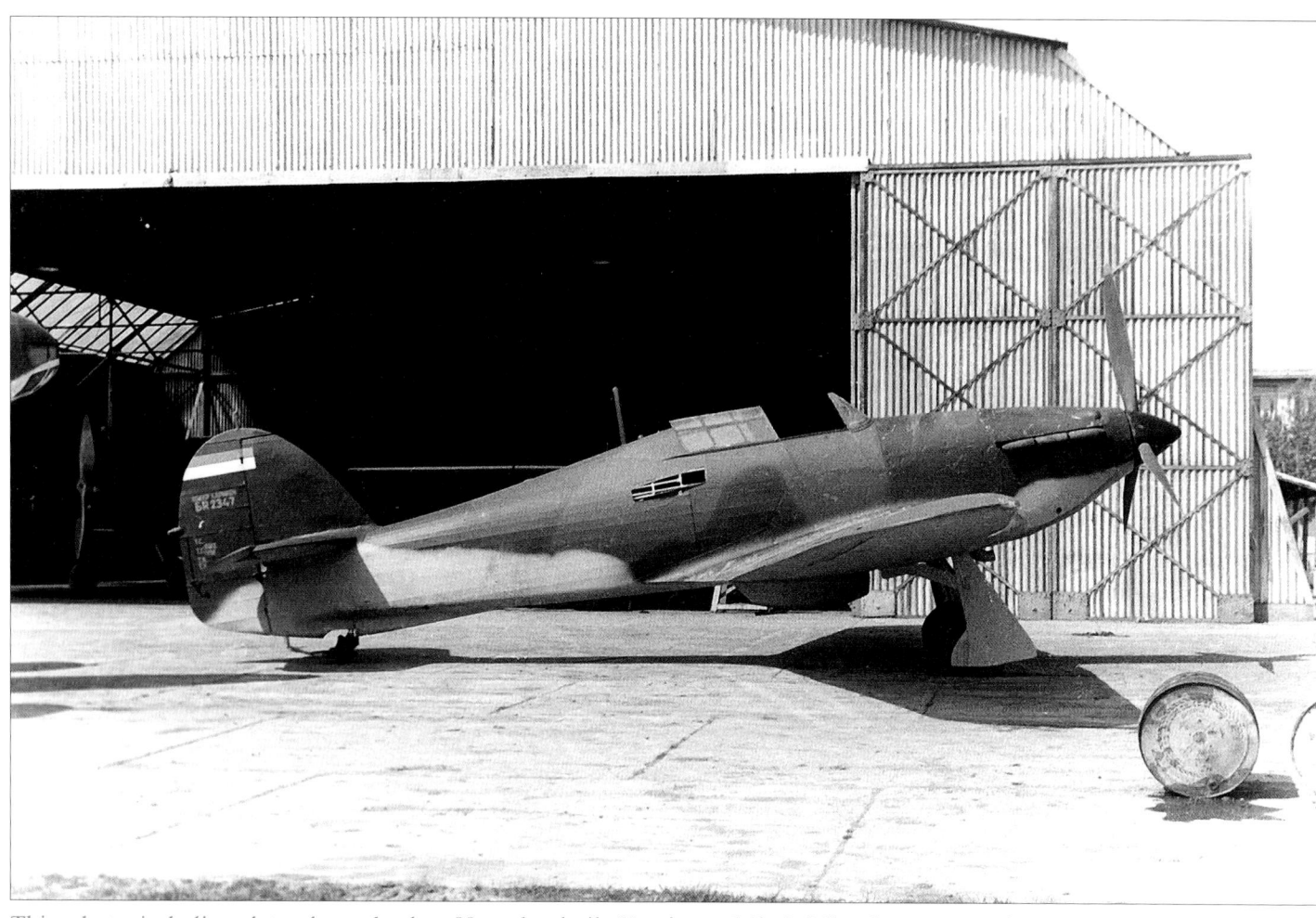

This photo is believed to show the last Yugoslav-built Hurricane Mk I following capture by German forces. *(Author's Collection)*

Yugoslavs as between December 1938 and February 1940 24 Mk Is had been delivered from the UK and the Hurricane had been licence-built in Yugoslavia until production ceased due to the war. Indeed one locally-built Hurricane, known as the LVT 1, (Lovac Vazduhoplovno Tehnički) had been flown with a Daimler Benz DB 601 engine as fitted to the Messerschmitt Bf 109.

In Yugoslav service LD975 was given the YAF serial 9539 and continued to serve until more modern, Soviet-supplied, aircraft became available, being finally retired on 18 August 1952. After withdrawal from service it was initially allotted to the Military Museum and displayed externally at Kalemagden Park, Belgrade, before being handed over to the Aeronautical Museum at Zemun in 1961. At that time it was coded 'T' and had traces of '319' on the wings. By the early 1970s it had been moved, together with many other aircraft, to Belgrade's Surčin Airport (since re-named Nikola Tesla Airport) and was subsequently restored in the markings of No. 351 Sqdn at the maintenance base of JAT (Yugoslav Airlines) before being put on permanent display in the new museum which opened in May 1989.

LF363
Hawker Hurricane Mk IIC

RAF Battle of Britain Memorial Flight, Coningsby, Lincs, UK

Despite the oft repeated claim that LF363 is "… the last Hurricane to enter service with the RAF …" nothing could be further from the truth; many Hurricanes were delivered after LF363 joined its first unit on 30 March 1944. Indeed four of the survivors, LF658, LF686, LF738 and LF751 were all taken on charge after LF363 and – if you want to be pedantic about it – PZ865 is actually the last Hurricane to enter service with the RAF as Duncan Simpson did not deliver it from the manufacturers until March 1972!

LF363 was ordered from Hawker Aircraft Ltd as one of the tenth production block (Contract No. 62305/39) and was built at Langley in the winter of 1943/44 as a cannon-armed Mk IIC. The aircraft in this block of 1,961 were a mixture of Mks IIB, IIC and IV with serials in the range LB542-LF956. LF363 fell into the serial batch LF359-LF405 (34 aircraft). It made its first flight on 1 January 1944 and was delivered to No. 5 MU at Kemble, Wilts, on 28 January. It was powered by a Merlin XX, engine number 142613/418645 and had 50 minutes flying time on it when readied for the delivery flight from Langley to Kemble, which took just 30 minutes. It remained at Kemble until 30 March when an ATA ferry pilot from No. 16 Ferry Pool at Kirkbride picked it up and delivered it to No. 63 Sqdn at Turnhouse near Edinburgh, the flight lasting 1hr 40mins.

No. 63 Sqdn had reformed in June 1942 from an element of No. 239 Squadron, initially equipped with the Mustang I and started undertaking tactical reconnaissance missions along the French coast in early 1943. It re-equipped with Hurricanes in March 1944, possibly due to issues with the Allison V-1710 engines of the early Mustangs, and had moved to Scotland from Odiham in January 1944. The Hurricanes were a temporary measure as the squadron converted to Spitfires in May; the squadron spent much of its time cooperating with either the army, taking part

LF363 showing off its latest colour scheme at the Shuttleworth Collection's Pageant at Old Warden on 7 September 2014. (*Gordon Riley*)

in training exercises, or with the navy, providing spotter aircraft for the naval bombardment on D-Day and during the Walcheren landings. The squadron also performed some tactical reconnaissance.

It was only as a result of a chance comment on an aero-modelling website in February 2015 that the author decided to re-check the Form 700 for LF363 and was astonished to note that on 7 April 1944 it was fitted with camera bearers in the rear fuselage and that two F.24 cameras were installed the following day. The aircraft continued to carry the blanked off camera ports for the rest of its life and they were even replaced during the complete restoration undertaken by Historic Flying Limited – although nobody realised what they were.

Although based at Turnhouse the squadron operated detachments at Dundonald and Ballyherbert during April and May 1944 before moving to Lee-on-the-Solent where it re-equipped with Spitfires. As a consequence LF363 joined No. 309 (Polish) Sqdn at Drem on 23 May, taking up the code 'WC-F'. Just like No. 63 Sqdn this squadron had previously been equipped with the Allison-powered Mustang I – also in the fighter-reconnaissance role – and

found the change to the Hurricane somewhat disappointing to say the least. They spent much of their time patrolling the east coast of Scotland and the Firth of Forth, after a solitary Ju 88 had dropped some bombs on Edinburgh. In September 1944, the unit converted back to Mustang Mk Is and LF363 was off on its travels again, re-joining its old unit, No. 63 Sqdn, on 2 November, now based at Manston and then North Weald, before moving to No. 26 Sqdn at Tangmere on 30 November 1944. No. 26 was also operating in the fighter-reconnaissance role but the Hurricane was not really suited to this and the squadron re-equipped with Mustangs in December 1944 – prompting another move for LF363, this time to No. 62 OTU at Ouston near Durham where it served for the remainder of the war. Its four 20mm cannon were removed on 20 April 1945. Despite an extensive search there is no mention of the cameras being removed but it is assumed that this took place when the aircraft was transferred to Ouston.

The aircraft's servicing logbooks (Form 700) indicate that it was air-tested following repairs at No. 22 MU, Silloth, on 4 July 1945, at which time it had logged a total of 144 hours 35 mins of flying time and had suffered no significant damage or accidents. It was then allocated to No. 5 MU, Kemble, on 14 August but was actually taken on charge by the Station Flight at Middle Wallop at the end of the month. Here it remained – possibly as the 'hack' of the station commander or another high-ranking officer – and was maintained in flying trim, although the Form 700 indicates that significant amounts of work had to be done to keep it flying – despite the fact that it was only three years old. The Form 78 (Aircraft Movements Card) has an entry dated 21 June 1947 which notes that LF363 was 'presumed struck off charge' which further backs up the theory that it was operating in a semi-official capacity at Middle Wallop; LF363 was certainly being flown regularly as the fuelling figures indicate the tanks being filled several times a month during the summer of 1947.

Seen at Hawker's airfield at Langley in 1955, LF363 has lost the air vice-marshal's pennant and also its cannon stubs. (*BAE SYSTEMS*)

There is a suggestion that by August 1947 LF363 had been transferred to the Fighter Command Communications Squadron at Northolt but the paperwork does not support this, the Form 700 confirming that it was still on charge at Middle Wallop but now with the Station Handling Flight. This state of affairs continued until 6 February 1948 when it was transferred to the Station Flight at Thorney Island, Hants, in accordance with a signal from HQ Fighter Command (Q 123) dated 5 February 1948. All of this coincides with the period when AVM Sir Stanley Vincent, DFC, AFC, held the position of Senior Air Staff Officer, RAF Fighter Command.

From 1948 he commanded 11 Group before requesting retirement in 1950. Vincent was the only RAF pilot to have downed aircraft in both world wars, firstly when flying with No. 60 Sqdn RFC during 1916-1917 and latterly when serving as station commander at Northolt during the Battle of Britain, when he often flew and fought alongside the Polish Hurricane squadrons under his command. Vincent's 'boss' Sir James Robb had a Spitfire LFXVIE, SL721, as his personal 'hack' at the time and Vincent 'acquired' LF363 as his.

Following the formation of the Battle of Britain Flight at Biggin Hill in 1957 LF363 was painted in green and brown camouflage, carrying these colours until 1968. (*Tony Clarke Collection*)

There is a tale that LF363 was found abandoned and awaiting scrapping and that Sir Sydney Camm personally arranged for it to be restored and presented to Vincent but that is stretching the facts somewhat. What the Form 700 records is that following its appearance in the 1948 Battle of Britain Flypast over London, in which it was flown by Vincent, a telephone call was made by W/Cdr Vatcher of HQ Fighter Command and the aircraft was ferried from Thorney Island to Hawker Aircraft at Langley on 29 October 1948 for significant amounts of rectification work to be carried out; by now it had 219 hours 55 mins flying time logged. During the Battle of Britain Flypast, on 15 September, the accumulator stowage panel (a large panel on the starboard side of the fuselage behind the cockpit) had detached in flight and Vincent had landed at West Malling where a temporary plywood panel was made and fitted in order to get him and 'his' Hurricane home.

Following the work at Langley LF363 was checked, on

20 April 1949, and judged to be serviceable for the ferry flight back to Thorney Island, subject to refuelling at Bovingdon – coincidentally where Robb's Spitfire was based with the Metropolitan Communication Squadron. On the morning of the flight, 22 April, the compressor was found to be not charging the air bottle to sufficient pressure so the bottle was charged on the ground and the flight plan amended to a direct flight to Thorney Island – where it landed with the undercarriage retracted when the gear failed to come down.

During filming of *The Battle of Britain* in 1968 LF363 carried a variety of different codes and serials; here it is seen in Polish markings as 'H3421/MI-D'. *(Peter R Arnold Collection)*

Repair work started immediately, the decision to carry out the work 'in house' being taken on 23 April and the Merlin XXII (which had only 22½ hours on it) was removed on 4 May for shock-testing and found to be within limits. The damage to the engine bay was repaired and the engine re-installed on 13 May with the team making excellent progress – replacing many components with serviceable units taken from stores – the final inspection taking place on 13 June when the aircraft was signed off for flight testing by S/Ldr E J Andrews. Following minor snagging a signal was received from Fighter Command HQ and on 27 June the aircraft was prepared for a re-spray in 'ice blue' with a red spinner, together with the air vice-marshal's pennant and the crest of 11 Group, Fighter Command, carried below the cockpit. Further touches were added on 10 September when a locally-made personal kit stowage box was fitted in the rear fuselage in order that Sir Stanley could pack a few items into the Hurricane when visiting airfields within 11 Group.

Vincent flew LF363 in the 1949 Battle of Britain Flypast over London, without incident, but he was soon to retire and the Hurricane was transferred to Hawker Aircraft at Langley on 28 November where the engine was inhibited and LF363 was stored until August 1950 when it was reactivated prior to delivery to Waterbeach in Cambridgeshire on 1 September (interestingly Vincent now lived in Bury St Edmunds, not far from Waterbeach). The following May saw LF363 flown to No. 19 MU at St Athan for servicing, many problems were discovered and the recommendation was made that '… this aircraft <u>not</u> flown at speeds exceeding 180 knots as vibration of cockpit section becomes excessive.' It was then flown to Langley where Hawkers removed the cannon mounting tubes and blanked off the leading edges of the wings before re-spraying it in temporary camouflage and markings for a flying role in the film *Angels One Five* which was filmed at Kenley during July 1951. LF363 was joined by Hawker's own PZ865 plus some Portuguese Air Force Hurricanes and flew at Kenley as 'P2617' – making life difficult for historians 60-odd years later trying to work out whether the actual P2617 (qv) had flown in the film or not (it didn't!). With the filming over the cannon tubes were re-installed on 18 August and LF363 returned to its ice blue colours by the simple expedient of washing off the temporary camouflage. It had been officially recorded as on charge to the Station Flight at Kenley during the filming but it now moved to Biggin Hill Station Flight and even No. 41 Sqdn – which was based at Biggin with DH Hornets at the time – before finding its way back to Waterbeach on 6 November 1951.

These markings – an approximation of those worn by Douglas Bader's Hurricane – were carried between 1969 and 1972. This photo was taken at Chivenor in August 1969. *(Gordon Riley)*

Between 1973–1978 the code letters were changed in style, as seen here in a photo taken at the Mildenhall Air Fete. *(Gordon Riley)*

LF363 remained at Waterbeach for the next four years, in the company of a motley collection of time-expired Hurricanes which had been gathered from other stations as a source of spare parts to keep it – now the last airworthy Hurricane on RAF strength – in the air. These three Hurricanes Z3687, LF751 and PG953 were progressively cannibalised until their remnants were used to build up a static gate guardian which took on the identity LF751 (qv). LF363's film career continued when it was used during the filming of a BBC television series *The War in the Air* and then, in August 1955, it returned to Kenley once more where it was utilised in the film *Reach for the Sky* – the life story of Douglas Bader. Following filming it was flown to Langley for another major overhaul in September 1955 and on 10 June 1956, resplendent in all silver and with the cannon tubes finally removed, it was delivered to Biggin Hill where it joined the Station Flight. The station CO was an ex-Battle of Britain Hurricane pilot, Wg/Cdr Peter Thompson, DFC, and Peter

hatched a plan to set up a Battle of Britain Flight at Biggin Hill with LF363 as its founding member.

Following the acquisition of three Spitfire PR XIXs and then three Spitfire LF XVIEs the following year Peter's idea became a reality and developed into what we now know as the Royal Air Force Battle of Britain Memorial Flight, the newly-camouflaged LF363 and Spitfire TE330 performing the Battle of Britain Flypast over London on 15 September 1957 as the flight's first official duty. More filming came the way of LF363 during 1957 when it was used in the film *The One That Got Away* about the German PoW Franz von Werra, Northolt doubling for the Rolls-Royce airfield at Hucknall where the real von Werra tried to steal a Hurricane.

Peter was posted from Biggin in February 1958 and, with the closure of the base, LF363 and the rest of the flight moved to North Weald the following month but that closed too so in May they moved to Martlesham Heath in Suffolk. Although the Spitfires experienced severe problems LF363 soldiered on, moving in November 1961 to a new home at Horsham St Faith, Norfolk, at which time it and Spitfire PR XIX PM631 were the only airworthy aircraft left on the flight – a situation which prevailed until 1964, by which time the flight had moved yet again, this time to Coltishall, Norfolk, on 1 April 1963, after the closure of Horsham St Faith.

The 'GN-F' markings of No. 249 (Gold Coast) Sqdn, 1940, were carried between 1979 and 1982, as seen here at Baginton when LF363 was sporting a Spitfire's four-bladed prop due to servicability issues. (*Gordon Riley*)

Following the acquisition of Spitfire AB910 in 1965 the Battle of Britain Memorial Flight started to establish itself more securely and LF363, in its green and brown camouflage with a red spinner, was a familiar sight at air displays and special events throughout the 1960s until it was 'called up' for duty in the epic film *The Battle of Britain* which was filmed at North Weald, Debden, Duxford, Hawkinge and other locations throughout the summer of 1968. During the film LF363 carried many different markings as the film unit only had three airworthy Hurricanes and once it was finished the aircraft was given a major overhaul and new fuselage fabric – probably by Simpsons Aeroservices Ltd, who had the contract to prepare and maintain all of the aircraft during the film and which had done the same to PZ865/G-AMAU (qv) at Bovingdon prior to its return to Hawker Siddeley at Dunsfold.

On its return to Coltishall, in all-silver, LF363 was quickly repainted in camouflage and coded 'LE-D' in honour of Gp/Capt Douglas Bader. The flight had now decided to change the markings on its aircraft whenever they received a major service and over the following seasons LF363 appeared in a variety of different markings – some more authentic than others. These were:

The dramatic all-black night-fighter scheme represenative of No. 85 Sqdn was carried between 1983 and 1986, as shown here at Greenham Common on 23 July 1983. (*Paul Thallon*)

1969–1972 'LE-D' of No. 242 Sqdn, Gp/Capt D R S Bader
1973–1978 'LE-D' thicker grey lettering than the previous version
1979–1982 'GN-F' of No. 249 (Gold Coast) Sqdn, 1940
1983–1986 'VY-X' all-black night-fighter scheme of No. 85 Sqdn, 1940
1987–1989 'NV-L' of No. 79 Sqdn, 1940
1990–1991 'GN-A' of No. 249 Sqdn, F/Lt James Nicolson, VC

The 1991 season saw a catastrophic accident befall LF363, the first in its 47-year life, when on 11 September it was

1987 saw a return to day-fighter scheme with the 'NV-L' code of No. 79 Sqdn; this photo was taken at Duxford. (*Gordon Riley*)

F/Lt James Nicolson, VC, flew the original 'GN-A' with No. 249 Sqdn during the Battle of Britain. LF363 carried these markings from 1990 until its horrific accident at Wittering in September 1991. (*Paul Marsh*)

flying from Coningsby to Jersey in a three-ship formation with the flight's Lancaster and one of the Spitfires. As they approached RAF Wittering the Hurricane's engine started to run rough and very soon smoke was pouring out of the exhausts. S/Ldr Allan Martin declared an emergency but, whilst attempting to land at Wittering, the Merlin gave up the ghost and LF363 slammed into the ground in a stall, sliding backwards along the runway in a shower of sparks. Martin escaped, despite a broken ankle, and sustained minor burns as the fully-fuelled aircraft burst into flames and was reduced to a charred wreck, despite the best efforts of the Wittering fire crew who were on the scene within seconds. The aircraft was returned to Coningsby on 13 September and the subsequent Board of Inquiry established that the engine had seized due to a broken camshaft.

After three years in store the decision was made to sell one of the flight's three Spitfire PR XIXs in order to raise the funds required to rebuild LF363, PS853 being selected for disposal. LF363 was then transported to Audley End, Essex, where Historic Flying Ltd were contracted to carry out a total rebuild to flying condition. Work started in early 1995 but the damage was so great that virtually everything had to be replaced, only six of the original fuselage tubes being re-utilised – the fuselage work being sub-contracted to Retrotec Ltd, whilst the centre section and wings were rebuilt by HFL using parts from LF363 and one of two ex-Russian recoveries as patterns. The 'Cranfield mod' to the tailplane spar was not repeated as Hawker Restorations now had the capability to build new spars to the original pattern, likewise a new fin, rudder and elevators were required as was totally new woodwork, cowlings and the majority of the aircraft's systems. During the wing rebuild the cannon mounts were removed and these are now fitted to PZ865 (qv) to enable LF363 to represent an eight-gun Hurricane IIA and PZ865 a cannon-armed IIC.

On return to the flight the 'US-C' markings chosen were very apt as they represented a Hurricane of No. 56 Sqdn, a unit then based at Coningsby but equipped with the Tornado

LF363 emerged in March 2006 as F/O Harold Bird-Wilson's 'YB-W' of No. 17 Sqdn during the Battle of Britain. (*Darren Harbar Photography*)

Following its restoration by Historic Flying LF363 returned in the 'US-C' markings of No. 56 Sqdn; this photo shows a nose-over at Duxford on 6 June 2004. (*David Whitworth*)

F.3, and whose squadron crest represents a phoenix rising from the ashes. LF363 was collected from Audley End by S/Ldr Paul Day on 29 September 1998 and flown to Cambridge Airport where a party from the flight checked it over before LF363 carried on to Coningsby and landed at 1730 hours – just over seven years from the date of the accident at Wittering. It made its first public display at Duxford on 11 October 1998, flown by Air Marshal Sir John Allison. The 56 Sqdn markings were retained until the winter of 2005-2006

when LF363 went to The Aircraft Restoration Company at Duxford for maintenance and emerged in March 2006 as F/O Harold Bird-Wilson's 'YB-W' of No. 17 Sqdn during the Battle of Britain. These colours were retained until the winter of 2013 when LF363 underwent a major overhaul at Coningsby from which it emerged in May 2014 in the markings of F/O Arthur Clowes' 'JX-B' of No.1 Squadron, making its first public appearance at the Shuttleworth Collection Pageant at Old Warden on 7 September 2014.

LF658
Hawker Hurricane Mk IIC

Musée Royal de l'Armée, Brussels, Belgium

LF658 was ordered from Hawker Aircraft Ltd as one of the tenth production block (Contract No. 62305/39) and was built at Langley in the winter of 1943/44 as a cannon-armed Mk IIC. The aircraft in this block of 1,961 were a mixture of Mks IIB, IIC and IV with serials in the range LB542-LF956. LF658 fell into the serial batch LF620-LF660 (41 aircraft). It was delivered to No. 22 MU at Silloth, Cumbria, on 3 March 1944 where it was prepared for squadron use and issued to No. 309 (Polish) Sqdn at Drem on 1 April as 'WC-E' – making it a contemporary of LF363 (qv). After an uneventful period patrolling the eastern coast of Scotland, September 1944 saw the unit converted back to Mustang Mk Is and LF658 is believed to have returned to No. 22 MU for a period of storage on 15 October – unfortunately the Form 78 is difficult to read. Whether it too was converted to carry cameras is not known but as it went directly to No. 309 Sqdn and not via No. 63 it is considered unlikely.

It looks as though it remained stored until 12 February 1946 when No. 22 MU delivered it to the Allied Flight Metropolitan Communications Squadron, then based at Hendon, now the site of the Royal Air Force Museum. This flight came into being in late 1944 to provide a fast communication service between London and Brussels once the Belgian capital had been liberated. LF658 carried out this role until transferred to the Belgian government on 2 September 1946.

LF658 was one of six former RAF Hurricanes acquired as fast communications aircraft but only three (LF345, PG554, PZ754) were actually operational with the 169th Air Transport Wing at Evere in 1946 while LF658 and the other two (PZ769, LF165) were used as instructional airframes. During 1947 all of the operational Hurricanes were withdrawn from service and on 8 August 1948 at least three were destroyed in a hangar fire at the Technical School at

LF658 is displayed painted as 'LF345 / ZA-P' in the Musée Royal de l'Armée, Brussels, Belgium. (*Ad Meskens*)

LF658 was not flown in Belgium but used for technical training, here it is fitted with a Spitfire propeller for display purposes at St Niklaas barracks. (*Daniel Brackx Collection*)

Saffraanberg. LF658 was subsequently sent to the Technical School at Tongeren where it was marked as 'RA-A/658' and fitted with a four-bladed Rotol propeller from a Spitfire for at least some of that time as evidenced by a photograph taken at a military barracks at Sint Niklaas.

Struck off charge during 1951, LF658 was moved to the Musée Royal de l'Armée, Brussels where it was repainted in a rather strange camouflage scheme and re-coded 'ML-B'. Here it remained, apart from the occasional outing to an external show, such as Brustem in 1965 when it was seen to be fitted with a roughly mocked-up canopy. During 1975-76 the aircraft was repainted and restored, although many internal parts were found to be missing, and put back on static display. The canopy now fitted came from one of the non-flying replicas built for the film *The Battle of Britain*. The colour scheme chosen is that worn by LF345, which had been coded 'ZA-P'.

LF658 is seen here at Brustem on 28 July 1965 at an air show commemorating the Golden Jubilee of the founding of the Belgian Air Force. *(The Peter Keating Collection © A Flying History Ltd)*

LF686
Hawker Hurricane Mk IIC

National Air and Space Museum, Steven F Udvar-Hazy Center,
Chantilly, VA, USA

LF686 was ordered from Hawker Aircraft Ltd as one of the tenth production block (Contract No. 62305/39) and was built at Langley in early 1944 as a cannon-armed Mk IIC. The aircraft in this block of 1,961 were a mixture of Mks IIB, IIC and IV with serials in the range LB542-LF956; LF686 fell into the serial batch LF674-LF721 (48 aircraft). It was delivered to No. 5 MU at Kemble, Wilts, on 14 March 1944 where it was prepared for use and issued to No. 41 OTU at Hawarden in Cheshire on 15 April where it served as an advanced trainer.

On 1 February 1945 the unit was split into two with No. 41 OTU Day Fighter Wing moving to Poulton, where it was re-designated No. 58 OTU on 12 March; the Hawarden element became No. 41 OTU Fighter Reconnaissance Wing, moving to Chilbolton on 23 March, where it disbanded on 26 April 1945, its job being absorbed by No. 61 OTU. LF686 probably moved to Chilbolton as it was here that it was reclassified as a maintenance training airframe, 5270M, on 27 June 1945, and transferred to RAF Maintenance Command.

In July 1948 LF686/5270M was issued to No. 7 School of Recruit Training, RAF Bridgnorth, Shropshire, where it was displayed outdoors opposite the guardroom, alongside Spitfire LF VB, BL614. It was probably still camouflaged on arrival (the Spitfire was) but by 1950 it had been repainted silver with post-war RAF roundels, its serial

LF686 on display at the National Air and Space Museum's Steven F Udvar-Hazy Center, Chantilly, VA. *(NASM)*

LF686 guarded the gate at RAF Bridgnorth until it closed in 1963. *(Richard Edgeler)*

eventually painted over. Bridgnorth closed in 1963, and LF686 was moved to Colerne, Wilts, where it was repainted in camouflage and displayed as part of the base's museum collection.

After Bridgnorth closed LF686 was moved to Colerne where it was repainted in camouflage, as seen here at an open day in 1968. *(David Grindley)*

During the late 1960s, the Royal Air Force Museum was being established and the curator, the late J. M. 'Jack' Bruce was trying to plug gaps in the collection. He was aware that the Smithsonian Institution's National Air and Space Museum had a Hawker Typhoon (MN235) in store at Silver Hill, Maryland, USA, and negotiated an exchange with LF686. An RAF C-130 Hercules delivered the Hurricane in 1969, returning with the sole surviving Typhoon. LF686 was stored at Silver Hill for many years until restoration at the renamed Garber Facility began in 1989, the project being completed eleven years later. The Hurricane is now on display at the National Air and Space Museum's Steven F Udvar-Hazy Center at Chantilly, Virginia.

LF738
Hawker Hurricane Mk IIC

RAF Museum, Cosford, UK

LF738 was ordered from Hawker Aircraft Ltd as one of the tenth production block (Contract No. 62305/39) and was built at Langley in early 1944 as a cannon-armed Mk IIC. The aircraft in this block of 1,961 were a mixture of Mks IIB, IIC and IV with serials in the range LB542-LF956; LF738 fell into the serial batch LF737-LF774 (38 aircraft). It was delivered to No. 22 MU at Silloth, Cumbria, on 19 March 1944 where it was prepared for use and issued to No. 1682 BDTF at Enstone, Oxon, on 10 April where it would have been coded 'UH-'. The Bomber Defence Training Flights were given the job of 'fighter affiliation' in other words they acted as attacking fighters to train air gunners from local

LF738 on show at the RAF Museum, Cosford, in May 2014 where it is coded 'UH-A' representing No. 1682 BDTF at Enstone, its first unit. *(Gordon Riley)*

LF738 on display outside St George's Chapel of Remembrance at Biggin Hill during 1965. *(Tony Clarke)*

bomber OTUs in the skills required to defend their aircraft from German fighters. No. 1682 was re-equipped in April 1944, replacing its outdated P-40 Tomahawks with slightly less obsolete Hurricanes.

The flight did not last much longer as it was disbanded on 21 August 1944 and LF738 was transferred two days later onto the strength of No. 22 OTU at nearby Wellesbourne Mountford, near Stratford-upon-Avon, where it probably carried on with fighter affiliation work but with the new unit code 'LT-'. The unit was mainly equipped with the Vickers Wellington, having 54 on strength at the end of 1944 together with six Hurricanes and a pair of Miles Masters. It operated its final course on 1 July 1945 and was disbanded on 24 July but LF738 had already been 'retired' as on 16 July it had been allocated the Maintenance Command serial 5405M as one of five Hurricanes dispatched to No. 12 School of Technical Training at Melksham, Wilts.

It remained at Melksham for the next nine years until 6 September 1954 when it was allocated to Biggin Hill where it was dedicated by the Bishop of Rochester, together with a Spitfire LF XVIE, SL674, at a drumhead service on 19

September 1954 as a permanent memorial and gate guard to St George's Chapel of Remembrance – the Battle of Britain Chapel – at the station. It was moved into place in front of the newly completed chapel the following year where it was displayed in a variety of different camouflage schemes and markings over the years. Fifteen years of service took its toll on the fabric-covered fuselage and during the summer of 1969 it was taken to No. 19 MU at St Athan for a full refurbish by the apprentices but was back on duty by Battle of Britain Day that September. Further work was carried out at No. 71 MU, Bicester, during 1974 but again it was back by September.

The likelihood of its continued long-term survival as an outdoor exhibit was getting critical and on 8 February 1984, LF738 was finally dismantled by a team from Bicester and transported to the Rochester premises of the Medway Branch of the Royal Aeronautical Society (now the Medway Aircraft Preservation Society) where an in-depth restoration commenced. At the time of arrival it was found to be missing many internal components, some would have been removed at Melksham whilst others were almost certainly

LF738 undergoing restoration at Rochester Airport. (*Andy Robinson*)

taken by the Battle of Britain Memorial Flight as spares for their flyable aircraft. During the survey it was found that it needed a replacement radiator and centre section inboard flaps, along with most aircraft systems, electrical, cooling and pneumatic. It had no fuel system pipework, controls or pumps, the rear fuselage woodwork had to be re-manufactured and all the fabric covering replaced. The fuselage had no surviving manufacturer's plates. A major help was the donation of a restored tailplane by Hawker Restorations.

The work took 11 years to complete and the formal handover to ACM Sir Michael Alcock took place at Rochester on 28 June 1995 with the Hurricane being moved by road to its new home in the Aerospace Museum at Cosford on 16 August – the move being sponsored by the *Wolverhampton Express and Star* newspaper. On arrival it was seen to have been restored as 'UH-A' of No. 1682 BDTF at Enstone, its first unit.

Ownership of LF738 was officially transferred to the RAF Museum by the Ministry of Defence on 3 August 1998 and it has remained on display at Cosford ever since, apart from a brief trip to Hendon in September 2007 when it acted as the centrepiece of a formal dinner to celebrate the 50th anniversary of the founding of the Battle of Britain Memorial Flight which was held on 4 October. It returned to Cosford on 10 October 2007.

LF751
Hawker Hurricane Mk IIC

Spitfire and Hurricane Memorial Museum, Manston, Kent, UK

LF751 was ordered from Hawker Aircraft Ltd as one of the tenth production block (Contract No. 62305/39) and was built at Langley in early 1944 as a cannon-armed Mk IIC. The aircraft in this block of 1,961 were a mixture of Mks IIB, IIC and IV with serials in the range LB542-LF956; LF751 fell into the serial batch LF737-LF774 (38 aircraft). It was delivered to No. 22 MU at Silloth, Cumbria, on 19 March 1944 (the same date as fellow survivor LF738) where it was

prepared for use and issued to No. 1681 BDTF at Pershore, Worcs, on 8 April. The Bomber Defence Training Flights were given the job of 'fighter affiliation' in other words they acted as attacking fighters to train air gunners from local bomber OTUs in the skills required to defend their aircraft from German fighters. No. 1681 had detachments at Honeybourne and Long Marston but was disbanded soon after LF751's arrival and its duties absorbed into No. 24

LF751, painted to represent BN230, displayed in the Spitfire and Hurricane Memorial Museum at Manston, January 2012. *(Gary Brown)*

OTU, to which the Hurricane was transferred on 24 August 1944.

No. 24 OTU had been formed at Honeybourne on 15 March 1942 as a 2/3 status unit within No. 7 Group, equipped with Whitleys and Ansons, and given the role of training night bomber crews. On 15 May 1942 it was transferred to No. 93 Group, under whose control it remained until disbanding on 24 July 1945, having been raised to full status in September 1942. It is reasonable to assume that LF751 was one of a small number of Hurricanes on strength to carry on fighter affiliation work. LF751 was 'retired' on 21 July when it was allocated the Maintenance Command serial 5466M and it is possible that it was dispatched to No. 12 School of Technical Training at Melksham, Wilts, alongside LF738.

LF751, showing the serial 5466M, out to grass at Waterbeach in 1952 where it was used as a spares source to keep LF363 airworthy. *(Noel Collier)*

It next appeared in the early 1950s as a derelict hulk at Waterbeach, Cambridgeshire, then home to the RAF's last airworthy Hurricane, LF363 (qv) which had been delivered to Waterbeach Station Flight in November 1951. It was painted overall silver, but with wartime type C1 roundels, and was kept company by 5708M (PG539) and a very historic example, the all-white Z3687 which had been used for experimental laminar-flow wing trials at Farnborough in 1945 and had a distinguished wartime record – having been flown by No. 43 Sqdn as 'FT-E' and suffered damage over Dieppe in August 1942. Its most momentous achievement was, however, on the night of 10/11 May 1941 when it was serving with No. 1 Sqdn. Czech pilot W/O Josef Dygryn

took off at night and proceeded to shoot down no less than three German bombers; the first was a Heinkel He 111 over London at 0035 hours, second was another Heinkel He 111 near Gatwick at 0150 and the third was a Junkers Ju 88 near Biggin Hill at 0325.

Unfortunately the historical significance of Z3687 was completely overlooked and its wingless fuselage sat with the other two until LF363 finally departed for Langley in 1955 and the remnants were combined into one aircraft which took on the identity of LF751 to become an all-silver gate guardian at Waterbeach, alongside Spitfire F.22 PK664.

With the closure of the base in August 1963 LF751 was moved to the old Fighter Command HQ at Bentley Priory where, repainted in camouflage colours, it stood in the grounds alongside a Spitfire (firstly SL574 and later TB252), although it did take a brief holiday, first to Henlow and then to Pinewood Studios, in 1968 when it was used to make the moulds for the static replicas which appeared in the film *The Battle of Britain*. It is interesting to note that one of those replicas was itself utilised to make a new set of moulds which are still in use today and have produced the gate guardians at Duxford and North Weald.

When LF363 departed Waterbeach the remnants of the spare airframes were combined to create a gate guard which took up the identity LF751/5466M, as seen here on 14 August 1960. *(George Trussell)*

LF751 continued to deteriorate in its outdoor position until the decision was taken to transport it to Rochester, initially to assist the restoration of LF738, and then to take its place in the workshop of the Medway Aircraft Preservation

Society. It arrived on 20 March 1985 and, owing to its past history as a 'spares ship' for LF363, it too was found to be in a dire condition with many missing parts. MAPS spent some 12,000 man hours refurbishing the aircraft before it was handed over to the RAF at an impressive ceremony at Rochester Airport on 22 April 1988. A Hurricane, Spitfire and a Phantom F-4 of No. 43 Squadron flew over the airport in salute. Oddly, despite the fact that parts from Z3687 are

probably contained within the airframe, the decision was taken to complete the aircraft as a totally different Hurricane of No. 43 Sqdn which had also taken part in the Dieppe Raid of August 1942. Whereas Z3687 was coded 'FT-E', LF751 has been painted to represent BN230, which was flown during the raid by a Belgian pilot, S/Ldr Danny Le Roy Du Vivier, and was coded 'FT-A'.

With the closure of Waterbeach LF751 was moved to Bentley Priory where is stood outside for over 20 years – this photo shows it in July 1977. *(Tony Clarke Collection)*

PZ865
Hawker Hurricane Mk IIC

RAF Battle of Britain Memorial Flight, Coningsby, Lincs, UK

PZ865 was ordered from Hawker Aircraft Ltd as one of the tenth production block (Contract No. 62305/39) and was built at Langley in the summer of 1944 as a cannon-armed Mk IIC. The aircraft in this block of 1,397 were a mixture of Mks IIB, IIC and IV with serials in the range LE121-PZ865, PZ865 falling into the final serial batch PZ848-PZ865 (18 aircraft) and was the final Hurricane ever built. It made its maiden flight at Langley in late July 1944, powered by Merlin XX No. 75283 and fitted with a Rotol RS5/10 propeller. The pilot was Hawker's chief test pilot, P W S 'George' Bulman, who had made the first flight of the prototype at Brooklands some nine years earlier on 6 November 1935. The following month an official 'christening' ceremony was held at Langley when it was named 'The Last of the Many' by Lady Spencer Spriggs, Bulman flying it again in company with Bill Humble in a Tempest V, EJ592, and the company's Hawker Hart, G-ABMR.

PZ865 running up at Duxford on 27 March 2013 following a ground-up restoration by The Aircraft Restoration Company Ltd. *(David Whitworth)*

Being such a significant aircraft the directors of Hawker Aircraft Ltd took the decision to purchase the aircraft back from the Ministry of Supply so it was not actually handed over

to the RAF (until March 1972) and was retained at Langley on CRD charge, where it was used as a communications aircraft until 9 December 1945. During that time it clocked up approximately 41 hours and 55 mins of flying time but its original logbooks were returned to RAF Uxbridge on sale to Hawkers and were subsequently destroyed, so this is an estimate.

The fuselage of PZ865 starting to take shape at Langley in the summer of 1944. *(BAE SYSTEMS)*

PZ865 was inhibited and stored at Langley in 1945, although it was brought out and transported by lorry through Kingston during a victory parade which was held on 8 June 1946. In 1950 Hawkers heard that there may be an embargo on flying military aircraft in civilian markings so the decision was made to bring it out of storage and civilianise it for 'racing, record and demonstration purposes'. To this end it received a Special Category Certificate of Airworthiness and was given the civil registration G-AMAU, being test flown at Langley on 12 May 1950 by the chief test pilot, T S 'Wimpy' Wade, DFC, AFC, for 25 minutes. Bulman took it up for 30 minutes the following day before Wade made a surprise appearance at the Royal Aeronautical Society's garden party at White Waltham on 14 May, where it was seen to be finished in an Oxford Blue and gold civilian colour scheme. The colours were adopted as Hawker's 'house colours' and later applied to the company Hawker Hart, G-ABMR, and Hawker Tomtit, G-AFTA. At this stage in its civilian career it retained the 'sword-type' aerial mast but had the cannon tubes removed and the wing leading edges faired over.

Now mounted on the centre section and undercarriage, the banner lists the major theatres of operations in which Hurricanes had fought. *(BAE SYSTEMS)*

Further test flights were carried out during May as the Hurricane had been entered in the King's Cup Air Race as the personal entry of HRH Princess Margaret. The pilot was to be G/Capt Peter Townsend, CVO, DSO, DFC and Bar – who had made his name as a Hurricane pilot with No. 85 Sqdn during the Battle of Britain and who was to become romantically linked to the young princess until her announcement that she did not intend to marry him was made in 1955. Townsend flew G-AMAU for the first time on 26 May and a Rotol four-bladed propeller was fitted on 1 June. The race was being staged at Wolverhampton and Townsend flew G-AMAU there and back on 2 June to test its performance with the new propeller. The speed increase was not considered sufficient to warrant the change so the original three-bladed prop was reinstalled on 5 June. It is interesting to note that G-AMAU/PZ865 was flown with a four-bladed Rotol propeller during the 1980s when the Battle of Britain Memorial Flight was experiencing issues with spares. The same being true of its stablemate, LF363.

The aircraft was then fitted with two additional 12.5-gallon fuel tanks in the armament bays outboard of the main wing tanks and was flight-tested with these on 12 June.

The King's Cup Air Race was held on 17 June and G-AMAU was delivered to Wolverhampton the day before by 'Wimpy' Wade, who flew it back to Langley on 18 June. The race consisted of three laps and Townsend averaged 283 mph in 50 minutes to come home second with an extremely low pass over the finish line. The fact that the race was won by Edward Day in his Miles Magister, G-AKRV, is a testament to the skill of the handicappers, who had set the Hurricane off last in the field of 36 competitors. The race also featured two Spitfires, G-AISU and G-AIDN, but the thrilling finish was marred by a fatal accident to W H Moss, who was flying the Moss MA1, G-AEST.

P W S 'George' Bulman takes PZ865 up for an early test flight from Langley in July 1944. *(BAE SYSTEMS)*

Its next air race was the Kemsley Challenge Trophy, held on 19 August at Fairwood Common, Swansea, over three laps of a 28-mile circuit. This time G-AMAU was flown by another wartime fighter pilot, S/Ldr Neville Duke, DSO, OBE, DFC & two Bars, AFC, who came third at an average speed of 295 mph. Its Merlin XX (No. 75283) had been replaced with a Merlin 24 (No. 309303) on 11 August, which may account for the slight performance increase. The final event of the year was the *Daily Express* International Air Race along the south coast from Hurn to Herne Bay, which was held on 16 September. No less than 75 aircraft were chasing the £2,350 prize purse on offer and G-AMAU was flown by Hawker

The fuselage is transported through Kingston as part of a Victory Parade held on 8 June 1946. *(BAE SYSTEMS)*

test pilot Frank Murphy with F/Lt Frank Bullen keeping him company in the Tomtit, G-AFTA. The most impressive sight must have been that of the Handley Page Halifax, G-AKEC, thundering around the course.

On 13 October a test flight was made to test the radio equipment which was probably to do with the removal of the 'sword-type' aerial mast, which had been replaced by a Type 147 'whip' aerial and which was signed off on 30 October 1950. Its last flights of the year were on 18 October when Neville Duke took it over to Farnborough and back during the afternoon, his 'commute' taking 10 minutes each way.

G/Capt Peter Townsend about to start in the King's Cup Air Race at Wolverhampton on 17 June 1950. *(Author's Collection)*

Between 18–24 July 1951 PZ865/G-AMAU was displayed at Hendon as part of the *Daily Express* Fifty Years of Flying exhibition. It is in the temporary camouflage and markings applied for making the film *Angels one Five* at Kenley. Note the whip aerial. *(Tony Clarke Collection)*

The C of A was renewed on 3 May 1951 and the Hurricane appeared at White Waltham three days later, Peter Townsend taking it up for a 30-minute local flight on 21 June and again on the 22nd in preparation for the Jubilee Trophy Air Race, part of the National Air Races, which was scheduled to be held at Hatfield two days later. Despite Frank Murphy flying G-AMAU to Hatfield on 22 June bad weather the next day caused the cancellation of the races – in which all three aircraft of the 'Hawker Circus' were entered – and Neville Duke flew the Hurricane back to Langley on 25 June.

The Hawker historic flight appeared at major air displays throughout the 1950s. Note the company's Hawker Hart, G-ABMR. *(Tony Clarke Collection)*

In 1960 it was repainted in its original camouflage scheme, although the civil registration was carried beneath the tailplane. Here it is seen at Farnborough in September 1962. *(The Peter Keating Collection © A Flying History Ltd)*

Filming of *Angels One Five* took place at Kenley during July 1951 and G-AMAU was painted in temporary RAF camouflage and markings as 'P2619/US-B', joining its latter-day stablemate LF363 and a group of Portuguese Hurricanes at the Surrey airfield on 2 July when it was flown over from Langley by Frank Murphy. The opening sequence of the film shows G-AMAU, with no squadron codes, being flown into the fictitious 'RAF Neethley' by John Gregson's character P/O 'Septic' Baird – the Hurricane used for the studio shots of the subsequent crash scene has never been identified. Filming took place at Kenley until 27 July, with G-AMAU being flown by Hawker pilots Bullen or Murphy and returning to Langley each night. The Hurricane 'took leave' during filming to take part in the Fifty Years of Flying exhibition which was sponsored by the *Daily Express* and held at Hendon, flying in from Langley in full film colours on 18 July and returning on 24 July, piloted by Frank Murphy. Although A W 'Bill' Bedford, OBE, AFC, FRAeS, is supposed to have also flown it during filming this is not borne out by the logbook entries, which show that his first flight in the aircraft was not until 24 September when he ferried it back from Shoreham to Langley after Frank

Murphy had competed in the *Daily Express* Trophy Race from Shoreham to Brighton, Newhaven, Whitstable, Hythe, Rye Harbour, Hastings, Eastbourne, Beachy Head and back to the finish at Brighton's West Pier on 22 September.

Bob Stanford Tuck on the wing of PZ865 during the press call for the film *The Battle of Britain*. *(The Peter Keating Collection (c) A Flying History Ltd)*

PZ865 'MI-G' leading LF363 'MI-D' during filming of *The Battle of Britain*. The whip aerial was replaced with a standard mast which sloped slightly backwards from the vertical, making it easy to identify again! *(W G Ramsey/After The Battle)*

Bedford then became one of its regular pilots and throughout 1952 his name appears frequently alongside his test pilot colleagues Frank Murphy, Frank Bullen and Neville Duke – the latter taking the Hurricane on its first flight outside of the UK on 8 June 1952 when he flew it from Dunsfold to Lympne to clear customs and then on to the RAF base at Celle, Lower Saxony, from where he returned by the reverse route the following day. The aircraft had been first flown to Dunsfold on 28 April when Frank Bullen made the 10-minute 'hop' from Langley and it seems to have been based there for the rest of the year, making visits to a variety of locations including Sywell, Boscombe Down, West Raynham, White Waltham, Brockworth and Baginton.

The pattern continued throughout 1953 although 'Bill' Bedford and Don Lucey were now the main pilots. 9 October was an interesting day as no less than nine different Fleet Air Arm pilots all took the controls for 10 minutes at a time – probably at the end of a course at Boscombe Down. Don Lucey flew it back to Langley on 16 February

1954 and its next flight was another overseas trip, Neville Duke flying to Schiphol, Amsterdam, via Lympne on 4 May and returning two days later. For the Battle of Britain Day events that year G-AMAU was loaned to the RAF, F/Lt Smith picking her up from Langley on 14 September and flying her to Waterbeach, from where he participated in the London flypast on 15 September, returning her to Dunsfold on 17 September. This may indicate that the Waterbeach-based LF363 was unavailable for the flypast and with G-AMAU the only other flyable Hurricane in the UK she was pressed into service. Two more test pilots from the Hawker team took their first flights towards the end of 1954, Duncan Simpson on 12 November and Hugh Merewether on 20 December. Meanwhile 19 August 1955 saw none other than G/Capt 'Sammy' Wroath, commandant of the Empire Test Pilots' School at Boscombe Down – and who had founded the school in 1943 – taking the Hurricane up for 25 minutes. Wroath had returned to the ETPS in 1953 and was commandant until 1957.

After delivery to the Battle of Britain Memorial Flight in 1972 PZ865 was almost immediately repainted in the markings of Bob Stanford Tuck's Hurricane, as seen here taxying past the tower at Duxford on 24 August 1975. *(Mark Miller via David Whitworth)*

Another familiar name to grace the logbook is none other than Wg/Cdr Peter Thompson, DFC, who founded the Battle of Britain Memorial Flight at Biggin Hill. LF363 was obviously u/s yet again so on 13 September 1956 he picked up G-AMAU from Dunsfold and flew her to his base at North Weald where he landed at 0935 hours and handed her over to G/Capt Jamieson who carried out two 50-minute flypasts, taking off at 1030 and 1500. Thompson returned her to Dunsfold on 14 September and 'Bill' Bedford took her off the following morning for displays at Wymeswold, Thorney Island and Benson – a somewhat circuitous trip!

June 1957 saw the start of G-AMAU's regular trips to and from the Hawker factory at Blackpool's Squires Gate airfield. The factory had originally been built by the Ministry of Aircraft Production during 1939-40 and was used by Vickers-Armstrongs to manufacture Wellington bombers during World War 2. In order to keep pace with orders for the Hunter, Hawkers leased the factory and re-opened it in the early 1950s and it was here that they also chose to set up a small facility to take ex-Fleet Air Arm Sea Furies and convert them for overseas use. To this end they received an order to convert a batch of two-seat Sea Furies into target tugs for the German company Deutsche-Luftfahrt Beratungsdienst and the Hurricane was the aircraft of choice for the Hawker test pilots to commute between Dunsfold and Blackpool to flight-test the Sea Furies, the trip generally taking David Lockspeiser just over an hour. The first trip

was for a local air display but by January 1958 they were a regular occurrence which continued until the end of May.

It is frequently stated that G-AMAU was used as a 'chase' aircraft during the early test flights of the Hawker P.1127, the logbook certainly showing many local flights during the period September 1960–October 1961, when the P.1127 was under development and test at Dunsfold, plus some flights to Filton where the Pegasus engine was manufactured but unfortunately nothing is logged with regard to the purpose of those flights. By the time of the test flights the blue and gold colour scheme had given way to grey/green camouflage with the name 'The Last of the Many' reapplied below the cockpit, the civil registration was carried in small black letters below the tailplane and during winter maintenance on 11 December 1962 the Merlin 24, which had been fitted in August 1951, was removed and replaced with a Merlin 502, serial number 212473.

In 1978 PZ865 was repainted as 'JU-Q' of No. 111 Sqdn; it is seen here at Duxford with a four-bladed Spitfire propeller installed due to serviceability issues. *(Gordon Riley)*

By now relegated to air show displays, and a small amount of air taxi work, G-AMAU continued flying throughout the mid-1960s until early 1968 when it had the C of A renewed as normal but was delivered from Dunsfold to Henlow on 29 March by John Farley. Here it was repainted in 1940s-style camouflage and markings and joined two other Hurricanes (LF363 and RCAF 5377/G-AWLW) to fly in the epic film *The Battle of Britain*. Initially flown with the 'whip' aerial this was soon replaced with a rigid sword-type mast – which sloped slightly backwards compared with the other

Hurricanes – a feature which it retained for several decades after the film and which helped to distinguish it from the other two Hurricanes used in the flying sequences. All of the aircraft carried a multitude of different codes and serials during the filming but some that are known for PZ865 are 'H3429 / KV-M', 'MI-B' and 'MI-G'.

Over the winter of 1981–82 the markings were changed and it flew in its original camouflage as 'The Last of the Many' until 1988. (*Andy Robinson*)

S/Ldr D W Mills delivered it from Henlow to the film set at Debden on 8 May 1968 and he and F/Lt Curry were its pilots at Debden, North Weald and Duxford until F/Lt Curry flew it from Duxford to Dunsfold on 7 June where John Farley used it for an air display on 8 June before F/Lt Curry flew it back to Duxford on 10 June for it to re-join the film unit at Debden the next day. The majority of the flying took place at Debden or Duxford but Curry flew it to Hawkinge on 2 July, where it filmed some scenes before he ferried it to Northolt – where it featured as AVM Sir Keith Park's personal Hurricane 'OK-1' between 5-8 July. Another diversion was the Hawker Siddeley Families Day held at Hatfield on 13 July, Curry performing the display having delivered it on the 12th from Duxford and returning to Debden on the 15th. Later that week all three Hurricanes were flown to Blackbushe, Hants, where they arrived on the 16th and left on the 18th – the nearby forest roads being used for the refugee sequences seen at the opening of the film. Most of August and September was spent filming at Duxford, the final sequences being shot at Sywell between 24 September and 1 October – on which day the Hurricane was ferried to Bovingdon by S/Ldr Mills.

Simpsons Aeroservices Ltd had moved from Henlow to Bovingdon when the lease on the hangars had expired and all of the aircraft were gathered there before they were returned or disposed of. Hawkers contracted 'Tubby' Simpson to overhaul G-AMAU and this took place during the winter months; in addition to normal rectification work the opportunity was taken to strip the fuselage and to recover it with new fabric, four coats of dope were applied before it was repainted in its grey/green camouflage scheme reverting to 'The Last of the Many'. The work was complete by 17 March 1969 and F/Lt Curry delivered it to Dunsfold where John Farley test-flew it and then carried out a display on 14 June.

Between 1988–1992 PZ865 represented 'RF-U', of No. 303 Sqdn, flown by Sgt Josef Frantisek. This photo was taken at West Malling. (*Tony Clarke Collection*)

G-AMAU / PZ865 then settled down to its last few years with the manufacturer, carrying out its air show displays in the hands of the Hawker test pilots – Hugh Merewether experiencing a tail oleo failure on 26 July 1969 when it sheared taxying across the grass after landing at Dunsfold following a display at Lee-on-the-Solent. The regular routine continued until 1971 when the directors of the company decided that it was appropriate to present the Hurricane to the newly-formed Royal Air Force Museum at Hendon, alongside their Hawker Hart, G-ABMR, and Hawker Cygnet, G-EBMB. It would seem that some discussion took place at a high level within the company and in the event the Hart and Cygnet went to Hendon but PZ865 was presented instead to the RAF Battle of Britain Memorial Flight. John Farley carried out a test flight at Dunsfold on 21 March

The next scheme change was between 1993–1997 when PZ865 flew as 'J', of No. 261 Sqdn, Malta, September 1940, its cannon had now been refitted. *(Andy Robinson)*

PZ865 flying at the Shoreham Air Show in the SEAC markings it carried between 1998 and 2004. *(Paul Blackah)*

1972 and the aircraft was flown from Dunsfold to Coltishall shortly afterwards by Duncan Simpson, thus becoming the last Hurricane delivered to the RAF.

Almost immediately the civil registration was cancelled, the colour scheme was changed and PZ865 emerged in the markings of Bob Stanford Tuck's 'DT-A' of No. 257 Sqdn at Debden in late 1940, markings which it retained until 1977. As with all of the flight's aircraft, the colour scheme was changed at each major overhaul and the markings carried by PZ865 during its time with the flight are:

1972–1977 'DT-A', of No. 257 Sqdn, 1940, W/Cdr Bob
            Stanford Tuck
1978–1981 'JU-Q', of No. 111 Sqdn
1982–1988 'The Last of the Many', its original colour
            scheme from 1944
1989–1992 'RF-U', of No. 303 Sqdn, Sgt Josef Frantisek
1993–1997 'J', of No. 261 Sqdn, Malta, September 1940
            (cannon refitted)
1998–2004 'Q', of No. 5 Sqdn, SEAC
2005–2010 'JX-E', of No.1 Sqdn, F/Lt Karel Kuttelwascher
2012–2015 'EG-S', of No. 34 Sqdn, SEAC, F/Lt Jimmy
            Whalen

Between October 2004 and March 2005, PZ865 underwent a deep-strip maintenance inspection and a brand new radiator was fitted alongside all new control cables, this work carried out by the Aircraft Restoration Company at Duxford. When it reappeared it was in the markings carried by BE581, flown by F/Lt Karel Kuttelwascher, DFC, and named 'Night

Reaper'. A further in-depth restoration was carried out by the same company between October 2010 and March 2012 in which the fuselage tubing – originally fitted at Langley in 1944 – was replaced with new material and a new centre section, supplied by Hawker Restorations, was installed. Up until that time PZ865 was essentially the same aircraft that had rolled out of Langley in July 1944. When it reappeared it was in the markings carried by Hurricane IIC HW840, coded 'EG-S', of No. 34 Sqdn, South East Asia Command during 1944, the personal aircraft of Canadian pilot, F/Lt Jimmy Whalen, DFC.

Over the winter of 2004-2005 a major overhaul was completed by the Aircraft Restoration Company which saw it appear as 'JX-E', F/Lt Karel Kuttelwascher's 'Night Reaper' of No. 1 Sqdn. This photo was taken at Duxford on 13 July 2008. *(Gordon Riley)*

CANADIAN-BUILT HURRICANES

During 1938, the British and Canadian governments reached an agreement to begin licensed production of the Hurricane in Canada. Production was undertaken by the Canadian Car and Foundry Company (CCF) at Fort William (now Thunder Bay) and was helped by the delivery of a pattern aircraft (L2144) together with two sets of production drawings on microfilm (a total of 82,000 individual items). 20 Mark I Hurricanes were also supplied to the RCAF at the same time and took up serials RCAF 310-330. The first Canadian-built Hurricane, P5170, made its first flight on 10 January 1940 and a further 1,450 examples were built – although only 1,449 unique serials have been confirmed. Initial production was of the Mk I – which soon became known as the Mk X to distinguish it from British-built aircraft – and further production was of the Mks II, XI, XII and Sea Hurricanes. The manner in which some aircraft designations were changed during their lifetime depending on engine fitted, user (RAF, FAA or RCAF) and other factors is beyond the scope of this book. The following is just a brief overview of those types represented by the surviving examples. As with the British-built survivors the aircraft are listed in serial order without reference to mark number.

Hurricane Mk I & X	The first 40 Canadian Hurricanes were built for the RAF to Contract No. 964753/38 as Merlin III-powered Hurricane Mk Is with serials P5170-P5209 and were delivered to the UK by sea between March and July 1940. Once issued to RAF squadrons they were indistinguishable from UK-built aircraft but the designation Mk X came into use from August 1940 onwards, probably to assist in ordering spares. It was subsequently used by the RCAF to identify Merlin III-powered Hurricanes.
Sea Hurricane Mk IA	Initially ordered for the Royal Navy, the Sea Hurricane Mk IA was intended for the catapult ships of the Merchant Ship Fighter Unit, as such it featured catapult spools but no arrester hook. The armament was the standard eight Brownings and they were powered by the Merlin III driving a de Havilland propeller.
Sea Hurricane Mk IB	Identical to the Sea Hurricane Mk IA but with an arrester hook fitted for deck operations from carriers.
Hurricane IIA/B/C	Identical to British production although the Rolls-Royce Merlin XX could be substituted with the Packard Merlin 28 or 29.
Hurricane XII and XIIA	Essentially the Hurricane IIB, armed with 12 .303 inch Brownings but powered by a Packard Merlin 28 or 29. Many early examples were flown without a spinner fitted to the Hamilton Standard propeller because the backplate on the spinner fouled the constant-speed unit on the front of the crankcase. Once a modified spinner was developed many were fitted with spinners.

Sea Hurricane XIIA	The eight-gun Sea Hurricane converted for land-based use (usually at No. 1 OTU, Bagotville) by the removal of the arrester hook and replacing the Merlin III with a Merlin 28 or 29 driving a Hamilton Standard propeller.

Identity Crisis

Just one Canadian Hurricane (RCAF 5584, c/n 52019) was selected for preservation at the end of World War 2, the remainder were disposed of from a variety of depots. The vast majority of those were scrapped but others were taken away by farmers who stripped them down for useful parts – one enterprising farmer using wings to level his fields by towing them behind a tractor! During the early 1960s Canadian and American enthusiasts started to collect Hurricane parts from farms, scrapyards and crash sites across the country, some like Bob Diemert, Neil Rose and Harry Wheratt, eventually got their aircraft flying whereas others intended them for static display. In those days the only way to rebuild these aircraft was to exchange components between airframes and as a result there was an enormous amount of 'horse trading' between individuals and groups which resulted in many of the surviving Canadian Hurricanes becoming composites with parts acquired and exchanged as the need arose.

One of the major players in the collection and redistribution of Hurricane parts and projects was the late Jack Arnold of Brantford, Ontario, who recovered many crashed Hurricanes in various states of completeness. These parts were then 'packaged' and sold as projects but there was no guarantee that the identity quoted for a specific project actually matched the parts supplied. Complications also arose due to misunderstanding the tie-up between the CCF construction number and the RAF or RCAF serial allocated to each airframe; this is further compounded when some projects were initially identified by using a major component number rather than the actual construction number.

As a consequence it is very difficult to be absolutely sure of the identities of some of the Canadian Hurricane survivors and these have been indicated by adding an asterix after the serial.

Z7015
Hawker (Canadian) Sea Hurricane Mk IB
The Shuttleworth Collection, Old Warden, Beds, UK

Z7015 was ordered from the Canadian Car and Foundry Company (CCF) against Contract No. BSB 166, which was for 100 Hurricane Mk Is with serials between Z6983-Z7162. Bearing c/n CCF/41H/4013, Z7015 fell into the serial block Z6983-Z7017 and is the oldest surviving Canadian Hurricane. Although assigned to No. 13 MU at Henlow, Beds, on 30 July 1940, it did not make its first test flight until 0920 hours on 18 January 1941, at the CCF plant at Fort William, in the hands of V J Hatton who took it up for 35 minutes. Due to the ground temperature that day being

-20 ºC part of the oil cooler had to be blanked off; the same pilot made a further 20-minute flight at 1400 that afternoon.

Originally completed as a Merlin III-powered Hurricane Mk I, it was subsequently re-designated as a Mk X and delivered to Henlow on 18 March 1941 being assembled by No. 13 MU before despatch to No. 5 MU at Kemble, Gloucestershire, on 20 April where it was placed in store. At this time some 400 Mk I and Mk X Hurricanes were being converted to Sea Hurricane configuration and Z7015 was one of those selected, being allocated to General Aircraft Ltd

Z7015 flying at the Shuttleworth Collection's Pageant at Old Warden on 7 September 2014. (Gordon Riley)

Taken shortly after it was delivered to Loughborough College, this photo shows the code 'Y1-L' of No. 759 Sqdn of the Advanced Fighter School. *(Shuttleworth Collection)*

at Hanworth on 27 June. Here it was modified with slinging points, catapult spools and an arrester hook – in addition to general strengthening – prior to delivery to RNAS Yeovilton (HMS Heron) in July 1941 where it was taken on charge by the Fleet Air Arm and allocated, on 29 July 1941, to No. 880 Sqdn, which on 29 June had moved from Arbroath to St Merryn, and was replacing its three Sea Gladiators and nine Hurricane Is with fully navalised Sea Hurricane IBs.

The squadron was due to embark on HMS *Indomitable* but, as the ship was still working up, four Sea Hurricanes of A Flight embarked on HMS *Furious* on 21 July 1941 to provide fighter cover for the strike on Petsamo in the Arctic, during which the CO, Lt/Cdr F E C Judd, RN, and Sub Lt R B Haworth, RNVR, shot down a Do 18 on 31 July 1941. The rest of the squadron, including Z7015, remained at St Merryn before moving to Twatt (Shetland Isles) on 14 August and then Sumburgh in the Orkneys on 15 September, where Sub Lt Hugh Popham flew it several times during September on convoy patrols and other duties. They left Sumburgh in early October, rejoining A Flight personnel at Machrihanish to embark on HMS *Indomitable* and sail to join the Eastern Fleet, via work-up at Bermuda and the West Indies. Z7015 became unserviceable at some stage of the flight between the Shetlands and Machrihanish over 7-11 October 1941, and did not join the ship before it departed from Greenock on 18 October 1941. It seems to have been retained in a training capacity and was next noted on 10 February 1942 when it was flown from Hatston (HMS Sparrowhawk) near

Kirkwall, Orkney, to RNAS Donibristle (HMS Merlin), near Rosyth, Fife, in Scotland by Sub Lt Peter Hutton of No. 801 Sqdn.

Z7015 was allocated to David Rosenfield Ltd (part of the Hurricane Repair Organisation) at Barton, Manchester, on 5 April 1942 where it underwent repairs to the centre section and undercarriage – which suggests a landing accident of some sort. It is interesting to note that when the aircraft was stripped for restoration in 1995 the centre section was found to have been built at Kingston in 1939 but as Hawkers supplied CCF with spar webs until they started local manufacture it is not conclusive that the centre section was replaced during this repair.

The repairs took some time to complete and it was not ready for collection from Barton until 26 November 1942, being taken on charge at Yeovilton (HMS Heron) on 8 December where it was allocated to No. 759 Sqdn, which was the Advanced Flying School component of the Fleet Fighter School, for operational training, taking up the code 'Y1L'. By May 1943, about 60% of the squadron strength of over 100 aircraft were Sea Hurricanes. Z7015 seems to have served with No.759 Sqdn at Yeovilton until August 1943 before it was retired and transferred, in November 1943, to Loughborough College of Technology, which had an aircraft engineering department which was training ground engineers for the Royal Navy. Here it was joined in 1945-1946 by another Hurricane (KX829, qv), a Spitfire (AR501) and a Grumman Martlet (AL246) all of which survive today.

All of the training airframes were eventually re-doped in all-silver with their original paintwork obliterated, note the DH propeller still fitted. *(Author's Collection)*

When Z7015 was reassembled at Old Warden in 1961 it initially retained the silver scheme but the propeller had been switched for the Dowty unit from Spitfire AR501 and the arrester hook was missing. *(Shuttleworth Collection)*

At Loughborough the aircraft retained the camouflage and markings from its time with No. 759 Sqdn until at least 1946 but it was then re-doped overall silver. On arrival at the college it was fitted with a de Havilland variable pitch propeller – normal for the Sea Hurricane IB, as it was found that the heavier metal blades of the DH prop helped counterbalance the combined weight of the arrester hook and catapult spools, and improved the aircraft's longitudinal stability in the air. On 21 February 1961 Loughborough College exchanged Z7015 and the Spitfire, AR501, with the Shuttleworth Collection, receiving the Hunting Jet Provost prototype G-AOBU in return – a far better airframe for training a new generation of engineers.

On arrival at Old Warden the Hurricane was reassembled by a team from Hawkers at Dunsfold and was seen to have acquired the Rotol propeller from AR501 and lost its arrester hook. It is interesting to note that following its restoration to flight the Pilot's Notes for Z7015 mention its longitudinal instability and the Airworthiness Approval Note (AAN), lodged with the CAA, mentions that in order to solve centre of gravity problems the original 20 lb hook had been replaced by a 6 lb aluminium reproduction – maybe the DH prop should have been reinstalled!

Although initially displayed at Old Warden in the silver finish with red spinner, Z7015 was soon repainted in green/brown camouflage and acted as a gate guard alongside the Spitfire PR XI, PL983, until the summer of 1967 when it

The aircraft was soon repainted in camouflage as seen in this photo taken in April 1965. *(Tony Clarke Collection)*

was moved into the blister hangar and the fabric stripped in order to survey it for a possible restoration to flying condition for the forthcoming film *The Battle of Britain*. The Merlin III was ground-run but an unserviceable radiator prevented any chance of a return to flight – a lucky break as the restoration team had no idea that the tailplane spar was so badly corroded that it would have broken up if flight loads had been applied to it. In the event Z7015 was used as airfield dressing at Duxford as 'H3428/L' and is seen in the early part of the film being doused with 'petrol' as the squadron abandon their French landing ground (it is lacking a propeller as its serviceable Rotol prop had been fitted to Spitfire TB382 at Henlow in May 1968).

With the filming over Z7015 returned to Old Warden for a further stint as a gate guard, the damp grass wreaking even more havoc on the steel tube structure and tailplane spar, and here it remained until Dowty at Cheltenham undertook to carry out a restoration to flying condition. On arrival at Staverton the true extent of the corrosion was discovered and the attempt abandoned, the fuselage and wing centre section being returned to Old Warden for storage whilst the outer wings were sent to British Airways at Heathrow where they were refurbished in 1980.

Z7015 was only used in static scenes of *The Battle of Britain*, its serviceable Rotol prop being fitted to Spitfire TB382 at Henlow in May 1968. *(Gary Brown Collection)*

The fuselage was moved to Duxford in 1982 and placed in what is now known as Hangar 5 where volunteers from the Duxford Aviation Society started yet another restoration attempt before lack of resources brought the project to a halt. It

was not until June 1986 that the project was put onto a formal footing with the Imperial War Museum agreeing to provide the funding to get the aircraft restored to flying condition, David Lee reforming the team that had previously restored Shuttleworth's ex-Loughborough Spitfire, AR501, with Keith Taylor as crew chief (and Merlin engine specialist), Steve McManus as deputy crew chief and Norman Gardiner as overall project manager.

The task was enormous, hampered by the previous attempts, and the first job was to catalogue how much of the airframe they had and what condition it was in. Norman Chapman was the licensed engineer on the aircraft and he oversaw all of the work – no stranger to Hurricanes, he had first worked on them in 1940.

Reconstruction work began in earnest in 1987 and one of the first requirements was the building of a tube-squaring machine to roll the square ends onto the circular section steel tubing used in the Hurricane's construction. Although much of the stainless steel and other fittings could be cleaned and re-used, the four main longerons and many of the other fuselage tubes were badly corroded and had to be replaced. The centre section was rebuilt first followed by the fuselage and engine bearer. The undercarriage, radiator and dog-house were sent off to specialist sub-contractors whilst the tailplane was dispatched to Cranfield where the College of Aeronautics had developed an approved modification for the tailplane spar which had already been utilised by the Battle of Britain Memorial Flight on its Hurricanes.

Over the next few years the various parts started to return, the dog-house from Maurice Bayliss, the radiator from Cambridge Radiators and the propeller – complete with new Hoffman blades – from Skycraft. The wings were inspected and found to be serviceable and in 1990 Keith Taylor started work on getting the Merlin III back to airworthy condition following an inspection by one of the Merlin's original design team, Alec Harvey-Bailey. The fuselage fabric was attached and doped by Chris Morris from Old Warden in early 1993, the Shuttleworth Collection being responsible for all the fabric work, and on 13 March 1994 the fuselage – resplendent in the markings of No. 880 Sqdn – was moved into the restoration hangar with the wings being fitted the following May. The long-missing arrester hook had been located and re-installed but it was modified for display purposes. Originally, once the hook was lowered it could

Coming to the end of its restoration, Z7015 in all-silver dope at Duxford in May 1993. *(Tony Clarke Collection)*

not be raised again until after the aircraft had landed. The modification allows retraction via a pneumatic spring brake actuator system, and a slide ensures that actuator loads cannot be transferred into the airframe if the hook remains latched when the actuator is operated. The CAA have not assessed the hook in use and the aircraft was therefore not approved for arrested landings.

The Merlin III was first run on 23 July 1994 but it took a full year of further work – including rebuilding the prop – before the aircraft was at long last ready for its first taxi tests with John Lewis at the helm on 23 July 1995. The

CAA signed off the paperwork on 5 September 1995 and the first flight, in the hands of Andy Sephton, took place at Duxford on 17 September – nine years, nine months and nine days after the restoration work began. For certification purposes the Hurricane was registered G-BKTH with the UK Civil Aviation Authority on 24 May 1983 but this is not carried externally. For the first few years after restoration Z7015 was based at Duxford, making literally flying visits to Old Warden, but it is now permanently based with the Shuttleworth Collection at Old Warden where it often flies in company with their Westland Lysander.

Z7059
Hawker (Canadian) Hurricane Mk I/Mk X

Indian Air Force Museum, Palam, New Delhi, India

The subject of much conjecture over the past 40 years, the correct identity of this Hurricane has at last been laid to rest. The first solid evidence of its true identity came when Peter Vacher, owner of R4118 (qv) had the opportunity to inspect the cockpit and managed to note the c/n carried on a small brass plate near the fuel cock. This confirmed that it was a Canadian-built Mk I Hurricane with the c/n CCF/41H/4026. Peter consulted a number of sources including Frank Mason's classic book on the Hawker Hurricane and assumed from the production figures therein that it was the 26th CCF-built Hurricane, which he took to be serial number P5202, which had been dispatched to Bombay, India aboard the

SS *Clan Forbes* on 24 November 1943. This aircraft was converted to an instructional airframe on 29 October 1944 and finally written off charge in 1947. The painted serial 'P5202' found inside the cowlings was the final piece of the jigsaw in Peter's eyes.

What many people do not know was that Frank Mason, and many subsequent authors who have based their work on Frank's, missed out some serials from his production list. When writing the history of the Shuttleworth Collection's CCF-built Hurricane, Z7015 (qv), the present author noted that its c/n (CCF/41H/4013) was very close in the production sequence to the Indian example. By simple correlation of

Seen here at Palam in October 2008, the inspection panels and cowlings were removed while the Hurricane was being inspected by engineers from the RAF Battle of Britain Memorial Flight. *(John Sanderson)*

c/n with serial it became clear that the Indian aircraft was probably Z7059, a fact confirmed by checking the Form 78 Movements Card of that aircraft which indicated that this too had been shipped to India, actually to Karachi via Bombay, and had been struck off charge at the end of June 1944. Obviously it must have crossed paths with P5202 at some point – probably during its time as an instructional airframe – which is how the cowlings came to be swapped. Existing research by Dr Jon Leake, Norman Malayney and Jerry Vernon – who have made a 30-year investigation into CCF Hurricane c/n sequences – confirmed that CCF/41H/4026 was indeed allocated to Z7059.

Z7059 was ordered from the Canadian Car and Foundry Company (CCF) against Contract No. BSB 166, which was for 100 Hurricane Mk Is with serials between Z6983- Z7162. Bearing c/n CCF/41H/4026, Z7059 fell into the serial block Z7049-Z7093 and is the second oldest surviving Canadian Hurricane. Originally assigned to No. 13 MU at Henlow, Beds, on 30 July 1940, before it was actually completed and possibly when the order was placed, it was built at the CCF plant at Fort William as a Merlin III-powered Hurricane Mk I, subsequently redesignated Mk X in RAF service, with engine number 174720 and a de Havilland 'bracket' propeller. It was finally delivered to Henlow on 14 March 1941 where it was assembled by No. 13 MU before despatch to No. 27 MU at Shawbury, Shropshire, on 6 April where it was stored until delivered to Abbotsinch, Renfrewshire, near Glasgow, on 2 May 1941, for reserve aircraft storage within RAF Maintenance Command. Approximately 130 aircraft were stored at the airfield in 1941, including about 50 Hurricanes & 30 Blenheims; No. 232 Sqdn received Hurricane Is at Abbotsinch in July 1941, en route to Ouston, Durham. Also a detachment of the MSFU was based at Abbotsinch, with Sea Hurricane IAs & Hurricane Is, from May 1941 onwards, for operations from CAM ships. Which unit it was assigned to is not recorded; the airfield operating jointly at the time on a shared basis between the Royal Air Force and the Royal Navy (HMS Sanderling), but it remained here until 5 November 1941 when it was allocated to No. 59 OTU based at Crosby-on-Eden in Cumberland, which had a total of over 70 Hurricanes on strength during the 1941-1944 period.

The life of an advanced training aircraft is often harsh but Z7059 managed to stay out of trouble for over a year until

Taken in August 1967, this was the first photograph to appear in print showing 'AP832' in the newly-opened Indian Air Force Museum. *(S N Simms)*

22 December 1942 when it suffered a Cat B (beyond repair on site) flying accident. As a result it was sent to Taylorcraft Ltd at Rearsby, Leicestershire, (part of the Hurricane Repair Organisation) on 10 January 1943; the repairs in works took three months and it was not ready for return to the unit until 17 April 1943. No. 59 OTU had moved to Milfield, Northumberland, on 2-10 August 1942 (main party arrived 5 August 1942), so it is reasonable to assume that the accident occurred either there or at the satellite airfield, at Brunton, Northumberland which opened on 4 August 1942.

Z7059 was delivered to No. 10 MU at Hullavington, Wilts, on 4 May 1943 and – although not documented on the Form 78 – it was then issued to No. 1623 AAC (Anti Aircraft Co-operation) Flight based at Roborough, Devon, as it was serving with the unit when it suffered another Cat B flying accident on 18 May. It was being flown by P/O W R S Davidson on a naval co-operation flight and when landing at 1540 hours it was apparently hit by a down-draught causing the undercarriage to strike the airfield boundary hedge. As it struck the ground it nosed over and the undercarriage collapsed causing damage which required repairs in works (RIW) at an unknown civilian repair organisation (CRO) unit. It was ready for collection following repairs on 16 July and dispatched to No. 5 MU at Kemble, Gloucestershire, on 9 August.

By August 1943 a Mk I Hurricane was obsolescent in the European Theatre (although No. 1 Sqdn, Indian Air

Force, had been flying them operationally in the tactical reconnaissance role in the Far East until April 1943) but Z7059 had been selected to be overhauled and sent to Air Command, South East Asia (ACSEA) as a training aircraft for Indian pilots. The Japanese army had invaded Burma and was advancing towards India so the plan was to boost pilot numbers in the region by sending Hurricanes as training aircraft. On 1 December it was sent to the packing depot of No. 52 MU at Pengham Moors, Cardiff, Glamorgan, where it was crated and on 13 March 1944 it was on board the cargo ship the SS *Malakand* en route for Karachi. (Owned by the Brocklebank Line, this was the third ship to carry the name, its immediate predecessor having exploded in Liverpool Docks on 3 May 1941 when it was set alight by enemy

By March 2005 the fuselage serial had been repainted as 'AB832' although the underwing serial remained 'AP832'. *(Peter R Arnold)*

bombs whilst being loaded with ammunition, destroying the entire Huskisson No. 2 Dock and killing four people.)

The ship sailed via Bombay on 13 March 1944 and arrived at Karachi on 18 April 1944, with Z7059 being taken on charge on 29 April. The RAF depot at Drigh Road, Karachi, initially known simply as 'Aircraft Depot, India', had been renamed No 1 (India) Maintenance Unit on 20 January 1942, and Group Captain J McFarlane assumed command. With the entry of the Japanese into World War 2, the role of Drigh Road expanded; it was now the main supply base not only for the RAF in India but also for all the squadrons and units engaged in the Burma and Malaya campaigns. No.1 (India) MU was re-designated No. 301 MU on 18 March 1942, No. 320 MU formed from the repair depot element of No. 301 MU on 1 November 1942 at Drigh Road, and No. 301 MU

became only an equipment depot in December 1942; Nos. 301 & 320 MUs remained at Drigh Road until 30 October 1947, when transferred to the Royal Pakistan Air Force. Records show that in the early months of 1942 the greater number of aircraft dispatched by the maintenance unit were Hurricane and Mohawk fighters. On 29 June 1943, work was started by the North Western Railway Company on a new rail siding in the dispersal area to expedite deliveries of aircraft which arrived by sea in crates, as well as to replenish the bulk fuel tanks. The new sidings were completed on 22 August and a test train was successfully operated. Since partition in 1947 the airfield has been within Pakistan and is now known as PAF Faisal, home to the PAF's Southern Air Command and the PAF Air War College.

Although Hurricanes, in the form of the later Mk II and Mk IV variants, were numerically still the most important fighters in service with South East Asia Command until the end of 1944, even in India a Mk I Hurricane was considered ancient, the MU at Drigh Road having been erecting and distributing P-47 Thunderbolts from March 1944 onwards, and in July 1944 an order was promulgated which gave instructions that all such aircraft were to be reduced to produce with any valuable items removed and returned to stock, the airframes being moved to the 'graveyard'. Z7059 had been struck off charge on 30 June so it possibly escaped destruction by being chosen – along with a small number of other Hurricanes including R4118 (qv) – as an instructional airframe. Whereas the latter aircraft was passed to Banaras Hindu University nothing is known about the subsequent movements of Z7059 until it was first noted in the Indian Air Force Museum in August 1967, painted all-silver and bearing the serial 'AP832'. Over the subsequent 40-odd years it has been repainted many times, now bearing a peculiar camouflage scheme, and carrying the serial 'AB832'.

Despite these indignities – and the loss of its undercarriage doors – it remains on display and is kept in good condition, having been recently surveyed for a possible restoration to flying condition with the Indian Air Force Historic Aircraft Flight. There was, some years ago, a suggestion that it could be exchanged with the Battle of Britain Memorial Flight's LF363, but that was when it was thought to be either P5202, or V6846, another Mk I sent to India in 1944, which were both genuine Battle of Britain veterans.

AE977
Hawker (Canadian) Hurricane Mk I/Mk X

Peter Monk, Biggin Hill, Kent, UK

AE977 was ordered from the Canadian Car and Foundry Company (CCF) against Contract No. BSB 166, which was for 340 Hurricane Mk Is with serials ranging from AE958 to AG684. Allocated the c/n CCF/41H/8020, it emerged as the 20th and final aircraft in the serial block AE958-AE977. On arrival in the UK these aircraft were re-designated as Hurricane Mk X to differentiate them from their UK-built cousins.

Although assigned to No. 13 MU at Henlow, Beds, on 1 September 1940, before it was actually built and possibly when the order was placed, it was not completed until March 1941 and not delivered until 21 April 1941. AE977 was assembled by No. 13 MU before despatch to No. 10 MU at Hullavington, Wilts, on 27 May where it was placed in store, probably at the dispersed site at Down Farm (a satellite landing ground for No. 10 MU) near Westonbirt, Glos, on 3 June 1941. At this time about 400 Mk I and Mk X Hurricanes were being converted to Sea Hurricane

configuration by General Aircraft Ltd at Hanworth where they were modified with slinging points, catapult spools and an arrester hook – in addition to general strengthening – prior to delivery to the Fleet Air Arm. Despite AE977 being noted as a Sea Hurricane on its Form 78 and the fact that it was one of around 80 operated by the Royal Navy from RNAS Yeovilton for training purposes, the records and wartime photographs do not show that it was ever physically converted into a Sea Hurricane. When the wreckage was examined by Hawker Restorations there was no sign of any catapult spools or strengthening plates, all of which point to the fact that AE977 was a Hurricane Mk I/Mk X operated by the Fleet Air Arm.

On 11 July 1941, AE977 was transferred from No. 10 MU to No. 20 MU, Aston Down, Glos, where it was prepared for service and issued to the RN Deposit Account on 17 July (this simply meant that it was a Royal Navy aircraft being stored at an RAF facility). It was delivered

Caught outside its home at the Biggin Hill Heritage Hangar on 18 November 2014, AE977 shows off its newly-applied markings during a night photoshoot. (*Tad Dippel*)

to RNAS Yeovilton (HMS Heron) where it was issued to Nos 759/760 Sqdns in August 1941 and coded 'S'. These units were shore-based operational training squadrons, part of the Fleet Fighter School, which prepared fighter pilots who were going to become carrier-based in due course. AE977 served without any serious mishaps until 11 July 1942 when it suffered a burst tyre on landing and taxied off the runway due to a jammed wheel; the pilot was Sub Lt A D R Webber of the Royal New Zealand Navy and the damage was classified as Cat X (made serviceable by local resources). It was soon back in action again but on 5 December 1942 it was involved in a mid-air collision with another non-navalised Hurricane Mk I, Z4702, of No.759 Sqdn, and crashed near Godney in the Somerset Levels near Glastonbury. The pilot was Lt D T Keene or Sub Lt D T King depending on the source material – whatever his name he was safe but the Hurricane was beyond repair, classified as Cat Z (likely to be struck off charge), and was written off.

AE977, coded 'S' and with 'Royal Navy' lettering on the rear fuselage, flying with five other Hurricanes from Yeovilton on 9 December 1941. (© *IWM*)

It seems that significant portions of the airframe remained at the crash site and were recovered in the 1960s, eventually coming into the possession of Malcolm Clube, well known in motor racing circles. When interviewed in February 2015, Clube explained that he had acquired it from a motorcycling associate, Julian Ide, whose father had overheard two farm workers discussing the crash in a Somerset pub many years

previously. Intrigued by the conversation Ide's father had asked them to show him the crash site and then arranged for the wreckage to be removed and taken to his home in Milford, Surrey, where it was stored for several decades. Clube himself stored it for several more years before it came to the notice of Tony Ditheridge – who was then forming his company, Hawker Restorations, in association with Sir Tim Wallis of New Zealand. A deal was struck and a very large chunk of battered Hurricane was delivered to Tony's workshop at Milden, Suffolk, in 1994. The aircraft was registered to Hawker Restorations as G-TWTD on 6 May that year, the registration incorporating the initials of the founders of the company Tim Wallis and Tony Ditheridge.

Over the next six years the recovered components were stripped and assessed to see if they could be re-utilised in the restored aircraft. It was possible to use all of the fuselage stainless steel plates and attachment brackets but the T50 tubular steel structure was corroded and had to be replaced with modern material of the same gauge. The same applied to the centre section and tailplane. A new radiator, new header tank and new oil cooler were manufactured by Anglia Radiators; the main undercarriage legs were stripped and salvaged where possible, with the outer casings and axles being replaced, whilst the Dowty tailwheel unit was stripped and repaired.

Hawker Restorations have a large supply of spares obtained from Russian crash sites and elsewhere and these proved valuable as both spares and patterns, the company's own engineers being highly skilled and able to recreate damaged or missing components as required in their on-site machine shop. Other parts – such as the outer wing panels – were subcontracted to specialist suppliers, the wings being built and assembled by Airframe Assemblies in their workshops at Sandown on the Isle of Wight. No armament is fitted to the rebuilt wings, the space being taken up by additional fuel tanks.

AE977 was originally fitted with a Merlin III and a DH 'bracket' prop when it was assembled by No. 13 MU in May 1941 but during the restoration it was decided to fit a Packard Merlin 224 with a Hamilton Standard three-bladed constant speed propeller. This engine is the Packard equivalent of the Rolls-Royce Merlin 24 and effectively brings AE977 up to Mk IV standard – as evidenced by the deeper radiator and oil cooler so characteristic of the later Hurricanes. The colour

Taxying in the Californian sunshine on 27 May 2007. *(Jim Buckel)*

scheme chosen was representative of Douglas Bader's LE-D of No. 242 Sqdn during 1940, although it retained its own serial. First engine tests were carried out at Milden before the aircraft was transported by road to the nearby military airfield of RAF Wattisham where Stuart Goldspink took it up for its first test flight on 7 June 2000 and it made its first public appearance at the Flying Legends air display held at Duxford the following month. AE977 thus became the first of Hawker Restorations' Hurricanes to fly in the UK, P3351 (qv) having flown in New Zealand the previous January.

Sold to American collector Tom Friedkin, AE977 left Duxford on 27 April 2001 and was transported to Southampton Docks from where it was shipped to Galveston, Texas, together with Tom's Spitfire, ML417, and then taken by truck to Houston where it was reassembled, the registration G-TWTD being cancelled on 25 September 2001. Registered in the USA to Tom's company, Chino Warbirds Inc, as N33TF the Hurricane was flown to Chino, California, where it was based and displayed with the Planes of Fame Museum until 19 April 2012 when it was re-registered to Tom's new company, Comanche Warbirds Inc, and flown to his private airfield near Houston. It was soon sold however and on 12 March 2013 it was re-registered in the UK as G-CHTK, joining Peter Monk's Biggin Hill Heritage Hangar Collection at the Kent Battle of Britain fighter base.

Once it had arrived at Biggin Hill AE977 was repainted in the markings of Hurricane Mk I, P3886 / UF-K of No.

601 Sqdn, which had been flown by American volunteers Billy Fiske and double ace Carl R Davis. It flew in this scheme as part of the Eagle Squadron demonstration team, commemorating US airmen who flew from the UK during World War 2, between March 2013 and October 2014 when the markings were changed to represent P2921 / GZ-L of No. 32 Sqdn which was flown from Biggin Hill by F/Lt Pete Brothers during July and August 1940. Convinced that he needed more speed, Brothers had the rear view mirror removed from his aircraft and fitted a car mirror inside the cockpit. By having his rigger file down rivet heads on the wings he managed to squeeze an extra 5 mph out of his aircraft.

Following sale to Peter Monk AE977 was initially repainted as 'P3886 / UF-K' as shown here at Duxford on 25 May 2013. *(Peter Green)*

AM274
Hawker Hurricane Mk IIB

Eric Vormezeele, Brasschaat, Belgium

AM274 was ordered from the Canadian Car and Foundry Company (CCF) against British Air Commission Contract C45 (British Supply Board Contract BSB 166), which was for 100 Hurricane Mk IIBs built with serials ranging from AM270 to AM369. As AM270 was retained in Canada, a further Hurricane was built with the serial AP138 to complete the 100 aircraft batch for delivery to Britain. The serial AM270 was allocated in error to both a Hurricane and a Catalina, but the duplicated serial on this Hurricane was not cancelled and replaced by AP138 on the same aircraft, as incorrectly implied elsewhere.

Following completion at Fort William, Ontario, AM274 was assigned to No. 13 MU, Henlow, Bedfordshire (probably on acceptance by the Air Ministry representative at CCF) and then crated and transported by rail to Halifax, Nova Scotia, where it was loaded on board a ship which probably sailed as part of Convoy HX191, which departed Halifax on 24 May 1942 and arrived without loss at Liverpool on 6 June 1942. From here it was transported to No. 13 MU at Henlow, where the vast majority of CCF-built Hurricanes were assembled in the UK, arriving on 3 July 1942. The assembly process was normally very efficient but AM274 is thought to have sustained damage in transit as it required repairs in works (RIW) at No.13 MU, under the authority of the civilian repair organisation, and was not awaiting collection until 28 November. During John Norman's strip-down prior to restoration various damage repairs were discovered in the centre section port side trailing edge and the starboard wing attachment points. The port main undercarriage door had also been replaced with a British-built unit, all of which points to damage having been incurred during the sea crossing.

Although a Packard Merlin 28 had been fitted at Fort William this was removed at Henlow – because of a fault with initial Merlin 28 engines which required rectification –

and she was re-engined with a Rolls-Royce Merlin XX (No. 41957 / A219526), remaining a Hurricane IIB. This engine had originally been dispatched from Derby to Langley on 23 August 1941 and fitted into a new Hurricane but it had been returned to Rolls-Royce at Glasgow for overhaul after 200 hours, which had been completed on 28 March 1942, a few days before AM274 arrived at Henlow. It is certain that AM274 then had a Rotol propeller fitted together with 12-gun wings with external hard points allowing it to carry bombs or long-range fuel tanks. Whether these wings were the original CCF wings or replacements fitted during the repairs is not known. All CCF-built Hurricanes from AG665 onwards, including AM274, were built as Mk IIBs with 12-Browning wings, except for Sea Hurricanes of the BW835-BW884 batch which had eight-Browning wings. Wings and centre sections of the latter aircraft were possibly exchanged on the production lines with aircraft having AG/AM serials, hence 24(---) major part numbers found on wing centre sections of Sea Hurricane survivors.

On 5 December 1942, AM274 was flown to No. 10 MU at Hullavington, Wilts, but five days later it moved on to the packing depot of No. 76 MU at nearby Wroughton where it was broken down and crated again – this time for shipping to Russia as part of the Lend-Lease agreement. The crated Hurricane was shipped from Wroughton to Hull Docks, probably by rail, and arrived on 28 December before being loaded on board the merchant vessel SS *Dan-Y-Bryn*, departing on 12 January 1943. The ship joined Convoy JW52 which left Liverpool for Gourock and then Loch Ewe before sailing to Murmansk on 17 January. Seven days into their journey, on 24 January 1943, the convoy was in the Barents Sea between Iceland and Norway when they became the target of an aerial attack by three Heinkel He 115 torpedo bombers. The *Dan-Y-Bryn* was in the lead row, second ship in from port. All three ships in the port column

With both wings attached AM274 was starting to look like a complete aeroplane again in June 2012. *(John and Heather Norman)*

were active in the battle, managing to shoot down one of the Heinkels and disable another. The third Heinkel was shot at but probably made it back to base. More attacks followed but the ship arrived safely in Murmansk on 27 January 1943.

Once in Russian hands AM274 was reassembled and fitted with Soviet-built armament. The 12 0.303 inch Brownings were removed, new gun mounts were fitted and parts of the wing structure were altered to accommodate the changes. Shell casing chutes and machine-gun exit holes were riveted over and new shell casing chutes and gun apertures were made in order to accommodate two ShVAK 20mm cannon and two UBT 12.7mm (0.50 inch calibre) heavy machine guns. AM274 was also fitted with a tropical cowling and Vokes air filter, probably during the work done by No.13 MU at Henlow as an estimated 20% of Hurricanes supplied

to Russia featured the Vokes filter. The initial deliveries to Russia, diverted from aircraft originally destined for the Middle East, had tropical filters but many later deliveries did not have them; Soviet personnel developed their own smaller dust filters which were fitted from 1943 onwards. In late February 1943, AM274 was put into service by the 2nd Sqdn, 78th Fighter Aviation Regiment of the Naval Air Force of the Soviet Northern Fleet (78 IAP, VVS-SF) based at Vaenga. This was the same airfield where the Hurricanes of 151 Wing RAF had operated some 18 months earlier.

In June 1943, Soviet anti-shipping sorties boiled over into fully-fledged aerial battles. A major operation against an enemy convoy was conducted on 19 June 1943, when Soviet Hurricane ace, Capt Vasiliy Adonkin of 78th IAP, claimed a victory whilst leading eight Hurricanes. Apart from Adonkin, fellow Hurricane pilots Lts Z V Bulat, F M Kochanov and V G Mitrofanov from his squadron (2./78 IAP) each claimed a Bf 109 destroyed. The eight Hurricanes of 78th IAP were accompanying four Il-2s, with six Yak-1s and eight P-39s providing the fighter escort.

At 0300, the attack aircraft swept in from 400m (1,300ft) to engage the enemy convoy, which was approaching its home port of Liinakhamari, with an escort of 13 Bf 109s and four Bf 110s circling overhead. The Soviet aircraft were still 8km (5 miles) from the target, when they were intercepted by a large force of enemy fighters. Some of the Messerschmitts engaged the Hurricanes, which in turn became separated from the Il-2s. The latter remained unprotected, as the 20 Yak-1s which should have been providing a fighter escort were still at high altitude, and eventually arrived over the convoy just as the battle was ending. By then, the Il-2s had managed to evade the fighters and fight their way to the ships. Making a single pass, the Shturmoviks strafed, rocketed and bombed the vessels from an altitude of 200m (650ft).

Fighting for their survival, the Hurricane pilots engaged in a fierce battle with the opposing fighters, which soon gained the upper hand. No fewer than five Hurricanes (including AM274) were shot down, mostly into the sea, resulting in the deaths of Jr Lts Vasiliy Nazarov (a flight commander), Petr Gaplikov and Nikolai Starosvetskiy. Lts Yuriy Maslennikov and Fyodor Kochanov bailed out of their burning aircraft, and were quickly rescued from the water by launches. Two more damaged Hurricanes made emergency landings at Pummanki, as did an Il-2, leaving the remaining attack aircraft (escorted by Yak-1s and P-39s) to fly back to Vaenga. The Hurricane pilots of squadron 2./78 IAP claimed four Bf 109s destroyed.

AM274 was being flown by Lt Maslennikov who, despite his aircraft being hit in the propeller, engine and starboard fuel tank – which was set on fire – managed to pull off a skilful wheels-up landing on the tundra at Heinäsaari on the Rybachiy Peninsula. Luckily for Maslennikov, the Rybachiy Peninsula was in Soviet hands. Though largely uninhabited, there were a number of Soviet units there, one of which rescued him. There are no further listings of Maslennikov being wounded or killed, so it is highly likely he survived the Great Patriotic War.

The wreck was re-discovered almost exactly 48 years after she crashed on 19 June 1943. It was on 15 June 1991 that the search group Podvodnik from Murmansk discovered AM274 and found the wreckage to be essentially complete. This group also detected wreckage of two other Hurricanes that day on the Rybachiy Peninsula. When translated, the name Podvodnik means 'Diver'. The group was comprised of Andrey Kopytkov, Leonid Aleksjutin, Michail Kazakevich, Valentin Hapaev and Aleksandr Kazakov. After discovering the wrecks and taking photos the group had to leave the wreckage on the tundra, in order to make arrangements for a helicopter, a pilot, a loader and operator, mechanics, trucks, drivers, etc, so they could carry out the actual salvage operation. Unfortunately, in the time that it took the group to organise the recovery *another* group descended upon the site and by the time they returned they discovered that the tail section and wings had already been salvaged, leaving just the forward fuselage and engine to be recovered. Years later it was discovered that the wings salvaged from AM274 are those acquired by Kermit Weeks for his Hurricane project, RCAF 5400 (qv).

The remains of the three wrecks were taken back to Murmansk but in 1992 they were sent to St Petersburg for restoration. This did not happen and the wreckage of AM274 surfaced in 1994 as one of a 'package' of three Soviet Hurricanes being offered for sale by Ben Kolotilin's company Kolair Inc of Roswell, Georgia, USA. Whether he acquired all three of the original Hurricanes recovered from the Podvodnik group or it was AM274 plus two different Hurricanes is not clear. Similarly it is not clear whether he acquired them directly from Russia or via an intermediary.

The three aircraft were bought by Ed and Rose Zalesky, operating as The Airplane Supply Centre of White Rock, BC, Canada, in 1995 but the aircraft were stored in containers at Blaine, WA, USA. Ed and Rose, together with Bill Thompson, Ron Stunden and Barry Jackson had formed the Canadian Museum of Flight and Transportation, based on the family farm at Crescent Road in Surrey, BC, Canada, in 1970 but Ed eventually separated his business interests from those of the museum. The package was advertised for sale as a whole and in June 2003 John Norman of JNE Aircraft Restoration Services of Burlington, WA, (about 40 miles south of Blaine) went to look them over and bought them on the spot.

Once all three wrecks were laid out in John's workshop

he discovered the identity of AM274 on the chin cowling of one of the airframes and decided that it would be the one he would restore. John is an inspector on the Boeing 787 Dreamliner production line at Everett, WA, where he works some 40 hours a week; JNE Aircraft Restoration Services has no staff apart from John and the Hurricane project was a massive undertaking. The plan was to work evenings and weekends on the project and to restore AM274 to its Soviet configuration complete with armament. He originally estimated that it would take 10 years to complete the work, after which the Hurricane would be sold. Registered in the USA as N274JW work progressed well, with many parts being repaired or remanufactured in-house, and by 2008 the newly built woodwork was being fitted to the restored fuselage and a new stainless steel firewall was in place together with a refurbished fin and rudder which had been sourced from the UK. Instead of buying in new centre section spars John used his contacts in the aerospace industry to find a local company which could heat-treat his own newly-built spars.

The wreck of AM274 lying on the Kola Peninsula. *(Peter R Arnold Collection)*

Although most of the components used in the restoration are from AM274, parts not available on that airframe – or ones which were too badly damaged – were taken from the other two wrecks, one of which was found to be Z2330 (qv) and the other an unidentified Gloster-built Hurricane Mk I. These two were eventually sold to Brian Davis of Hamilton, Ontario who has passed on the Mk I project to Darrell Brown of Oshawa. The centre section from Z2330 was less damaged than that from AM274 but rather than

switch centre sections John used it as a jig to ensure that AM274's structure retained its shape and dimensions. The rebuilt centre section was completed during 2010 and on 6 September the fuselage was attached to it, the engine mount and Merlin were refitted and the following day the rebuilt main undercarriage was successfully lowered to allow AM274 to stand on her own legs once again.

The wings from AM274 had been salvaged and sold separately and are now known to be with Kermit Weeks in Florida so John set about rebuilding the damaged pair which had been part of the 'package deal'. The skins had been removed in 2005 but then work was suspended to concentrate on the fuselage. With the fuselage mounted on the centre section and the undercarriage in position, John turned his attention back to the wings in late 2010 and by March 2011 it was time to start the re-assembly process. Things went smoothly until May when John and his wife Heather decided it was time to work on their house rather than the Hurricane. By May 2012 it was time for the port wing to be offered up to the centre section and on 5 May it was gently slotted into place, the starboard wing following in June. There was still much work to be done but this was a major milestone in the restoration.

John had always intended to sell AM274 and in January 2014 he was visited by Eric Vormezeele and his family from Brasschaat, Belgium, who were interested in adding the Hurricane to their impressive collection of warbirds. An agreement was reached and Eric's sons Frédéric and Alex returned on 28 February to assist John and Heather with the task of packing the Hurricane into two shipping containers. The containers finally left on 3 March and after a very arduous journey, which included leaving Halifax, Nova Scotia, on 14 April, on board the container vessel *Charles Dickens*, she docked in Southampton on 22 April before finally arriving at Rotterdam the same day. The containers arrived at Brasschaat, Belgium, on 2 May 2014 where the Vormezeele family will continue the restoration to flying condition.

BW853
Hawker Sea Hurricane Mk IB/ Mk XIIA
Kevin Wheatcroft, Cotswold Airport, Kemble, Glos, UK

BW853, c/n CCF R30019, was part of a Canadian Car and Foundry production batch comprising 50 aircraft with serials between BW835-BW884. They were built in 1941 and all to Sea Hurricane Mk IB standard with eight-gun wings and Merlin III engines, but with the longer nose of the Hurricane Mk II airframe. They were originally intended for use by the Fleet Air Arm so they featured catapult spools and arrester hooks and the first three were ferried from the factory to RCAF Station Dartmouth, where the Royal Navy and the Merchant Ship Fighter Unit of the RAF had aircraft servicing facilities, by MSFU pilots in November 1941. The second three aircraft, flown by the same pilots in worse weather 10 days later, crashed short of fuel on or near the Nova Scotia coast (two Cat B and one lost) and all subsequent deliveries were made by rail. Following the Japanese attack

on Pearl Harbor on 7 December 1941 all the CCF-built Sea Hurricanes were transferred onto RCAF charge to be issued to east coast units to provide air defence for the port of Halifax, and to help plug gaps in the Canadian fighter defence caused by Kittyhawks being transferred to the west coast to face what was believed to be an impending Japanese attack.

The RAF Form 78 shows BW853 being taken on charge by the RCAF in Nova Scotia on 3 December 1941, followed by an official transfer on 14 December, but the RCAF record card states that it was brought on charge by RCAF Station Dartmouth before being issued to the British Admiralty at the Royal Navy base at Halifax, Nova Scotia, so was intended to be transferred to the Fleet Air Arm not the MSFU. RCAF records indicate that RCAF Eastern Air Command took it on charge on 17 December 1941 when it was assigned

The fuselage of BW853 seen at William Tassell's farm in August 2008. *(William Tassell)*

to the Hurricane Flight of No. 118 (F) Sqdn at Dartmouth, Nova Scotia, until it was transferred to No. 126 (F) Sqdn at Dartmouth, which was formed from No. 118 Sqdn Hurricane Flight as a fighter unit at Dartmouth on 27 April 1942 for east coast air defence, with Canadian-built Sea Hurricanes (designated Sea Hurricane Mk Is by the RCAF) on its strength. The squadron CO was S/Ldr H de M Molson, a member of the Canadian Molson brewing family, who had served in the Battle of Britain on Hurricanes with No. 1 (F) Sqdn of the RCAF, the only Canadian squadron to serve in the battle. An odd coincidence is that Molson crashed during the Battle of Britain just three miles from where BW853 was kept for 19 years by William Tassell at Ulcombe, near Maidstone, Kent. Whilst serving with No. 126 it was coded BV-L.

BW853, coded 'TF-L', being loaded onto a railway wagon for transport to the CCF factory at Amherst following Sgt Brant's accident on 24 July 1942. *(Dr Jon Leake Collection)*

A second Hurricane squadron, No. 127 (F), was formed at Dartmouth on 1 July 1942 and BW853 was transferred to this unit, keeping its individual code letter when it was re-painted as TF-L. It did not survive intact for long however as at 2055 hours on 24 July 1942 Sgt J W Brant, on his first solo flight in a Hurricane, undershot the runway by 100 ft in conditions of poor visibility due to oil on the windscreen, the undercarriage collapsed and the aircraft slid onto the turning apron on its belly. BW853 sustained Category B damage and was transferred to No. 4 Repair Depot at Scoudouc, New Brunswick and dispatched to the CCF factory at Amherst, Nova Scotia, for repairs on 6 August 1942. Sgt Brant was sent back for more dual time on Harvards.

How long the repairs took is unclear as on 1 February 1943 it was re-allocated to CCF at Fort William, Ontario, where it was scheduled for conversion to Mk XIIA standard with a Packard Merlin 29 engine, and was finally returned to Eastern Air Command, when conversion to Mk XIIA was completed, on 5 July 1943. The RCAF had no Hurricane Mk IIA designation, and aircraft with Packard Merlin 29s and eight-Browning wings were referred to rather awkwardly as 'Mk IIBs except with eight Browning machine guns', until they were re-designated Mk XIIAs in August 1943.

In July 1999 BW853 was reunited with Mike Bailey, who had hit a tree in it on 14 June 1944. *(William Tassell)*

The aircraft was issued to No. 1 (F) Operational Training Unit at RCAF Bagotville, Quebec, and received minor damage when an RAF trainee, P/O Mike Bailey, hit a tree during a low-flying exercise on 14 June 1944. He was uninjured and the aircraft was repaired on unit. Further damage was inflicted on 1 August 1944 when Sgt Brown was forced to make an emergency landing in a field two miles south of St Gedion (Saint Gédéon), one mile east of the firing range, whilst on an air to sleeve gunnery exercise, after apparent engine failure at 1830 hours. BW853 sustained Category B damage in the accident and was designated as having been sufficiently damaged to require return to the repair depot. Sgt Brown was uninjured. On 11 August the aircraft was allocated for repairs at No. 9 Repair Depot (St Jean, Quebec), however, it had been decided to close the OTU and wind down further pilot training, so the repair card was altered to

The static restoration starting to take shape in May 1999. *(William Tassell)*

'write off' (Cat A), as it was no longer necessary to maintain the level of Hurricanes previously needed.

The OTU's last course finished on 6 October 1944 and the Hurricanes were all ferried away for storage. Aircraft with even minor damage were all written off, as there was no reason to repair them. BW853 was struck off strength on 12 October 1944, as were three other Hurricanes, BW862, BW881 and RCAF 5666, on 12 Oct, 29 Sept and 20 Dec 1944 respectively – all of which somehow managed to survive (see individual entries).

BW853 and BW881 (qv) arrived in England in the summer of 1987, both having been purchased by Tony Ditheridge (later to form Hawker Restorations) from Matt Sattler who had probably obtained them from Jack Arnold of Brantford, Ontario. It is possible that Arnold acquired them from Tex Lavallee, who had a collection of Hurricane wrecks said to include BW862, BW881 and RCAF 5666 in his 'Cultural and Aeronautical Collection' at St Chrysostome, Quebec, or Arnold may have obtained BW853 directly from a farmer or scrapyard near Bagotville during the period 1982-1983. The Hurricane was placed on the UK civil register as G-BRKE on 6 October 1989 but cancelled on 22 December 1995 during a register clean up by the Civil Aviation Authority (CAA).

At the time Tony's company, AJD Engineering Ltd, had a track record of having restored or rebuilt 21 World War One aircraft plus several World War Two aircraft including a Corsair, Wildcat, two Yak-11s and a two-seat Spitfire. However, once he looked at the Hurricanes in depth he realised

"… they were a metallurgist's nightmare. It became obvious very quickly that to get the material and the tooling made was well beyond our budget. We needed several million pounds to get it done properly. So we sold our two Hurricanes and walked away completely."

BW853 and BW881 were purchased jointly by William Tassell and Henry Pearman. The pair had shared several exotic cars together over the years and felt this was not only an extremely rare opportunity, but also an exceptionally rewarding and exciting project to get involved with. William's initial enthusiasm included the construction of a welded steel tube rear fuselage, plywood fuselage formers, together with the acquisition of a Russian fin, rudder, tailplane and elevators (from Tony Ditheridge) and a Merlin crankcase from a museum in the northeast of England. Although the aircraft was only ever intended to be a static reconstruction, the pair soon realised that further restoration was beyond them and the project was stored on William's farm at Ulcombe, Kent.

In July 1999 BW853 was reunited with Mike Bailey, who had hit a tree in it on 14 June 1944, and this was featured in the press at the time. BW853 was eventually entered into an auction held at the Goodwood motor racing circuit and aerodrome on 19 September 2008 where it was sold to Kevin Wheatcroft for the remarkably low price of £8,050 – a reflection of the amount of work needed to restore the aircraft. It has since been stored on behalf of the owner by Retro Track and Air at their facility at Cotswold Airport, the former RAF Kemble, Glos, where many Hurricanes were stored and maintained during World War Two.

BW862
Hawker Sea Hurricane Mk IB/Mk XIIA

Brian Davis, Hamilton, Ontario, Canada

BW862, c/n CCF R30028, was part of a Canadian Car and Foundry production batch comprising 50 aircraft with serials between BW835-BW884. They were built in 1941 and all to Sea Hurricane Mk IB standard with eight-gun wings and Merlin III engines, but with the longer nose of the Hurricane Mk II airframe. They were originally intended for use by the Fleet Air Arm so they featured catapult spools and arrester hooks and the first three were ferried from the factory to RCAF Station Dartmouth, where the Royal Navy and the Merchant Ship Fighter Unit of the RAF had aircraft servicing facilities, by MSFU pilots in November 1941. The second three aircraft, flown by the same pilots in worse weather 10 days later, crashed short of fuel on or near the Nova Scotia coast (two Cat B and one lost), and all subsequent deliveries were made by rail. Following the Japanese attack on Pearl Harbor on 7 December 1941 all

The cockpit area and centre section of BW862 seen in early 2015 after the engine mount had been removed for renovation. *(Brian Davis)*

the CCF-built Sea Hurricanes were transferred onto RCAF charge to be issued to east coast units to provide air defence for the port of Halifax, and to help plug gaps in the Canadian fighter defence caused by Kittyhawks being transferred to the west coast to face what was believed to be an impending Japanese attack.

The RAF Form 78 shows it being taken on charge by the RCAF in Nova Scotia on 3 December 1941, followed by an official transfer on 12 December, but the RCAF record card states that it was brought on charge by RCAF Station Dartmouth before being issued to the British Admiralty at the Royal Navy base at Halifax, Nova Scotia, so was intended to be transferred to the Fleet Air Arm not the MSFU. RCAF records indicate that Eastern Air Command took BW862 on charge on 30 December 1941 when it was assigned to the Hurricane Flight of No. 118 (F) Sqdn at Dartmouth, NS. It may have been operated for a short period in May and June 1942 by the Saguenay Fighter Detachment of No. 118 Sqdn at Saguenay (Bagotville), Quebec, which was equipped with two Sea Hurricanes and a Lysander for protection of the Alcan factory at Arvida, Quebec, providing fighter defence and anti-aircraft co-operation respectively, before joining No. 1 (F) Operational Training Unit, also at Bagotville, which had been formed on 6 June 1942. It was sent back to Canadian Car and Foundry at Fort William on 23 June 1943, for conversion to Mk XIIA by the removal of the catapult spools, arrester hook and associated equipment and the replacement of the Merlin III with a Merlin 29.

Following conversion it was returned to Eastern Air Command on 8 September 1943 and re-issued to No. 1 (F) OTU for pilot training. It suffered Category C/D damage on 6 July 1944 as a result of a forced landing near Lac St Jean, (Lake St John in contemporary RCAF documents), and was issued on 18 July 1944 to No. 9 RD, St Jean, Quebec. The OTU's last course finished on 6 October 1944 and the Hurricanes were all ferried away for storage. Aircraft with even minor damage were all written off, as there was no reason to repair them. BW862 was struck off strength on 12 October 1944, as were three other Hurricanes, BW853, BW881 and RCAF 5666, on 12 Oct, 29 Sept and 20 Dec 1944 respectively – all of which somehow managed to survive (see individual entries).

Sometime around 1980 the wingless fuselage centre section of BW862, still sitting on its undercarriage, was obtained by Tex Lavallee, a country and western singer, cowboy movie actor and World War 2 aircraft enthusiast, who collected together a ragged band of aeronautical 'junk' as his 'Lavallee Cultural and Aeronautical Collection' at St Chrysostome, Quebec. Lavallee eventually disposed of the collection and BW862, together with the remains of RCAF 5666, was sold to the Canadian Museum of Flight and Transportation which had been established in association with the Zalesky family at Surrey, British Columbia. Redevelopment of the museum's original site meant that in 1996 the museum moved to Langley Airport and in the spring of 1998 it legally changed its name to the Canadian Museum of Flight Association.

Following these changes Ed and Rose Zalesky, operating as The Airplane Supply Centre of White Rock, BC, took 5666 (qv) with them and the museum retained BW862, which was in far worse condition. The museum eventually decided to rationalise its collection and BW862 was put up for disposal, being acquired by Brian Davis of Hamilton, Ontario, who also purchased John Norman's spares holdings, comprising the remains of Z2330 (qv) plus those of an anonymous Gloster-built Mk I. Brian is now concentrating on acquiring parts for BW862 and Z2330 for eventual airworthy restorations whilst the anonymous Mk I centre section has been passed on to Darrell Brown of Oshawa, Ontario.

BW874
Hawker Sea Hurricane Mk IB/Mk XIIA

Karl-Friedemann Grimminger, Munich, Germany

Although the RCAF serial number 5487 has been quoted as the identity of this aircraft, which would have been one of a batch of aircraft built by Canadian Car and Foundry at Fort William (Thunder Bay) for the Royal Canadian Air Force with serials between 5376-5675 the identity plate acquired by Classic Aero Engineering Ltd with the damaged airframe is from CCF R30040 which makes it BW874. It is assumed that the paperwork got muddled up by one of its previous owners.

BW874 was built to Sea Hurricane Mk IB standard, brought on charge by RCAF Station Dartmouth for issue to the British Admiralty at Halifax, but taken on strength by the Hurricane Flight of No. 118 (F) Sqdn at Dartmouth on 8 January 1942. It was almost certainly transferred to No. 126 Sqdn RCAF at Dartmouth, which was formed from No. 118 Sqdn Hurricane Flight on 27 April 1942 for east coast air

defence, with CCF-built Sea Hurricane Is. It was returned to Canadian Car and Foundry at Fort William on 23 June 1943 for conversion to Mk XIIA standard and issued to No. 1 (F) OTU at Bagotville, Quebec, on 20 September. It went missing on a training flight from Bagotville on 15 November 1943. Five aircraft were up on a local formation flying exercise when a very sudden heavy snowstorm covered the entire area with zero zero conditions. An extensive search was made for Sgt Raymond W Bailey, RAFVR, and his aircraft and it was thought at the time that he had crashed through the ice of a lake 30 miles ESE of Bagotville. The real crash site was not found until a logging crew discovered the wreck, and the body of its pilot, in dense woodland during 1973. Bailey was buried at Chicoutimi (St Francois Xavier), Quebec, but his Hurricane, BW874 appears in lists supplied by both Tex Lavallee and Jack Arnold. Lavallee said it was recovered in

Clive Davidson gently touching down at Thruxton on 12 October 2014. *(Gordon Riley)*

poor condition following a crash whilst Arnold says it was recovered from northern Quebec on the side of a hill near Bagotville. It is known that Jack Arnold acquired some of Lavallee's collection of Hurricane parts and that the crash site was visited several times following its initial discovery which has led to salvaged parts from BW874 being offered for sale on internet auction sites and elsewhere.

A damaged Hurricane centre section was sold by Jack Arnold to Matt Sattler of Carp, Ontario, and he in turn sold it to Tony Ditheridge, then trading as AJD Engineering Ltd. This, together with other parts and the c/n plate from CCF R30040, was subsequently sold by Hawker Restorations to Classic Aero Engineering at Thruxton aerodrome, Hants,

and was registered G-CBOE on 24 May 2002. Classic Aero was owned by Peter Tuplin and the late Paul Portelli; chief engineer Bruce Ellis was concentrating on rebuilding Paul's Spitfire Tr 9, SM520 / G-ILDA, so work on the Hurricane was subcontracted to Hawker Restorations who rebuilt the fuselage. The registration was transferred into Peter and Paul's ownership on 24 February 2005 but, following Paul's death in May 2007, all efforts were focused on completing and selling the Spitfire.

By this time Phil Lawton had acquired a Hurricane project, Z5207/G-BYDL (qv), which he had placed with Classic Aero for restoration but as that company started to wind down its operation Phil was faced with a dilemma –

The damaged centre section as received by Classic Aero Engineering Ltd. *(Phil Lawton)*

G-CBOE taxying in its temporary Finnish colours during the Oulu International Airshow, 9 August 2014. *(Jouni Saari)*

how would he get Z5207 completed? The solution came in 2011 when he purchased the Classic Aero Hurricane project, G-CBOE, and some workshop machinery, setting up Phoenix Aero Services Ltd in order to complete both aircraft. As G-CBOE was much more advanced it was decided to concentrate all efforts into getting it flying and, as a consequence, work on Z5207 ceased in March 2011.

In addition to these two Hurricanes Phil had another project, G-RLEF, which he had purchased from Maurice Bayliss, some parts from the tail group from that project being used on G-CBOE. The engine fitted is a Merlin 500-29 which was previously installed in a Spanish Air Force CASA 2.111 and which was overhauled by Retro Track and Air; the propeller is a Hamilton Standard 23EX, as originally fitted to Canadian-built Hurricanes, the spinner uses an original backplate but the cone was newly-manufactured. The wings were assembled at Thruxton using a kit manufactured by Bob Cunningham at Bournemouth in a wing jig loaned by Retro Track and Air.

The registration was transferred to Phoenix Aero Services on 30 January 2013 and on 30 April 2013 it was changed to Phil Lawton's name. It had always been Phil's intention to sell this Hurricane to fund the completion of Z5207 and to that end he chose a colour scheme which could be easily painted over. The all-silver colours represent a CCF-built Hurricane, AG244, which was operated by the Central Flying School, Royal Rhodesian Air Force, based at Norton Air Base, Rhodesia in 1945.

The first flight took place at Thruxton on 16 July 2014 and just a few days later the all-silver colour scheme was put to the test when Peter and Faye Medley of Flying Colours Contracts Ltd applied a temporary Finnish Air Force camouflage scheme to represent HC-465, formerly Z2585, which was operated by the Finns having been captured from the Soviet Air Force in February 1942. Phil is married to a Finn and lives in Helsinki and the colours were applied for the Hurricane to appear in the 'Tour de Sky', the Oulu International Airshow, which was held on 9-10 August 2014. On its return the washable paint was removed and the silver finish was gleaming when the author visited Thruxton in October 2014 to witness a short flying display by Clive Davidson. Both G-CBOE and Z5207, together with the assets of Phoenix Aero, were sold to Munich-based collector Karl-Friedemann Grimminger in December 2014.

BW881
Hawker Sea Hurricane Mk IB/ Mk XIIA

Flying Heritage Collection, Paine Field, Everett, WA, USA

BW881, c/n CCF R32007, was part of a Canadian Car and Foundry production batch comprising 50 aircraft with serials between BW835-BW884. They were built in 1941 and all to Sea Hurricane Mk IB standard with eight-gun wings, Merlin III engines and DH propellers, but with the longer nose of the Hurricane Mk II airframe. They were originally intended for use by the Fleet Air Arm so they featured catapult spools and arrester hooks and the first three were ferried from the factory to RCAF Station Dartmouth, where the Royal Navy and the Merchant Ship Fighter Unit of the RAF had aircraft servicing facilities, by MSFU pilots in November 1941. The second three aircraft, flown by the same pilots in worse weather 10 days later, crashed short of fuel on or near the Nova Scotia coast (two Cat B and one lost), and all subsequent deliveries were made by rail. Following the Japanese attack on Pearl Harbor on 7 December 1941 all the CCF-built Sea Hurricanes were transferred onto RCAF charge to be issued to east coast units to provide air defence for the port of Halifax, and to help plug gaps in the Canadian fighter defence caused by Kittyhawks being transferred to the west coast to face what was believed to be an impending Japanese attack.

The RAF Form 78 shows BW881 being taken on charge by the RCAF in Nova Scotia on 17 January 1942, but the RCAF record card states that it was brought on charge by RCAF Station Dartmouth before being issued to the British Admiralty at the Royal Navy base at Halifax, Nova Scotia, so it was intended to be transferred to the Fleet Air Arm not the MSFU. RCAF records indicate that Eastern Air Command took it on charge on 22 January 1942 when it was assigned to the Hurricane Flight of No. 118 (F) Sqdn at Dartmouth, NS. It was almost certainly transferred to No. 126

A close-up shot of the 'Bulldog' artwork of No. 135 Sqdn RCAF. (*Chris Chapman*)

Sqdn RCAF at Dartmouth, which was formed from No. 118 Sqdn Hurricane Flight on 27 April 1942 for east coast air defence, with CCF-built Sea Hurricane Is, but may have later served with the other Sea Hurricane squadrons in Eastern Air Command. Nos. 126, 127 and 129 Sqdns flew Sea Hurricanes until March 1943, based respectively at Dartmouth (with an initial detachment at Bagotville), at Gander (in Newfoundland), and at Dartmouth again. It remained with Eastern Air Command until 23 June 1943 when it was returned to CCF at Fort William, Ontario, where it was converted to Hurricane XIIA standard by the removal of the arrester hook and catapult spools whilst the Merlin III was replaced with a Packard Merlin 29 driving a Hamilton Standard propeller.

The aircraft was returned to Eastern Air Command on 20 September 1943 and issued to No. 1 (F) Operational Training Unit at RCAF Bagotville, Quebec. Just after take-off on 10 December F/Sgt E E Whitehead was climbing through 4,000 feet about three miles northwest of St Anne, Quebec, when the aircraft suffered engine failure. Whitehead was uninjured in the subsequent wheels-up landing and an investigation determined that the engine had thrown oil through the breather, possibly as a result of a failure of the scavenge pump. BW881 suffered Cat D damage but was dispatched for repair and returned to the unit. On 7 September 1944, with only a month to go before the OTU's final course was due to finish, F/O E L Banks was testing a new Merlin in BW881 when a con-rod failed and Banks brought it down to another wheels-up landing behind the hospital at Chicoutimi, Quebec. Banks was not harmed but the aircraft suffered Cat B damage and was allocated to No. 9 Repair Depot at St John / St Jean, Quebec, where on 28 September 1944 it

BW881 making a low pass over Paine Field on 25 August 2012. *(Chris Chapman)*

was written off as 'spares and produce'.

BW881 next appeared in the collection of Tex Lavallee whose 'Cultural and Aeronautical Collection' at St Chrysostome, Quebec, numbered several Hurricane hulks amongst a variety of aeronautical junk. When Lavallee sold his collection BW881 and BW853 (qv) were acquired by Matt Sattler of Carp, Ontario, who sold them to Tony Ditheridge in the summer of 1987 (see BW853 page 162)

BW853 and BW881 were purchased by William Tassell and Henry Pearman and moved to Tassell's farm at Ulcombe, Kent. Restoration work was started on BW853 but BW881, owned solely by Henry Pearman, remained untouched and after several years in storage the project – complete with the all-important CCF construction plate – was sold to Maurice Hammond of Eye Tech Engineering Ltd and registered as G-KAMM on 23 February 1995. Hammond did no work on it either and it was returned to Tony Ditheridge at Milden in Suffolk where on 10 December 1998 it was re-registered to The Alpine Deer Group Ltd of Wanaka, New Zealand.

Tony had formed a new company, Hawker Restorations, in partnership with Sir Tim Wallis, specifically to remanufacture Hawker Hurricanes, and Wallis's own Mk I Hurricane, P3351/DR393 (qv) was the first to fly, followed by AE977, 'KZ321', and R4118 so by the time that BW881 came along they were well-versed in the technique. The Flying Heritage Collection acquired BW881 from Sir Tim

Wallis in August 1998 as part of a four-aircraft package including a Messerschmitt Bf 109E, Polikarpov I-16 and Spitfire F VB. Restoration continued until 2006 when the completed aircraft, now fitted with a Packard Merlin 224 driving a Hamilton Standard Hydromatic propeller, was taken by road to Wattisham, Suffolk, where it made its first flight in the hands of Stu Goldspink on 15 March. The colour scheme chosen is representative of RCAF 5429, which served with No. 128 (F) Sqdn, an east coast air defence unit within Eastern Air Command, equipped with Hurricane XIIs from December 1942, at Sydney, Nova Scotia, until disbanded in March 1944, at Torbay, Newfoundland; however, RCAF 5429 was no longer on the active strength of the Home War Establishment from January 1944 onwards, and served with No.1 Advanced Tactical Training Detachment at Greenwood, Nova Scotia, during the February-December 1944 period. Following further test flights BW881 was shipped to Arlington, WA, USA, in August 2006 where it was re-assembled by John Norman of JNE Aircraft Restoration Services – owner and restorer of AM274 (qv) – before its final move to the Flying Heritage Collection's new home at Paine Field, Everett, WA, where it is regularly flown. The UK civil registration G-KAMM was cancelled on 23 August 2007 and it is now registered in the USA as N54FH.

RCAF 1374
Hawker Hurricane Mk I/ Mk XIIA

Hanger 11 Collection, North Weald, Essex, UK

Although originally thought to be RCAF 5403, recent research has shown that this aircraft is actually RCAF 1374, c/n CCF/R20023, which was originally laid down for the RAF as a Hurricane Mk I, AG287, but which was part of a batch of aircraft which were transferred to the RCAF and given new serials in the block RCAF 1351-1380.

AG287 was almost certainly the first Hurricane built by CCF to RAF Mk II standard, with eight-gun wings and the longer nose of the Hurricane Mk II airframe, but was transferred on to RCAF charge as RCAF 1374, without its intended Packard Merlin engine, for future issue to an east coast unit. Like other Hurricanes of the RCAF 1351-1380 batch (from the AG287-AG332 range) it was fitted with

a Merlin III and DH propeller which had been removed from an RCAF Fairey Battle trainer, and in this form was designated a Hurricane Mk I in RCAF service. It entered service with No. 125 Sqdn, Eastern Air Command, on 30 April 1942 at Sydney, Nova Scotia, transferring to No. 128 Sqdn when the latter unit formed at Sydney on 7 June 1942, for east coast air defence.

1374 suffered a Cat C accident on the runway at RCAF Station Sydney, at 1335 hours on 1 July 1942 when being flown by Sgt W S Fowler and was issued to No. 4 Repair Depot at Scoudouc, New Brunswick, on 24 July for repair, after which it was allocated to the war reserve at RCAF Station Sydney on 5 September. It returned to active service

Peter Teichman in 'BE505' formates with the camera ship on a flight from North Weald on 25 October 2009. *(Darren Harbar Photography)*

with EAC on 7 June 1943, possibly serving with No. 125 Sqdn at Sydney again. It was sent to Canadian Car and Foundry at Fort William on 2 September 1943 for conversion to Mk XIIA standard and following this it was issued to No. 1 (F) OTU at Bagotville, Quebec, on 18 November 1943. The conversion to Mk XIIA standard (with Packard Merlin 29) was not noted on the RCAF record card until 22 April 1944, when it was allocated to No. 9 Repair Depot at RCAF Station St John/St Jean (Cap de la Madeleine), Quebec, for salvage and disposal action after a crash at Bagotville which resulted in its eventual write-off. It was finally written off on 6 September 1944 just weeks before No. 1 (F) OTU ran its final course.

This was one of several Hurricanes sold by Jack Arnold to David Tallichet and Bob Schneider in the late 1980s. Schneider, trading as RRS Aviation, had a business relationship with Tallichet's Military Aircraft Restoration Corporation and restored several aircraft at his workshop in Hawkins, Texas, including the P-40 and Bristol Beaufort in the RAF Museum at Hendon. All of his work involved static museum aircraft, none of them being restored to fly. Schneider built two static Hurricanes, using welded steel tubing as the main fuselage structure; one of these is now displayed in the Pima Air & Space Museum, Tucson,

Arizona, and the other is at the National Museum of the US Air Force at Wright-Patterson AFB, Dayton, Ohio. The latter aircraft was subsequently rebuilt by Hawker Restorations using non-airworthy fuselage tubing.

When RRS Aviation closed down the remaining Hurricane parts, drawings and other material, comprising at least three aircraft, were sold to Hawker Restorations and transported to Milden, Suffolk, where the best components were selected to re-build the aircraft, utilising the centre section of RCAF 1374 which still carried the manufacturer's data-plate stamped CCF/R20023. As with all of the Hurricanes restored by the company, as much of the original material that could be salvaged was retained and refurbished with some of the fuselage tubing being replaced. The wings were then restored by Bob Cunningham and his team in Bournemouth in the correct 12-gun configuration and uniquely incorporated full gun mounting fittings, ammunition boxes and feed chutes. As a Hurricane XIIA it would have been fitted with a Packard Merlin 29 and an example was sourced and rebuilt by Maurice Hammond of Eye Tech Engineering to be paired with a Hamilton Standard propeller which was overhauled by California Propellers in the USA.

The aircraft was placed on the UK civil aircraft register

by Hawker Restorations as G-HRLO on 26 September 2005 but following the sale of the partially completed project to Peter Teichman's Hangar 11 Collection the registration was amended and on 5 April 2007 the aircraft became G-HHII. The decision was made to complete the restoration as a fighter-bomber in order to represent an important aspect of the Hurricane's extensive operational career. As such the wings feature the distinctive faired bomb racks, together with a full set of ten Browning 0.303 inch machine guns and ammunition belts (the third gun in each block is deleted as the space is occupied by the bolts which secure the bomb racks).

The comprehensive restoration was completed in January 2009 and saw it rolled out resplendent in the markings of 'BE505', a Manston-based Mk IIB fighter-bomber operated by No. 174 (Mauritius) Sqdn in the spring of 1942. Her first post-restoration flight took place from North Weald on 27 January 2009 and she is now a firm favourite on the UK and European air show circuit.

RCAF 5389
Hawker Hurricane Mk XII

City of Calgary, Wetaskiwin, Alberta, Canada

RCAF 5389, c/n CCF 42024, was part of a batch of aircraft built by Canadian Car and Foundry at Fort William (Thunder Bay) for the Royal Canadian Air Force with serials between 5376-5775. They were built in 1942-43 and all as Hurricane Mk XIIs with 12-gun wings and Merlin 29 engines[1]; 5389 was taken on charge on 23 June 1942 although a note on its record dated 10 June 1942 stated 'aircraft to be modified before being placed in service', possibly because of a fault with initial Merlin 29 engines which required rectification.

It was delivered to stored reserve with No. 4 Training Command, BCATP, with headquarters at Calgary, Alberta, and on 3 July 1942 was issued to No. 133 (F) Sqdn at Lethbridge, Alberta, where it was coded FN-M. RCAF 5389 was transferred to Western Air Command (WAC) on 26 October 1942, after the squadron moved, via the Spokane-Yakima route, to the nearly-completed RCAF Station Boundary Bay, BC, on 4-5 October 1942, where it was stationed for Home Defence duties. There was an accident and several near misses as the unit arrived and hastily landed at Boundary Bay, all trying to stop before they ran into a fog bank moving in down the runway. The squadron relocated on 30 June-1 July 1943 to RCAF Station Tofino, BC, and on 15 July 5389 suffered a crash initially reported as Category C (RCAF record card incorrectly logging unit and location as '123 Sqdn, Dofino'), which resulted in it being dispatched to Coates Limited at Vancouver for repairs on 22 July 1943, where it was assessed as a Cat B accident. The repairs were not completed until 28 February 1944, when it went back into stored reserve with WAC. No. 133 Sqdn was on the point of re-equipment with Kittyhawks in March 1944.

After six months in store it was transferred from WAC, in the Western Hemisphere Operations organisation, to No. 2 Training Command, BCATP, with headquarters at Winnipeg, Manitoba, on 4 August 1944, before amalgamation of Nos. 2 and 4 TCs to form No. 2 Air Command on 1 December 1944. RCAF 5389 was placed into stored reserve with No. 2 AC on 12 February 1945, but returned to active service with No. 2 Air Command on 5 March 1945, within the WHO Home Defence organisation, for interception of Japanese balloon bombs over the prairies. Between November 1944 and April 1945, the Japanese launched approximately 10,000 balloons across the Pacific, carried by the jetstream at about 30,000 ft, to attack North America with incendiary and explosive devices. As the 'Prairie Hurricanes' were required to climb to altitude quickly to intercept Japanese fire balloons, they only carried two of their normal 12 Browning machine guns in order to save weight, and were distributed by No.2 AC, WHO, at various RCAF stations in Alberta and Saskatchewan for balloon-bomb interception operations. RCAF 5389 was based either at Lethbridge, Alberta, or at Moose Jaw, Saskatchewan, from 5 March 1945 (joined later by RCAF 5447 at the base) until 12 July 1945, when the No.2 AC Hurricanes were retired from active service, due to a large decline in the reported balloon-bomb incidents.

5389 was made available for disposal with No.2 AC from 12 July 1945, allocated to No. 3 SEHU (Surplus Equipment Holding Unit), RCAF Station Swift Current, Sask, when it had 447:30 airframe time logged (engine number 4687/19631), and was finally struck off charge to the War Assets Corporation for sale on 20 August 1946. Like many surplus aircraft 5389 was purchased by a farmer for its parts and for the glycol still filling the radiator and coolant system. Here it remained until 1962 when it was purchased by Lynn Garrison and transported to McCall Field (Calgary Airport), courtesy of Wolton Lumber, where it and another Hurricane, RCAF 5424 (see RCAF 5711), were stored in Hangar 4. At the time Garrison was a member of No. 403

---

[1] All Hurricane Mk XIIs, built in 1942–43 by this company were similarly constructed (see pages 145–146)

Fuselage and centre section of RCAF 5389 in January 2013 following the move to Wetaskiwin. (Richard de Boer)

(City of Calgary) Sqdn, RCAF, and he began to collect a wide range of historic aircraft; he personally purchased Lancaster FM136 and started the Lancaster Memorial Fund to see the aircraft as a memorial to those who trained under the British Commonwealth Air Training Plan of World War 2. Despite collecting an impressive array of aircraft and holding fund-raising air shows between 1963 and 1965, the support base was lacking and Garrison moved to Ireland where he set up his Blue Max Aviation facility to provide aircraft for films such as *The Blue Max, Darling Lili, Zeppelin* and others.

In 1964 Garrison established The Air Museum of Canada but it would seem that title to his aircraft was never transferred to the museum and during that year the museum stated that both Hurricanes were to be restored by members of the Calgary Ultra-Lite Aircraft Association. 5389 found its way into a small building occupied by No. 403 (City of Calgary) Sqdn which was used as their pilot's room, where it remained until 1966 when it was relocated to RCAF Station Lincoln Park, Alberta, where the local air cadet squadron attempted a restoration project, starting with the fuselage woodwork. The other Hurricane, 5424, languished at McCall Field until its partial fuselage and a pair of stripped wings, plus other parts, were moved to Regina, Saskatchewan, to assist Rem Walker and his group's attempt to rebuild an airworthy Hurricane (see 5711).

During 1972 RCAF 5389 became the property of the City of Calgary and was moved to the Calgary Centennial Planetarium where it remained stored until 1988 when stewardship was transferred to the Aero Space Museum of Calgary. There was a planned restoration as 'LE-A', of No. 242 Sqdn RAF in honour of Calgarian William 'Willy' McKnight but no work was accomplished. 1990 saw ownership of the City of Calgary's vintage aircraft collection challenged in court by Lynn Garrison, who claimed that the sale to the city by Peter Norman in 1972 had been without his knowledge or consent. The court ruled in favour of the city and in 2000 the Hurricane was placed into offsite storage, along with a de Havilland Mosquito and a Cessna Crane.

In 2007 an offer was made to restore the Hurricane in exchange for ownership of the city's Mosquito but this came to nothing and on 15 July 2010 both the Hurricane and the Mosquito were moved to another city-owned warehouse. By now there was considerable local discussion and debate about the future of the Hurricane and the Mosquito. On 8 December 2010 the Community and Protective Services Committee of the City of Calgary voted to retain ownership of both aircraft and on 14 February 2011 the full Calgary City Council confirmed the decision.

The Calgary Mosquito Aircraft Society was created in 2008 to prevent the sale of the Mosquito and to see to

The port outer wing showing wartime paint still in good condition in April 2014; this may well be the wing obtained by Rem Walker's group from Shaunavon, Sask. *(Richard de Boer)*

its restoration and eventual display. During this campaign it became expedient to include the Hurricane under the society's offer to the city to restore both aircraft. At the 8 December 2010 meeting the city, in making its decision to retain both aircraft, recognised their responsibilities as owners and offered to pay half the projected cost of restoring both aircraft on a matching dollar basis, with the Calgary Mosquito Aircraft Society having to raise the other half within two years of signing the contract with the city on August 1, 2012. The CMAS fulfilled this requirement in June 2014 meaning that funding for both the Mosquito and Hurricane restorations was secure.

On 21 December 2011 the City of Calgary awarded the restoration of RCAF 5389 to the Calgary Mosquito Aircraft Society and on 27 October 2012 the aircraft was moved to Historic Aviation Services in Wetaskiwin, Alberta,

to begin its restoration. This organisation is located at Wetaskiwin Alberta Airport, and had previously carried out the restoration of Hurricane RCAF 5418 (qv). The Merlin 29, along with the Mosquito, was restored at the Bomber Command Museum of Canada and the rebuild was due to be completed by May 2015 at which time it will be transported to Wetaskiwin to be mated to the airframe. Projected completion for the aircraft is May 2016. The Hurricane will be restored as it served with No. 133 Sqdn and it will be brought up to a runnable and taxyable status, though HASI has informed the society that it could easily be brought to flying status, though the city has not chosen this as an option. Upon completion Hurricane 5389 will be returned to its owners, the City of Calgary, and in all likelihood placed on display at the Aero Space Museum, located at the south end of Calgary International Airport.

RCAF 5400*
Hawker Hurricane Mk XII

Kermit Weeks, Polk City, Florida, USA

There has been some debate as to the identity of the composite Hurricane project owned by Kermit Weeks and which is currently stored at his Fantasy of Flight Museum at Polk City Florida. The partially-restored fuselage was acquired from Don Bradshaw of Saskatoon, Saskatchewan, Canada, together with the logbook which gives the identity as that of RCAF 5400. Don had obtained a derelict centre section from fellow Hurricane-restorer Harry Whereatt of Assiniboia, Saskatchewan, in the early 1980s, which had been cut through in many areas with a blowtorch so, to provide the missing parts, he purchased three more derelict Hurricanes from Jack Arnold of Brantford, Ontario, around 1983. These were transported halfway across Canada on the same truck which delivered a Packard Merlin 29 from Arnold to the Reynolds Museum at Wetaskiwin, Alberta. The hulks were stored on a farm and Don began building a composite Hurricane by utilising the best parts from all four, together with new-build components. All steel materials were unusable, so all-new steel tubes were fabricated by Don as well as the 12-sided upper and lower centre section spar caps; new spar webs, and numerous steel end fittings also had to be remade. The Hurricane cockpit has two stainless steel tubes which form a V between the lower cockpit area and the corner brackets of the top longerons,

The centre section and cockpit area of Kermit Weeks' Hurricane project in store at Polk City in January 2013. *(Gordon Riley)*

The wings from AM274 which form part of the project, in store at Polk City in January 2013. *(Gordon Riley)*

near the instrument panel lower corners; Don was able to salvage a good pair of these from the three centre sections obtained from Jack Arnold.

Amongst the items purchased from Jack Arnold was the logbook from RCAF 5400 so this became the identity associated with the project. Don continued to rebuild the Hurricane and as parts became surplus they were traded on to other restorers, two of the centre sections obtained from Jack Arnold were passed on to Harry Whereatt and another was sold to the BCATP Museum at Brantford to become the basis of their Hurricane project which has taken on the identity of RCAF 5461 (qv).

RCAF 5400 was part of a batch of aircraft built by Canadian Car and Foundry at Fort William (Thunder Bay)

for the Royal Canadian Air Force with serials between 5376-5775. 5400 should have been taken on charge by Eastern Air Command on 7 June 1942 but it seems it was used for 'special tests' at the Test & Development Establishment at RCAF Station Rockcliffe, Ontario, so it was not actually taken on strength until 18 January 1944 when it was allocated to No. 3 Training Command, and later to No. 1 Air Command, when Nos. 1 and 3 TCs were disbanded and amalgamated to form No. 1 AC on 15 January 1945. It was noted as 'stored reserve' on 14 May 1945 before finally being made available for disposal from 13 April 1946. On 3 July 1947 the aircraft was struck off strength (SOS) at No. 5 REMU (Reserve Equipment Maintenance Unit), Picton, Ontario.

5400 may have been one of the 72 or more Hurricanes

The same centre section under reconstruction in Don Bradshaw's workshop before the sale to Kermit Weeks. (*Don Bradshaw*)

acquired by Cameron Logan which were taken to his farm at Scotland, Ontario, where they were broken up for scrap, although the distance of over 180 miles between Picton and Scotland, Ontario, seems to make this an unlikely scenario. Many of Logan's Hurricanes are known to have been obtained from No. 401 REMS (Reserve Equipment Maintenance Satellite) at Dunnville, Ontario, which is only about 42 miles from his farm. Although the majority of the 200+ aircraft scrapped by Logan were all gone by the mid-1950s a few Hurricane hulks remained into the 1970s and several collectors and enthusiasts visited the farm to seek out parts. It is assumed that Jack Arnold, from nearby Brantford, Ontario, was one of those collectors.

Although Don made good progress with the reconstruction of the fuselage he was persuaded to part with the project and it was sold to Kermit Weeks and moved to the original Weeks Air Museum which was situated at Tamiami Airport, some 13 miles southwest of downtown Miami, Florida. After the devastation caused by Hurricane Andrew in 1992, the museum was relocated to Polk City, between Orlando and Tampa Bay, Florida. Wings for the project were obtained from Jim Pearce in the UK and these are known to have come from AM274 (qv), which was restored by John Norman and which has now been sold to Eric Vormezeele in Belgium. When the author was shown the project in January 2013 it remained in store with no immediate plans for further restoration.

RCAF 5418
Hawker Hurricane Mk XII

Reynolds-Alberta Museum, Canada's Aviation Hall of Fame,
Wetaskiwin, Alberta, Canada

RCAF 5418, c/n CCF 44013, was part of a batch of aircraft built by Canadian Car and Foundry at Fort William (Thunder Bay) for the Royal Canadian Air Force with serials between 5376-5775.

It was taken on strength on 5 August 1942 and delivered to No. 4 Training Command for No. 135 (F) Sqdn at Mossbank, Saskatchewan on 5 August 1942. The unit had been established at Mossbank as part of No. 4 Training Command on 15 June, six months after the Japanese attack on Pearl Harbor, and was constituted to provide air defence of the west coast of Canada against possible attack by Japanese forces. The unit remained and trained at Mossbank, Saskatchewan, for the next four months. It was one of three Hurricanes taken on strength (TOS) that day which were flown from the CCF factory at Fort William and which brought the unit strength up to 19 Hurricanes, the full complement of 24 not being achieved until 10 August. RCAF 5418 was transferred to Western Air Command on 1 October 1942, when No. 135 Sqdn moved to the west coast.

Although their first home was on the prairie, the unit

RCAF 5418 on display in Canada's Aviation Hall of Fame, Wetaskiwin, Alberta, in July 2008. *(George Trussell)*

was destined to relocate to a new facility at RCAF Station Patricia Bay, near Victoria, BC, at the southern tip of Vancouver Island. The RCAF's Secret Movement Order No. 2, dated 10 September 1942, covers the relocation to Pat Bay, and states in part, 'The relocation of No. 135 Squadron at Patricia Bay, B.C. is to be considered an expedient only, for an unspecified period, pending the availability of accommodation at No. 135 Squadron's ultimate war station.' The fact that the facilities at Pat Bay had not been finished meant that they formed up and began training at Mossbank on the prairies. On 30 September 19 Hurricanes and two Harvards of No. 135 Sqdn flew from Mossbank to Lethbridge, Alberta, where they stayed overnight with their sister unit, No. 133 Sqdn. The planned overnight stay turned into a two-day stay due to weather, but on 2 October they staged through Spokane, Washington, USA, and over to Yakima, Washington, en route to Pat Bay. They arrived at Yakima on the 3rd, but bad weather forced them to sit where they were for two more days. After a long journey, they arrived in Pat Bay from Yakima on 5 October 1942.

The squadron would remain for almost a year at Patricia Bay but on 14 August 1943 they moved to Annette Island, Alaska, remaining there until 17 November 1943. Western Air Command Operation Order No. 12WAC/43, dated 4 November 1943, initiated the relocation of No. 135(F) and No. 149(Bomber) Squadrons from Annette Island, Alaska, to the newly-built RCAF Station at Terrace, British Columbia, in the interior of the province, which was intended at that time to be their 'permanent location'. A training flight of No.135 Sqdn with three Hurricanes was detached to Smithers, BC, during the period between 20 January and 9 March 1944.

On 11–12 March 1944, No. 135 Sqdn moved from Terrace to Sea Island, BC, re-equipped with different Hurricanes, and ferried them back to Patricia Bay. On 19 May 1944, they re-equipped with Kittyhawks, which they flew until the end of the war. No. 135 Sqdn was the last squadron to fly Hurricanes on the west coast, although No. 126 Sqdn continued to fly Hurricanes on the east coast until 30 May 1945, after the war against Germany had ended.

5418 had been involved in a fatal mid-air collision with Hurricane 5419 on 30 May 1943, during a formation low flying exercise four miles north of Sydney Island, BC. 5419 was No. 2 in formation, flown by F/O Richard H Pallen. The

propeller of the No. 3 aircraft, RCAF 5418, flown by F/Sgt T E Jackson, cut off the tailplane of 5419, causing it to dive straight into the water. The propeller of 5418 was severely damaged, but the pilot managed to return to base safely and was uninjured. The body of F/O Pallen was recovered from the wreckage of his aircraft on 6 June 1943.

RCAF records indicate that 5418 suffered a Category C accident on 9 July 1943, while serving with No. 135 Sqdn, and another on 25 October 1944, apparently during ferrying by No. 124 (Ferry) Sqdn whilst en route to No. 8 Repair Depot, Winnipeg, Manitoba. Repairs were carried out between 2 November 1944 and 16 February 1945, when it was transferred to stored reserve in No. 2 Air Command, and was at last ready for an air test. Presumably the test did not go too well as on 17 February it underwent an engine change! 5418 was then selected for 'balloon intercept' modifications which were carried out between 3–16 April at No. 8 Repair Depot. The modifications involved taking excess weight out of the aircraft so that it could climb to intercept the high-flying balloons and this included the deletion of 10 of the 12 Browning machine guns.

RCAF 5418 was returned to active service with No. 2 Air Command on completion of the mods. No. 2 AC had been the result of a merger of Nos. 2 and 4 Training Commands on 1 December 1944, to facilitate the wind-down of BCATP operations in Western Canada, but took on a more warlike role within the Western Hemisphere Operations Home Defence organisation during March-July 1945, for interception of Japanese balloon bombs over the prairies (see RCAF 5389 page 175). RCAF 5418 was based at Saskatoon, Saskatchewan, from 16 April 1945 until 12 July 1945, when the Hurricanes were retired from active service due to a large decline in the reported balloon-bomb incidents. 5418 was made available for disposal with No. 2 AC from 12 July 1945, with 476:55 airframe time and allocated to No.3 Surplus Equipment Holding Unit (SEHU) at Swift Current, Sakatchewan, to await its fate.

The last date on 5418's RCAF records is 20 August 1946 when it was struck off to the War Assets Corporation for sale, following which it was sold to Gunther Thompson, a farmer, of Parkside, Saskatchewan, who took delivery at Swift Current and dismantled it before transporting it back to his farm.

The Reynolds Museum of Wetaskiwin, Alberta, purchased

The fuselage and centre section being loaded following its purchase from the Thompson family of Parkside, Saskatchewan, in November 1960. *(Byron Reynolds via Norman Malayney)*

the aircraft from the Thompson family in November 1960. Although disassembled, 5418 was remarkably complete when purchased by the museum, requiring only replacement elevators and rudder due to damage from a snowplough on the Thompson farm. The odd minor item that they were not able to locate at the time was sourced prior to and during the restoration. Stan Reynolds was a wartime Mosquito pilot who, on returning to Wetaskiwin after World War 2, established a large motor vehicle and farm machinery business in addition to founding Wetaskiwin Airport. He was an enthusiastic collector of anything mechanical and by 1955 the size of his collection had grown to the point where he could open a private museum to the public. He had collected 2,000 cars, 1,100 tractors, 500 trucks, 200 steam engines, 300 threshing machines, 800 stationary engines and 125 aircraft as well as military artefacts, Native American artefacts and toys.

Knowing that his collection represented an important part of Alberta's social and technological history, Reynolds initiated discussions with the Alberta government in 1974 about donating his collection to them so that it could

be preserved. In 1981, Reynolds donated 851 machines to the Alberta government. This donation provided the foundation of the Reynolds-Alberta Museum, which opened on September 12, 1992 and is one of Alberta's provincial historic sites. The donation that Reynolds gave to the province of Alberta for all the artefacts in the museum was the single largest donation in Canadian history.

The museum was built on a 156-acre site on the west side of Wetaskiwin Airport. The government also erected an 18,300 square feet (1,700 m²) hangar, which became the home of Canada's Aviation Hall of Fame. Reynolds continued to make donations over the years to the facility. In 1999, he made his second large contribution by donating 60 aircraft. It was the largest donation of vintage aircraft by any individual in Canadian history and gave the Reynolds-Alberta Museum the second largest collection of aircraft in Canada behind the National Aviation Museum. As of February 2000, Stan had donated a total of $11.5 million worth of artefacts to the museum.

The replacement Merlin 29 (engine number 233/19213) which had been fitted to 5418 at Winnipeg in February 1945

Byron Reynolds running up the restored Merlin 29 on 12 December 1988. Although restored to airworthy condition it will not be flown. *(Byron Reynolds via Norman Malayney)*

had less than 40 hours total time since new. It was inspected, repaired as necessary and reinstalled in the restored airframe allowing 5418 to be ground run in June 1988 and all systems indicated normal for the type. The restoration was carried out to an airworthy standard and, with very little work, it could be flown but museum policy then (as now) precludes this so the aircraft is displayed as a static exhibit and painted in the 'Bulldog' markings of No. 135(F) Sqdn, its first unit.

RCAF 5447
Hawker Hurricane Mk XII

Vintage Wings of Canada, Gatineau Executive Airport, Quebec, Canada

RCAF 5447, c/n CCF 46002, was part of a batch of aircraft built in 1942-43 by Canadian Car and Foundry at Fort William (Thunder Bay) for the Royal Canadian Air Force. With serials between 5376-5775.

RCAF 5447 was taken on strength by No. 1 Training Command (but apparently within the Home War Establishment) on 29 September 1942, having suffered a Category B accident following an engine failure, at 1055 hours on 4 September 1942, on its ferry flight by No. 124 (Ferry) Squadron from the CCF plant at Fort William to

No.1 OTU at Bagotville, its intended first unit. It was then sent back to CCF at Amherst, NS, for repairs between 2 October 1942 and 5 July 1943, being delivered to Eastern Air Command when they were completed. It probably served with No. 129 Sqdn, based successively at Goose Bay (Labrador), Bagotville (Quebec), Dartmouth (Nova Scotia) and Gander (Newfoundland), in the July 1943–September 1944 period, and may have been in the detachment of No. 129 Sqdn at Quebec City during 2–23 September 1944 covering the Quebec Conference of war leaders. It was then possibly

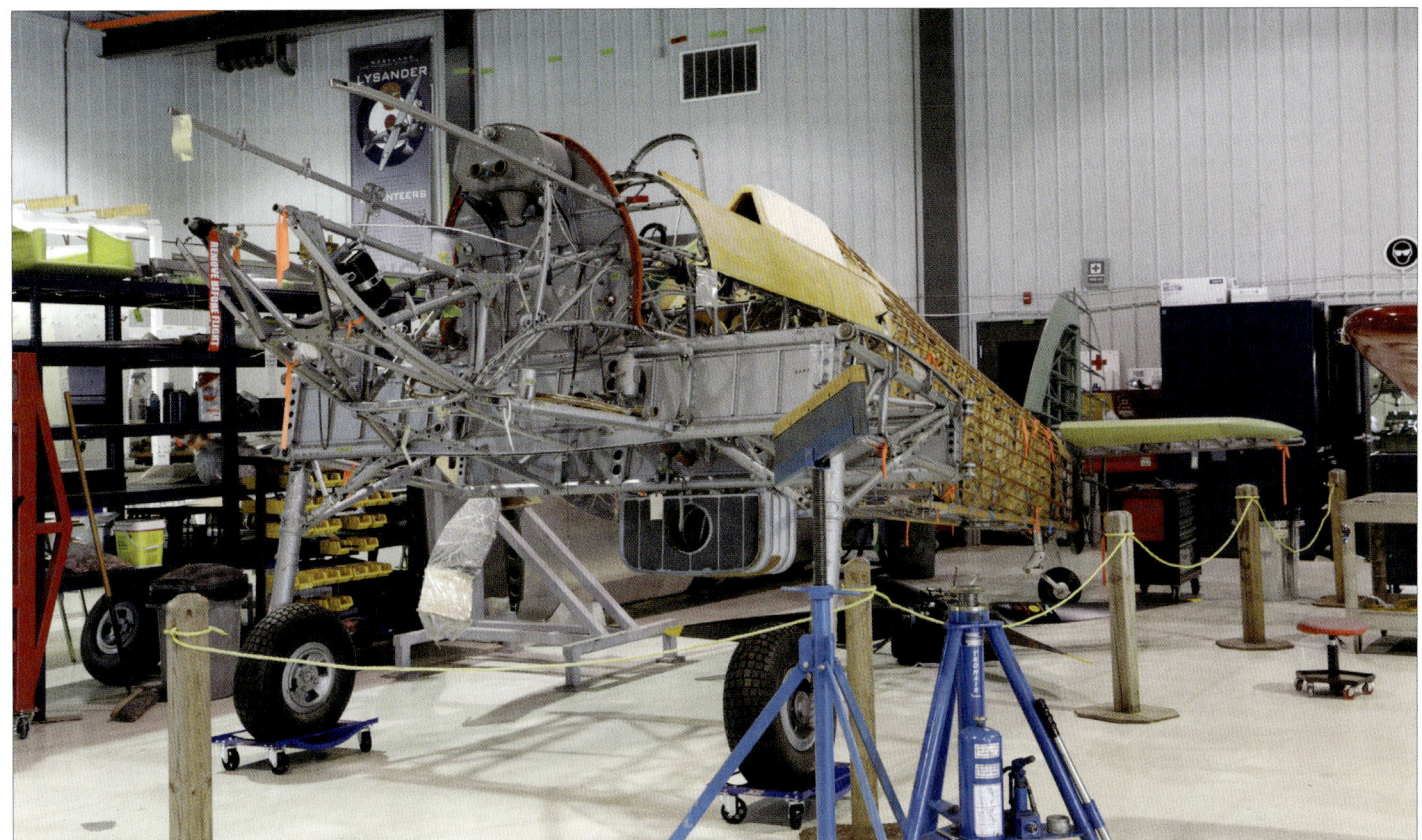

Fuselage and centre section of RCAF 5447 in August 2014 stripped and undergoing further restoration work. *(Jim Buckel)*

transferred to No. 1 OTU at Bagotville, as it seems to have served with its offshoot, No. 1 Advanced Tactical Training Detachment, to train pilots for ground-attack missions, low-level flying and evasive manoeuvres, at Greenwood, NS, until 29 November 1944, when the unit disbanded and dispensed with its aircraft. It was next sent for stored reserve with No. 3 Training Command on 29 November 1944, then on to No. 1 Air Command, still in storage, when Nos. 1 and 3 TCs were disbanded and amalgamated to form No. 1 AC on 15 January 1945, and finally on to No. 2 AC on 9 May 1945, again in stored reserve.

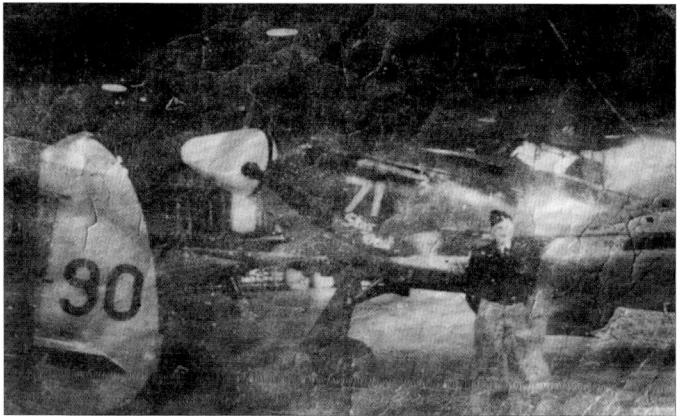

RCAF 5447 seen at RCAF Station Yorkton, Saskatchewan, in spring 1945 following conversion as one of the fire balloon defence 'Prairie Hurricanes'. The name 'StarDust' and the unit code '71' is visible in this photo. *(Dennis Bergstrom)*

RCAF 5447 was returned to active service with No. 2 Air Command on 4 June 1945, within the Western Hemisphere Operations Home Defence organisation, for interception of Japanese balloon bombs over the prairies (see RCAF 5389 page 175). RCAF 5447 was based either at Lethbridge, Alberta, or at Moose Jaw, Saskatchewan, from 4 June 1945 (joining RCAF 5389 already at the base) until 12 July 1945, when the No. 2 AC Hurricanes were retired from active service, due to a large decline in the reported balloon-bomb incidents, to await disposal.

RCAF 5447 was allocated to No. 3 SEHU (Surplus Equipment Holding Unit), at RCAF Swift Current, Saskatchewan, awaiting disposal from 12 July 1945, with 312:40 hours airframe time. It was struck off strength on 20 August 1946, and issued to War Assets for sale at Swift Current. Several aircraft sold out of No. 3 SEHU at Swift

Ernie Oakman of Stewart Valley with a Hurricane which was initially obtained by Rem Walker's Regina group but passed on to Harry Whereatt; this is believed to have been RCAF 5455. *(Rem Walker)*

Current to prairie farmers in the immediate post-war period survived and are now in museums and collections in Canada, the USA and the UK.

5447 was eventually purchased from a farmer by Harry Whereatt of Assiniboia, Saskatchewan, in the late 1960s. When acquired there was a short section of the rear fuselage missing which had been removed by the farmer, and the wings were found in the basement of an abandoned building having been used in an attempt to flatten rough earth by being towed behind a tractor! They were in a remarkable state of preservation considering this harsh treatment and only needed partial reskinning. All of the woodwork needed replacing and Harry later provided tracings of his woodwork to Bob Schneider of Hawkins, Texas who was rebuilding several to static display condition.

Brought up in Assiniboia, Harry's interest in flying was heightened during World War 2 when the British Commonwealth Air Training Plan's No. 34 Elementary Flying Training School was opened on the edge of the family farm. He bought a Tiger Moth in 1951, at the age of 23, and over the next few decades he owned many aircraft at various times, ranging from a Barkley-Grow airliner though RCAF trainers (Fleet Fort, Harvard, Tiger Moth) to a Bristol Bolingbroke, Westland Lysander and the Hawker Hurricane – the latter two he eventually sold to Michael Potter's Vintage Wings of Canada. At the time he acquired the Hurricane there was no evidence of any identity, which led to many different serials being published in different books and journals over the years and which has resulted in confusing accounts of Harry's Hurricanes.

Although 5447 was basically complete, Harry was undertaking the restoration at a time when companies such as Hawker Restorations Ltd did not exist and the only way to obtain essential spares was from other airframes. To that end Harry amassed a collection of Hurricanes and components to assist in his ambition of getting 5447 airworthy. Aircraft known to have passed through Harry's ownership include one which was found on Ernie Oakman's farm at Stewart Valley, Sask, in relatively intact condition complete with a Merlin 29 still installed. Another Hurricane used in the restoration of 5447 became the basis of Geoff Rodwell's restoration for Brian Angliss as G-HURR. This flew at Blackbushe in January 1996 as 'BE417' and passed through several UK owners until it was destroyed in a fatal accident at Shoreham on 15 September 2007. Other parts for 5447 were obtained from Jack Arnold in Brantford, Ontario, in addition to exchanges between Harry and other restorers including Neil Rose (5667), Don Bradshaw and the Regina group (5711). An entire centre section was passed to Don Bradshaw in 1980 which became the basis of his '5400' restoration (qv) and two of Don's centre sections which he had obtained from Jack Arnold in 1983 ended up with Harry. No identities were recorded as these were simply considered to be spares.

After some 30 years work the Hurricane was registered as C-GGAJ on 7 April 2000 and its maiden flight, with Harry at the controls, was made in May 2000. Painted as 'AE-W' of No. 130 (F) Sqdn it flew at least once – Harry was by now over 70 – but the flight was marred by it nosing over on landing due to brake problems. Following a stroke Harry decided to disperse his aircraft holdings, many Hurricane spares had already been sold and both 5447 and the Lysander were shipped to Vintage Wings of Canada at Gatineau Executive Airport, Quebec, in August 2006. Harry died on 25 June 2012 at the age of 83.

5447 is now in the middle of an extensive restoration programme at Gatineau and when it emerges it will be painted in the markings of the aircraft flown by F/O 'Willie' McKnight of No. 242 Sqdn. He was the first Canadian ace and Canada's fifth-highest scoring ace of World War 2. He joined the RAF in early 1939 and served in No. 242 Squadron RAF during the final phase of the Battle of France, covering the Allied retreat from Brittany, and later

Harry and his wife Anna standing with their Hurricane during a visit by members of the Canadian Aviation Historical Society.
(Angie McNulty)

RCAF 5447 at Gatineau in August 2006 showing the original untouched cowling panels still carrying the original paintwork from 1945. *(Oliver Lacombe)*

the Battle of Britain. His aircraft wore the distinctive cartoon of a jackboot kicking Hitler on the port side of the engine cowling. His Hurricane also carried a human skeleton image which held a sickle in its hand under the cockpit, on both sides of the aircraft. McKnight scored 17 victories, as well as two shared and three unconfirmed kills. He was shot down and killed on 12 January 1941 during a fighter sweep over Calais.

RCAF 5461*
Hawker Hurricane Mk XII

Commonwealth Air Training Plan Museum, Brandon, Manitoba, Canada

Precise details about this aircraft have proved very difficult to come by but as far as can be ascertained it is a partial replica built up around a genuine centre section from RCAF 5461, which was one of a batch of aircraft built by Canadian Car and Foundry at Fort William (Thunder Bay) for the Royal Canadian Air Force with serials between 5376-5775.

The centre section and other parts for this exhibit were sold to the museum by Don Bradshaw of Saskatoon, Sask, as parts surplus to his own project, 5400 (qv). Further parts are believed to have been obtained from Harry Whereatt which were leftovers from his airworthy restoration of 5447 (qv). Both of these men had obtained parts from Jack Arnold and elsewhere; Don Bradshaw had obtained three centre

sections from Jack Arnold to assist in the restoration of his project, 5400, and it is assumed that this was one of them, although it does not appear on the list of Hurricanes that Arnold claimed he had recovered over the years.

5461, if it is that aircraft, was taken on strength by Eastern Air Command in the Home War Establishment on 12 September 1942 and served with No. 130 (F) Sqdn based at RCAF Station Bagotville, Quebec, on east coast defence duty, coded AE-Y. The unit gave up its Hurricanes when it disbanded at Goose Bay, Labrador on 15 March 1944 but 5461 had already been transferred to stored reserve with EAC on 15 January. It was allocated to No. 1 (F) Operational Training Unit, also based at RCAF Station Bagotville,

The fuselage of RCAF 5461 under reconstruction at Brandon in June 1992. *(Steven Smart)*

Quebec, on 24 April 1944 and as it was reported as rocket equipped it may have served with No. 1 Advanced Tactical Training Detachment at Greenwood, Nova Scotia.

With No. 1 OTU's final course finishing in early October 1944, 5461 and other Hurricanes were allocated to stored reserve with No. 3 Training Command on 26 October 1944, then with No. 1 Air Command, when Nos. 1 and 3 TCs were disbanded and amalgamated to form No. 1 AC on 15 January 1945, still in storage. It was marked as available for disposal from 21 April 1945, with 581:50 airframe time and was stored post-war at No. 4 Reserve Equipment Maintenance Unit at Brantford, Ontario, although following the closure of that establishment it was assigned to No. 6 Repair Depot at Dunnville, Ontario, when struck off on 30 June 1947, to the War Assets Corporation for sale.

The Commonwealth Air Training Plan Museum had its beginnings in 1980 when a local group headed by Ed Baker became concerned that several trainer aircraft owned by Wes Agnew of Hartney, Manitoba, would be sold to foreign interests. Wes had been a RCAF flight instructor in the BCATP and had a desire to see a museum formed to honour the men and women who trained under 'The Plan'. A deal was struck and five of his aircraft formed the nucleus around which the museum was formed. The CATPM was incorporated in the province of Manitoba as a non-profit, charitable organisation on 4 March 1981 and opened that year in Hangar No. 1 at Brandon Airport. Located one mile north of the city, the airfield was the site of No. 12 Service Flying Training School operated by the BCATP during World War 2. During the formative years a concerted effort was mounted by volunteers to retrieve and store over fifty airframes and hundreds of parts from various aircraft from farms on the prairies. This cache of parts has enabled the museum to rebuild several aircraft and will serve as a source of restoration material for many years to come. Wes and Joyce Agnew moved into Brandon in 1982 and became founding members of the museum. Wes held the position of CATPM curator for five years and continued to volunteer at various tasks around the museum until his death in March 2000 at the age of 78.

The Hurricane was reconstructed by Jack Leonard using new material and is now displayed as 'YO-J' of No. 401 Sqdn RCAF. Although externally convincing, close examination reveals that some parts – such as the main undercarriage legs – are not genuine and some internal components are not to the original specification. The long-term aim is to get the aircraft capable of taxying under its own power.

RCAF 5481*
Hawker Hurricane Mk XII

Privately owned, Scone, NSW, Australia

RCAF 5481 was one of a batch of aircraft built by Canadian Car and Foundry at Fort William (Thunder Bay) for the Royal Canadian Air Force with serials between 5376-5775. It is one of Jack Arnold's Hurricane recoveries, this being the one which he attempted to restore to flying condition at Brantford, Ontario. As with many of his recoveries, there is some degree of confusion regarding its precise identity – the c/n quoted as '60372' is probably a part number as the c/n of 5481 would have been CCF 46036, but this was not known to Arnold at the time. Jack Arnold claimed that this Hurricane was found in or near "Bush near a lake" in northern Quebec in 1980.

RCAF records relate that 5481 was taken on strength by No. 3 Training Command on 7 October 1942 and flown to No. 1 WS at Debert, NS, to be used in the Third Victory Loan Campaign. This would be a reference to No. 1 Wireless School, but that was situated at Montreal, Quebec. Debert was the home of No. 31 OTU, later re-designated as No. 7 OTU. It was then transferred to Eastern Air Command and taken on charge by No. 1 (F) Operational Training Unit at RCAF Station Bagotville, Quebec, on 4 November 1942. After 11 months of hard flying it was assigned to No. 9 Repair Depot at St Jean, Quebec, between 22 October 1943 and 24 June 1944 for an overhaul before being issued to No. 3 Training Command. Allocated to No. 9 Bombing and Gunnery School at Mont Joli, Quebec, on 6 July 1944 it remained in service until 3 November when it was returned to No. 9 Repair Depot at St Jean for write off and was allegedly 'stored in field' after being struck off on 29 November 1944.

Whatever its origins this Hurricane underwent a long period of 'restoration', first at Jack Arnold's workshop and

Restoration work on RCAF 5481 was progressing well in July 2015; an aerial mast has now been fitted. First flight is scheduled for December 2015. (*John Parker*)

Jack Arnold with his Hurricane project before he sold it to Terry Dieno in 1984. The writing on the spinner reads 'From Hurricane 5585 for 5481'. *(Don Bradshaw)*

later in his hangar at Brantford, using parts taken from several of the other Hurricanes that he had recovered and utilising a lot of new steel tubing. Following an accident in which a Harvard fell onto him, Jack started to dispose of his aircraft collection and in 1984 the project was acquired by Terry Dieno of Davidson, Sask, who continued the rebuild using new 4130 aircraft grade steel tubing. Terry is the proprietor of Fast Toys for Boys and had acquired his pilot's licence in 1973 when he began a lengthy career in commercial crop spraying, pipeline patrol and aerobatics, the latter with a Yak and a Pitts Special. He and his sons are currently restoring a damaged P-51D Mustang 'Lou IV' which they acquired in 2007 following a landing accident at Camarillo, California.

The Hurricane project was sold to Charles Church of Micheldever, Hants, in 1986 and shipped to the UK where the restoration was started once again, this time by Paul Mercer at the premises of RGC Aeronautical Engineering at Sandown on the Isle of Wight. As the 4130 grade steel tubing previously used was not appropriate, the fuselage was completely taken apart and rebuilt with new T50 tubing which was squared to fit between the salvaged assembly plates, load bearing gussets and engine support mounts. The centre section was restored by RGC Aeronautical Engineering using modern materials to the original drawings and jigs. Completely new woodwork was made up whilst the construction of a new set of outer wings was subcontracted by RGC to Airframe Assemblies Ltd, the leading and trailing edges being completed by Dick Melton

Aviation at Roundwood Farm. The tailplane was overhauled by RGC using the original spars and webs from the BBMF Hurricane LF363 with the cross-brace members and inter-spar ribs fabricated by RGC. The Merlin 29 originally installed was replaced with a Merlin 500/224. The engine, serial no. 306773, was overhauled and test-run by Mike Nixon of Tehachapi, California, USA.

Following Charles Church's death in the crash of his Spitfire, 'EE606', on 1 July 1989 the Hurricane project was registered as G-ORGI on 20 November 1989 in the name of Charles Church Displays Ltd and transferred to Dick Melton's workshop on the Church estate at Roundwood Farm, Micheldever, Hants, where it was completed and test-flown, with a four-bladed Spitfire propeller and in silver dope and yellow chromate finish, for the first time on 8 September 1991. The correct Rotol RX5 three-bladed unit was installed when it was returned from overhaul by Dowty.

The Hurricane had been sold to David Price of Santa Monica, California, and the UK registration was cancelled on 31 January 1992, the aircraft being shipped by sea to California where it arrived in March 1992 and, following assembly at Chino by Craig Charleston, it was issued with a US Certificate of Airworthiness on 10 April prior to its first flight from US soil on 17 April. The markings chosen were representative of Geoffrey Page's No. 56 Sqdn Hurricane during the Battle of Britain, 'P2970 / US-X', and it was unusual in that it was rebuilt and flown with no aerial mast.

Painted as 'P2970 / US-X', RCAF 5481 also carried the registration C-FDNL under the tailplane when owned by the Russell Group in Ontario. Note the lack of an aerial mast. *(Eric Dumigan)*

RCAF 5481 being rebuilt at Sandown on the Isle of Wight. Paul Mercer was chief engineer on the project from 1986 onwards. *(Chris Michell)*

Registered NX678DP, the Hurricane was initially based at the Museum of Flying at Santa Monica but was later loaned to the Camarillo-based Southern California Wing of the Commemorative Air Force, to which it was delivered by air on 1 April 2003.

David Price parted with the Hurricane the following year, the US registration being cancelled on 27 April 2004 following sale to Ed Russell of Niagara Falls, Ontario, although it was not registered in Canada until 30 May 2005, the civil registration, C-FDNL, being applied beneath the tailplane. The Hurricane became a firm favourite at Canadian and US air shows for the next few years but in 2013 Ed Russell decided to part with his collection and on 16 December the Hurricane was cancelled from the Canadian civil register following sale to a group of private owners in Australia.

5481 was shipped to Scone, NSW, where it was unpacked at Pays Air Service on 7 April 2014, following which the fuselage was sent to Matt Webber and the team at Luskintyre Aircraft Restoration. This is so that the fuselage woodwork could be refurbished and new fabric applied, as it had been some time since the aircraft was fully restored. This work has been extensive as all the woodwork had to be replaced and the rear upper cockpit framing rebuilt. The wings and tail surfaces were stripped of paint and inspected at Scone whist the fuselage was being worked on. Although there are lots of options for a new colour scheme, as of August 2015 no decision had been made as to its final finish, although we are quite sure there will be an Australian connection.

RCAF 5584
Hawker Hurricane Mk XII

Canada Aviation and Space Museum, Rockcliffe, Ottawa, Ontario, Canada

RCAF 5584, c/n CCF 52019, was part of a batch of aircraft built by Canadian Car and Foundry at Fort William (Thunder Bay) for the Royal Canadian Air Force with serials between 5376-5775.

It was test-flown at Fort William by Victor 'Shorty' Hatton before being taken on strength by No. 2 Training Command on 6 November 1942 and was among 120 Hurricanes, RCAF 5503-5622, stored at RCAF Souris, Manitoba, between October 1942 and March 1943, before being issued to stored reserve with Western Air Command on 24 March 1943, as one of 10 Hurricanes taken out of storage at Souris and transported to No. 3 Repair Depot, Vancouver, for service with squadrons of Western Air Command on the Canadian west coast. It was issued to No. 163 (AC) Sqdn at RCAF Station Sea Island, Vancouver, BC, on 1 July 1943. This unit had been formed as an army co-operation unit on 1 March 1943 and initially flew Bolingbrokes on west coast photographic work and Harvards in close air support training for Canadian troops at Wainwright, Alberta. It converted to Hurricanes in June 1943, when six Hurricanes were taken on

strength, and was re-designated as a fighter squadron, No. 163 (F) Sqdn, on 14 October. It eventually re-equipped with Kittyhawk aircraft in November 1943, and was employed on west coast air defence until disbanded at Patricia Bay, British Columbia on 15 March 1944. RCAF 5584 remained on the active strength of Western Air Command units until 4 August 1944.

5584 was sent back to No. 2 Training Command on 4 August 1944, for use with the BCATP, before amalgamation of Nos. 2 and 4 TCs to form No. 2 Air Command on 1 December 1944. It was placed into stored reserve with No. 2 AC on 12 February 1945 but was transferred to No. 8 Repair Depot (8 RD) at Winnipeg, Manitoba, for a few days in March 1945. RCAF 5584 was returned to active service with No. 2 Air Command on 5 March 1945, within the Western Hemisphere Operations Home Defence organisation, for interception of Japanese balloon bombs over the prairies (see RCAF 5389 page 175). RCAF 5584 was based either at Moose Jaw, Saskatchewan, or at Lethbridge, Alberta, from 5 March 1945 until 12 July 1945, when the No. 2 AC

RCAF 5584 shortly after it was restored for display having been delivered to Rockcliffe in 1964. *(Bill Ewing)*

RCAF 5584 as displayed in the Canada Aviation and Space Museum, Rockcliffe, in December 2013. *(Mike Henniger)*

Hurricanes were retired from active service, due to a large decline in the reported balloon-bomb incidents, to await disposal with No. 2 AC.

RCAF 5584 was allocated to No. 3 SEHU (Surplus Equipment Holding Unit), at RCAF Swift Current, Saskatchewan, awaiting disposal, having flown 196:55 hours. Its RCAF records state that on 18 April 1946, still within No. 2 AC, it was '…to be retained in the RCAF for purposes of public display'. Initially the RCAF stored two examples of each type for museum display at RCAF Station Portage la Prairie, Manitoba, but with the re-activation of that base in 1950 a party under Bob Moore from RCAF Station MacDonald (near Portage la Prairie) selected just one of each type (Hurricane 5588 was sold to Ajax Aircraft Parts and scrapped in 1953) and moved them to storage at RCAF Station Chater, Manitoba. Here they remained until 1960-61 when they were relocated to RCAF Station MacDonald, Manitoba, before being moved to Calgary, Alberta, in 1963

and then finally to the museum at RCAF Station Rockcliffe, Ottawa, Ontario, on 6 February 1964.

According to its RCAF record card, Hurricane 5584 was located successively at RCAF Lincoln Park (Alberta), No. 6 RD Trenton (Ontario), No. 6 RD Detachment Mountain View (Ontario), and RCAF Uplands (Ottawa South, Ontario), between 1950 and 1964, when moved to RCAF Rockcliffe (Ottawa North, Ontario). In 1965, aircraft of RCAF Collection, Canadian War Museum and Uplands Museum were merged into the National Aeronautical Collection.

Since 1964 this Hurricane has been displayed at Rockcliffe and it is still technically owned by the Canadian government having never been disposed of by the War Assets Corporation.

RCAF 5662*
Hawker Hurricane Mk XII

Pima Air and Space Museum, Tucson, Arizona, USA

Although the identity RCAF 5662 has been quoted for this aircraft there is no evidence whatsoever that this is connected in any way with this airframe – much of which consists of welded steel tubing.

What is known with certainty is that five Hurricane hulks were sold by Jack Arnold to David Tallichet and Bob Schneider during the mid-1980s and these were transported to Schneider's workshop in Hawkins, Texas, where he operated as RRS Aviation. This company had a contract with Tallichet's Military Aircraft Restoration Corporation

(MARC) to rebuild static aircraft for museum displays. Schneider obtained tracings of the fuselage woodwork from Harry Whereatt (RCAF 5447) and set to work rebuilding two of the Hurricanes for museum display. In both cases the primary fuselage structure was built up using welded square section tubing instead of bolted round section tubes as used in the original. Despite this deviation from originality the aircraft displayed in Tucson retains a lot of original Hurricane structure – as was noted by the author when he examined it in detail in December 2014. The cowling shape

The fuselage of this aircraft is built of welded steel tubing and it can therefore be considered to be 50% replica, although there are many original parts in it. The cowlings are the wrong profile and there are many other issues with it. *(Gordon Riley)*

Taken inside Bob Schneider's workshop in the early 1990s, this shows one of the static Hurricane projects under reconstruction. *(Rob Mears)*

is clearly incorrect, as is the shape of the fin, but the wings were very convincing and the main undercarriage legs were original units.

The real RCAF 5662 would have carried the c/n CCF 56017 and was one of a batch of aircraft built by Canadian Car and Foundry at Fort William (Thunder Bay) for the Royal Canadian Air Force with serials between 5376-5775. They were built in 1942-43 and all were built as Hurricane Mk XIIs with 12-gun wings and Merlin 29 engines. 5662 was taken on strength by Eastern Air Command on 28 January 1943 but crashed at Carter Basin, Labrador, and the wreckage was not recovered. It was subsequently allocated to No. 4 Repair Depot at Scoudouc, New Brunswick, on 25 September 1943 for write off and struck off charge on 25 November 1943. Jack Arnold claimed to have recovered the wreck of this aircraft from Labrador in September 1988 stating it was "hard to find – water's edge" . This date is believed to be after the five aircraft were shipped to Texas and further suggests that there is little to prove the link with the identity.

Once it had been completed and painted in the markings of Bob Stanford Tuck's 'V6864/DT-A' the aircraft was displayed at the Cavanaugh Flight Museum at Addison, Texas, but after some years it was moved to the Pima Air and Space Museum, adjacent to Davis-Monthan AFB at Tucson, Arizona, where it is one of a number of aircraft on loan from David Tallichet's estate. It is possible that this is the aircraft placed on the US Civil Aircraft Register as N2009N but it is certainly not capable of flight.

RCAF 5666
Hawker Hurricane Mk XII

Mark Zalesky, White Rock, BC, Canada

RCAF 5666 carries the c/n CCF 56021 and was one of a batch of aircraft built by Canadian Car and Foundry at Fort William (Thunder Bay) for the Royal Canadian Air Force with serials between 5376-5775. Taken on strength by Eastern Air Command on 3 February 1943, 5666 was initially issued to No. 126 Sqdn at RCAF Station Dartmouth, Nova Scotia, with which it served until 24 July when it was transferred to No. 127 Sqdn, based at RCAF Station Torbay, Newfoundland, returning to Dartmouth and No. 129 Sqdn on 30 December 1943, all based at RCAF Station Dartmouth. It continued to serve with No. 129 Sqdn in EAC until May 1944 when it was transferred to No. 1 Operational Training Unit (still within EAC), at RCAF Station Bagotville, Quebec, from 3 May 1944. As it was fitted with a rocket projectile installation and used for rocket-firing training it was possibly operated at some stage by No. 1 ATT Detachment, at RCAF Station Greenwood, Nova Scotia, which specialised in rocket and gunnery training.

On the Canadian east coast, operational units served in Eastern Air Command, as part of Home War Establishment, renamed Western Hemisphere Operations organisation in spring 1944, i.e. EAC (HWE) or EAC (WHO), and training units served in Eastern Air Command, as part of the Commonwealth Training Establishment or BCATP organisation, i.e. EAC (CTE) or EAC (BCATP).

It is known to have suffered a Cat C forced landing near Moose Head Lake, Maine, USA, on 29 October 1944, while on a ferry flight with No. 1 OTU from Bagotville to Dartmouth, becoming lost and running out of fuel when flying around a snowstorm, and was subsequently transferred to No. 9 Repair Depot at St Jean, Quebec, on 15 November 1944 for write off. It was officially struck off by No. 9 Repair Depot on 20 December 1944. By 1980 its damaged remains had been acquired by Tex Lavallee for his 'Lavallee Cultural & Aeronautical Collection' located in St.

Chrysostome, Quebec, but it was sold later that year to Ed and Rose Zalesky of Surrey, BC.

Ed and others had become concerned about the drain of Canadian historic aircraft out of the country. So in 1970 Ed and Rose, together with Bill Thompson, Ron Stunden and Barry Jackson formed the Canadian Museum of Flight and Transportation, based on the family farm at Crescent Road, Surrey, BC. (The original vintage car interest never took off and efforts were concentrated on aircraft, although only many years later was the official title changed.) In 1985 Surrey Municipality, as part of a major plan for the north shore of the Nicomekl River, expropriated the site. Ed and Rose led the fight, supported by many members, to at least remain as part of a tourist attraction but to no avail. In 1995 Surrey finally evicted the museum which found a new home at Langley Airport.

Ed, Rose and their family decided to withdraw from the running of the museum, now re-named the Canadian Museum of Flight, and there was a separation of artefacts, 5666 being retained by the Zalesky family whilst BW862 (qv), which had been obtained at the same time, was retained by the Canadian Museum of Flight. The family went on to found the Airplane Supply Centre in White Rock and continued to trade in parts and accessories – including three ex-Soviet Hurricanes which are described elsewhere in this book. Ed died on 3 September 2009 but the remains of 5666 are still stored by the Zalesky family in White Rock, British Columbia.

The engine bearer, firewall, cockpit area and wing centre section are all that remain of RCAF 5666, which is now believed stored by Mark Zalesky. This photo was taken when it was in open store with the Canada Flight and Transportation Museum. Parts of BW862 can be seen in the bottom right of the photo. *(Norman Malayney)*

RCAF 5667
Hawker Hurricane Mk XII

Military Aviation Museum, Virginia Beach, Virginia, USA

RCAF 5667 carries the c/n CCF 56022 and was one of a batch of aircraft built by Canadian Car and Foundry at Fort William (Thunder Bay) for the Royal Canadian Air Force with serials between 5376-5775. As with 5666 (qv) it was taken on strength by Eastern Air Command on 3 February 1943 and was initially issued to No. 126 Sqdn at RCAF Station Dartmouth, Nova Scotia, with which it served until 24 July when it was transferred to No. 127 Sqdn, based at RCAF Station Torbay, Newfoundland, returning to Dartmouth and No. 129 Sqdn on 30 December 1943, all based at RCAF Station Dartmouth.

Neil Rose called at Harry Whereatt's farm at Assinboia, Sask, to show him the remarkably complete Hurricane in September 1965, unfortunately it came with two starboard wings. *(Norman Malayney)*

It continued to serve with No. 129 Sqdn of EAC until May 1944 when it was probably transferred to No. 1 Operational Training Unit at Bagotville, Quebec, possibly at its spin-off unit of No. 1 ATT Det, Greenwood, Nova Scotia, and was transferred again, from EAC to No. 3 Training Command, to be sent to Ottawa on 23 October 1944 for use in a Victory

Loan Drive, probably as a static display, before returning on 15 November 1944 to stored reserve, firstly with No. 3 Training Command, then with No. 1 Air Command, when Nos. 1 and 3 TCs were disbanded and amalgamated to form No.1 AC on 15 January 1945.

It was allocated to No. 2 Air Command on 9 May 1945, still in storage, but taken onto the active strength of No. 2 Air Command on 4 June 1945, within the Western Hemisphere Operations Home Defence organisation, for interception of Japanese balloon bombs over the prairies (see RCAF 5389 page 175). RCAF 5667 was based at RCAF Station Yorkton, Saskatchewan, from 4 June 1945 until 12 July 1945, when the No. 2 AC Hurricanes were retired from active service, due to a large decline in the reported balloon-bomb incidents.

Neil Rose's Hurricane nearing the end of its restoration. *(Norman Malayney)*

RCAF 5667 was noted as pending disposal with No. 2 AC from 12 July 1945, being allocated to No. 3 SEHU (Surplus Equipment Holding Unit), at RCAF Swift Current, Saskatchewan, from where it was sold as surplus on 1

Jerry Yagen's Hurricane, RCAF 5667, painted as 'V6793 / DZ-O', taxying after a display at the Military Aviation Museum, Virginia Beach, on 16 May 2013. *(Jim Buckel)*

October 1946. According to its RCAF record card, it had been fitted with a rocket projectile installation possibly indicating previous usage by No.1 ATT Det, and had 615:55 airframe time when struck off to the War Assets Corporation for sale on 1 October 1946.

The Hurricane was bought by a farmer named Pitsano of Gravelbourg, Sask, some 80 miles southeast of Swift Current, but he ended up with two starboard wings rather than a port and a starboard. Here it remained until discovered by Neil M Rose who bought the aircraft in June 1965 and took it back to Vancouver, Washington, USA, for restoration. During the course of the restoration Neil obtained parts from a number of other Hurricanes, including half of the centre section from 5409 – the centre section was simply cut in half with a blow torch as it was seen as nothing more than a source of vital spares. The problem of the two starboard wings was solved in August 1970 when a swap was arranged with the Rem Walker group in Regina, Sask, who had acquired two port wings from the Songh brothers' farm at Shaunavon, Sask, for their project which eventually became 5711 / G-HURI (qv).

After 29 years the Hurricane, which had been registered N2549 since the mid-1980s, made its maiden flight on 10 May 1994 but was damaged when landing at Yakima, Washington, a few days later on 22 May. The aircraft was swiftly repaired and then offered for sale or trade with 27 hours flown since the first flight. Neil was prepared to accept a Learjet 24, Cessna Citation or P-51 Mustang as a trade but in the end it was purchased by Jerry Yagen of Fighter Factory / Training Services located at Virginia Beach, Virginia, USA, on 1 June 2001 and flown to its new home at the owner's Military Aviation Museum. Although initially flown in RAF camouflage with the name 'Churchill's Chicks' on the cowling the aircraft was re-registered N943HH and is now flown as 'V6793 / DZ-O' with the civil registration carried below the tailplane.

RCAF 5667 was originally restored without squadron codes as shown here. *(Doug Fisher)*

RCAF 5708
Hawker Hurricane Mk XII

Lone Star Flight Museum, Fort Collins, Colorado, USA

RCAF 5708, c/n 72033, was built by the Canadian Car and Foundry Company at Fort William as part of the batch 5706-5775 and taken on charge by Eastern Air Command on 5 January 1943. Due to a shortage of radiators – which were supplied by sea from the UK – it was placed into stored reserve at Halifax pending their delivery and not issued to Home War Establishment until 29 July. The aircraft served with No. 129 (F) Sqdn based at Gander but on 20 July 1944, whilst being flown by P/O Robert MacDonald in the 'low flying area', the Merlin 29 (Serial No. 19542/A330) lost power and the aircraft crashed. Despite being only 300-400 feet above the ground and with his airspeed rapidly diminishing, MacDonald carried out a successful forced landing. He was not injured but the Hurricane sustained sufficient damage to rate it a Category A crash and it was deemed beyond further aeronautical value. On 9 November it was allotted to No. 4 Repair Depot at Scoudouc, New

Brunswick, and it was written off on 29 November 1944. The cause of the engine failure was later determined to be burned out flame traps in 'A' and 'B' banks. This caused some particles from the flame traps to stick between the valves, valve seats and in the cylinders leading to a loss of power to the engine. It was subsequently recommended that the flame traps be removed and cleaned every 160 hours.

The airframe was partly covered by canvas, possibly in order to shelter it for future recovery, but in the event it was abandoned and left where it lay. During the 1960s Ken Beanlands, who held a commercial pilot's licence in addition to a degree in forestry, was based near Gander, Newfoundland, with the Department of Natural Resources and became increasingly interested in the many wrecked aircraft that he saw from the air, his particular interest being aerial photo interpretation. To assist his work he leased and flew a Cessna 180 floatplane to ferry crews to remote areas

RCAF 5708, painted to represent Lance Wade's Hurricane, BG974, following its restoration and before the accident which crippled it in April 2010.
(Bill Strouse)

Ken Beanlands with his forest inventory crew and family members on recovery day, September 1972. *(Ken Beanlands)*

The Bell JetRanger was operating at the limit of its lifting capacity when 5708 took to the air once more. *(Ken Beanlands)*

which allowed him to conduct his own aerial surveys of crash sites. Following visits to Ottawa to get copies of the accident reports and squadron diaries he was able to identify 21 Hurricanes scattered across the region and visited many of them on foot or by truck. The only site that revealed anything resembling an aircraft was located approximately 10 miles east of Gander and Ken established that this was RCAF 5708 which had force-landed there on 7 July 1944. Although he did have thoughts of recovering sufficient parts to rebuild a Hurricane he knew that the job was more than he could handle and did not pursue the idea.

In 1969 Ken was approached by Duane Egli, a Texas-based pilot and engineer, who had been involved with Connie Edwards and others in making the film *The Battle of Britain*. During this he had made the acquaintance of Bob Diemert who had rebuilt and flown his own Hurricane which was used in the film (RCAF 5377 / CF-SMI / G-AWLW). Egli had heard that Ken had salvaged a Hurricane and wanted to buy it but at that time Ken was not interested and the idea did not progress further. It was not until Duane and Ed Jurist ferried a de Havilland Mosquito, RS709, from England to Texas in December 1971 that the idea was revived – the sight of the Mosquito flying over Ken's apartment to land at Torbay Airport at St Johns, Newfoundland, prompting Ken to drive to the airport where he met Duane and Ed – who were missing an exhaust stack from the Mosquito! They met at a hotel that night where Ken showed his photos of 5708 to Duane whilst Ed pointed out that the Hurricane would be nothing more than a "pile of rust!" Duane explained that

he wanted to find eight Hurricanes, rebuild them, sell seven and keep one back for himself. He was not deterred by the state of the wreck and simply asked what Ken would like in exchange for it if he could recover it. Duane said he had a 'basket case' Boeing Stearman in his workshop in Texas which he agreed to tow to Newfoundland in exchange for the Hurricane and the deal was sealed with a handshake.

Ken had already sought and received permission to recover 5708 and began work during 1972 to dismantle it and prepare it for a helicopter recovery. Whist retrieving the tail section of another Hurricane from Lake Melville, Labrador, Ken heard from a helicopter charter pilot that Bob Diemert was also interested in recovering Hurricane wrecks

and had claimed he too had been given permission to recover 5708! Bob and his wife had visited and photographed 5708 where it lay and when Ken heard of this he swung into action and one Saturday morning in September he assembled his forestry inventory crew and several of his in-laws to pull the wreckage out of the bog where it lay. He had made several trips to the site over the summer and partly cut a road to the nearest lake some two miles away. They were about to start moving it on a slide of freshly peeled logs when the helicopter charter pilot turned up in a Bell 206 JetRanger. It was a cool overcast day with little wind and they hooked the rear fuselage and centre section up to the helicopter, luckily a gust of wind helped it get airborne just as the lift began and having safely deposited it at the lake shore the JetRanger made three more trips to collect the wings and other parts. With the wreckage collected together they made a barge out of two aluminium boats and towed it to the town of Benton from where it was trucked to Ken's father-in-law's home in Trinity.

Ken and Duane Egli agreed that instead of the Stearman – which was not suitable for float operations – Duane would obtain a Citabria and, true to his word, on 28 October 1972 he and his son landed at Gander in CF-KJB. Duane was so amazed at the quantity of Hurricane parts that Ken had managed to salvage from various crash sites that he later restored a damaged Cessna 180 for him.

The wreck of 5708 was substantially complete but missing various parts so Ken had scoured the other 20 sites

that he had surveyed in order to complete the package. The radiator air scoop came from a wreck at St Johns whilst the radiator itself and the flaps came from BW854 which had been recovered from Pine Lake by the Atlantic Canada Aviation Museum using a Canadian Coast Guard Bell 212 helicopter.

Duane took the Hurricane back to his workshop in Fabens, Texas, where he started work on the Hurricane but his main work was rebuilding P-51 Mustang wings and 5708 was eventually sold to Len Tanner who moved it to his premises at New Braintree, Connecticut. Tanner did a fair amount of work on the project, including fitting a Merlin and getting it mounted on a pair of Harvard main undercarriage legs, before selling it, in 1991, to the Lone Star Flight Museum of Galveston, Texas.

Although some work was performed at Galveston it was soon realised that this was a very specialist job and it was dispatched to Ray Middleton of QG Aviation and rebuilt over an 18-year period at Fort Collins, Colorado. The Hurricane made its maiden flight – registered as N96RW – in the hands of Stewart Dawson on 12 May 2006 and was then ferried from Fort Collins to Hooks Airport, Houston, where the camouflage paint scheme was applied by John Stewart of Space City Aircraft Finishes. The colour scheme chosen represents 'BG974 / RS-W' a Hurricane flown by Wg/Cdr Lance 'Wildcat' Wade, DSO, DFC & two bars, a Texan, who flew with No. 33 Sqdn RAF in North Africa and in which aircraft he shot down a Ju 87 Stuka and a Macchi

RCAF 5708 undergoing restoration in Ray Middleton's workshop at Fort Collins, Colorado, during the 1990s. *(San Diego Air & Space Museum Archive)*

MC 202 on the same day, 28 May 1942. Wade is usually listed with 25 victories but official RAF records show that he had 22 solo victories and half each of two more for a total of 23, not counting one probable. Regardless of whether his score is 25 or 23 victories he is believed to be the leading American fighter ace to have served exclusively in any foreign air force. He was killed in a flying accident on 12 January 1944 at Foggia, Italy.

Tom Gregory delivered N96RW to Galveston on 1 November 2007 and it took part in its one-and-only air display, the 'Spirit of Flight' Air Show at Galveston, at the end of April 2008. On finishing its display it was badly damaged by the propeller of Bill Greenwood's Spitfire Tr 9, TE308, which demolished the Hurricane's tail section after a collision on the runway during a formation landing roll.

The Hurricane remained in the museum at Galveston but was further damaged when the hangar was flooded by seawater during Hurricane Ike, which hit the area the following September. It has now been returned to QG Aviation at Fort Collins where it is stored awaiting a decision on its future.

RCAF 5711*/G-HURI
Hawker Hurricane Mk XII

Historic Aircraft Collection Ltd, Duxford, Cambs, UK

This aircraft was brought to the UK in 1982 by Stephen Grey as an unfinished project which he had bought from a group based in Regina, Saskatchewan, Canada. That group comprised four members, Rem Walker, Bob Hamilton, Gary Rice and Laurie Wright, who, prompted by Bob Hamilton's discovery of a Rolls-Royce Merlin III on a farm east of Regina, harboured aspirations of finding and rebuilding a Spitfire. In the late 1960s Spitfires were a rarity in Canada but Hurricanes were not and they soon started to locate and acquire large quantities of Hurricane components. Much of the following account is based on Rem Walker's unpublished manuscript written in March 1974.

RCAF 5711 was repainted by Clive Denney in the spring of 2015; the markings chosen are those of 'P3700 / RF-E' which was flown by No. 303 (Polish) Sqdn and abandoned by Sgt Kazimierz Wünsche over Poynings, Kent, on 9 September 1940 having sustained damage from a Bf 109 during combat over Beachy Head. *(Gordon Riley)*

Bob Hamilton, Laurie Wright and Gary Rice pondering over two port wings that they discovered on the Songh brothers' farm at Shaunavon, Sask, 23 May 1970. *(Rem Walker)*

On 24 January 1970 the four visited Shaunavon, Saskatchewan, following up a lead given to them by Dave Klaiman, a member of the Experimental Airplane Association, who told them he had a tailplane, elevators, fin and rudder from a Hurricane which he had intended using on a homebuilt project he was working on. Having collected the parts the group made further enquiries which led them to a local farm, operated by the Songh brothers, to the south of Shaunavon. Here they found a pair of Hurricane wings buried under two feet of snow behind the chicken coop, the only problem – besides the snow – was that they were both port wings. The wings were in very good condition and showed little damage so they agreed to return the following May when the snow should have melted. The Songh brothers explained that the fuselage had been sold on to Ed Kronberg who had towed it on its undercarriage, complete with engine and prop, to his own farm further to the south and west. The hunt was on.

On arriving at Kronberg's farm the group were surprised to learn that Ed had put the fuselage into his workshop and systematically taken it apart, very carefully, down to the last nut and bolt. Nothing remained that resembled a Hurricane fuselage although it was mainly still there – just in a different form. Examples of his ingenuity included a main undercarriage leg which had been converted into a working

drill press and the centre section spars which had been cut and welded to build a small trailer. All of the valves, brackets, special fittings, bolts, etc were stored in two large boxes. The Merlin had been disassembled and the block cut up to be melted down for aluminium whilst the rest of the airframe – apart from the tail which had started the whole search in the first place – was in a snow-covered scrap pile. When Ed learned what the group planned he apologised for dismantling the Hurricane but he was consoled by the fact that many of the parts were usable due to the care that he had taken. In the end his farm provided many fuselage parts and other fittings including three good propeller blades, hub parts, radiator, one main undercarriage leg, canopy, windscreen, hydraulics, switches and many other components.

The group returned to Shaunavon on 23 May to start the process of loading up the parts and on 8 June they left the Songh brothers' farm with the two port wings on a trailer. It took several trips to transport all the parts back to Regina. The identity of the Shaunavon Hurricane has never been established but it is assumed to have been one sold as surplus from RCAF Station Swift Current, Sask.

The problem of the two port wings was solved when they learned that Neil Rose of Vancouver, Washington, USA, had two starboard wings with his Hurricane project so a trade was arranged and in August 1970 Neil and Harry Whereatt

Gary Rice tries out the cockpit of RCAF 5424 for size at Calgary's McCall Field on 20 September 1970, Bob Hamilton looks on. *(Rem Walker)*

delivered a starboard wing on a trailer and the exchange was made. The group continued to make many trips throughout Saskatchewan, Manitoba and Alberta in an effort to locate fuselage and other parts but these were not successful.

The breakthrough came in early September 1970 when they received a call from the air museum in Calgary who wanted to exchange the ex-Neil Rose starboard wing for a forward fuselage and centre section (no undercarriage or tail) plus two de-skinned but rebuildable wings and other miscellaneous parts. The exchange took place over the weekend of 19-20 September 1970 and the group brought back to Regina the partial fuselage from RCAF 5424 which had been part of the original Lynn Garrison collection dating back to 1962. Two Hurricanes had been acquired at that time and were transported to McCall Field (Calgary Airport), courtesy of Wolton Lumber, where they were stored in Hangar 4. A start had been made on restoring 5389 (qv) but 5424 was in far worse shape and was used as spares until exchanged for a good starboard wing to go onto 5389. The Air Museum of Canada disbanded in 1971 and its aircraft and assets were eventually turned over to the

By 22 September 1976 the fuselage was well on the way to restoration and it was moved to Laurie Wright's workshop where it was mated to the centre section with main undercarriage. *(Rem Walker)*

City of Calgary to be housed at the city's Planetarium for safekeeping and display. In 1975 the Aero Space Museum Association of Calgary was registered as a non-profit, charitable, organisation and assumed the care and upkeep of these artifacts. At the time of the sale to Stephen Grey this association made a legal attempt to claim title to the Regina Hurricane project on the basis that it had only been leased to the Regina group but this claim was not successful.

At this point Rem Walker's account becomes contradictory, one version noting that 'the tubing had weathered very well' and that 'less than half a dozen pieces needed to be replaced' whilst his photo album states that there was 'much corrosion, pipes frozen and burst, many sections damaged beyond repair. Needed replacement.'

Things were now moving swiftly and on 5 October 1970 a large wooden crate arrived containing a complete Hamilton Standard propeller, spinner and hub which had been purchased from Len Ariss of Guelph, Ontario. With a diameter of 12 feet it was quite a crate!

Whilst work on the fuselage and wings continued in Regina the group was still looking for more parts to complete the puzzle and in 1972 they visited Cameron Logan's farm at Scotland, Ontario, in order to locate more hard-to-find components. Logan had purchased over 200 surplus aircraft in the immediate post-war period including two Halifaxes and a Messerschmitt 262, all of which were scrapped on his property. Amongst the aircraft were no less than 72 Hurricanes but by 1972 the few remaining hulks were badly corroded due to having been left in open fields of alfalfa. Luckily Logan had stored some components in a building on the property and the group found a good pair of main undercarriage legs, a set of wheel spindles, brakes, pitot tube, wobble pump, a set of wheels and a flap jack. All were in very good condition and when cleaned up they were as good as new.

In September 1972 they were amazed to find another Hurricane centre section, comprising the wing centre section and partial cockpit, right under their noses in Schraag Steel's scrapyard in Regina. Needless to say this was acquired to join the growing collection of essential parts needed to create a flyable Hurricane. This was followed by another trip to Calgary when on 11 November 1972 the group collected a Merlin 29, still inhibited and in its original crate, which had been located in Kelowna, BC, the existence of which

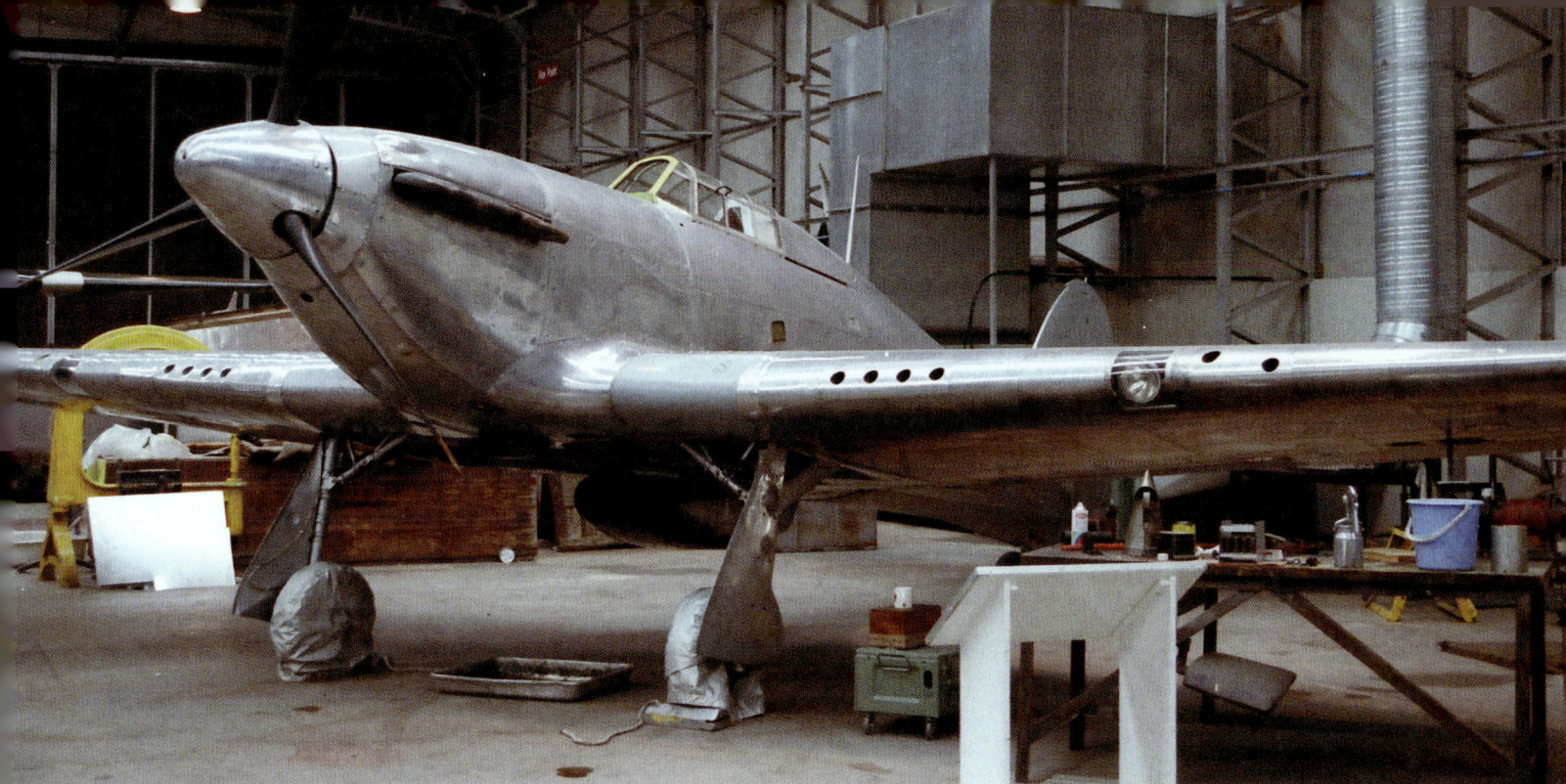

RCAF 5711 undergoing final assembly and systems fit-out at Duxford in the summer of 1988. *(Gordon Riley)*

was passed on to the group by the Calgary Centennial Planetarium.

It must be taken into account that during this period (1970-1985) most restorers were not at all interested in the identities of the aircraft they obtained. They were just seen as sources of spares. With companies like Hawker Restorations decades away from being formed the only way to get a flyer was to cannibalise the good parts from many hulks. In doing so the identities got mixed and matched, not only between airframes but also between owners. When and if they got a flyable aircraft that was when they worried about an identity and even this was purely for paperwork purposes. It is for this reason that the identities of the projects rebuilt at this time – including this one – have been called into question by modern-day historians anxious to pin down an evidence trail. Unfortunately this is not a simple matter.

The Regina group spent 12 years working on rebuilding an airworthy Hurricane from the best components that they had to hand until they eventually realised that the task was beyond their means so in 1982 they made it known that the project was available for sale. Stephen Grey telephoned Rem Walker on a Tuesday, arrived in Regina the following Friday and a forty-foot container was subsequently loaded at Gary Rice's premises with the main Hurricane project, plus

parts from at least six other aircraft. Most of the unwanted parts were eventually passed on to Maurice Bayliss to form the basis of his Hurricane project which was eventually sold to Phil Lawton and finally abandoned in September 2014 (see G-RLEF).

On arrival in the UK the container was initially stored in Coventry, where Stephen Grey was the managing director of the Coventry Climax company, before moving on to Coningsby, Lincs, where Paul Mercer had been contracted to carry out the restoration to flying condition. Mercer, assisted by Peter Rushen, had just completed rebuilding Spitfire F VIII MT719 / I-SPIT for Franco Actis in Italy and was later responsible for the rebuild of 5481 / G-ORGI (qv) on behalf of Charles Church Displays Ltd.

The project was registered to Stephen Grey as G-HURI on 9 June 1983, quoting the RCAF serial '5547' as its previous identity. Where this came from is not known as that aircraft had been shipped to India or the Soviet Union with a serial in the PJ range during 1943 and had never returned to Canada but it is known that Harry Whereatt mis-identified his Hurricane variously as 5445, 5455 and 5545 so it is possible that this was a simple transcription error. When the civil registration was amended on 10 January 1989 with the owner now being listed as Patina Ltd – the operating company behind The Fighter Collection – the identity that had originally been mis-quoted to the CAA was amended to CCF c/n 72036, which equates to a very late production aircraft with the RCAF serial 5711, one of the last 200 Hurricanes built at the Fort William plant. 5711 was almost certainly one of the 72 Hurricanes which were sold to Cameron Logan and was presumably one of the derelict wrecks which were still present when Rem Walker and others visited the farm in the 1970s.

When first restored it was painted to represent 'Z3781', coded 'XR-T' of No. 71 'Eagle' Sqdn – although the serial was partly obscured by the fighter band around the rear fuselage. It carried these markings from 1989 to 2004. *(Andy Robinson)*

In a letter dated 13 October 1988 Stephen Grey clearly stated that: 'This centre section and fuselage structure very definitely and permanently carried 72036 so that is the correct historical identity of my aircraft.' Unlike many of the more recent restorations G-HURI is, without doubt, one of the most original Hurricanes flying today having been rebuilt in the early 1980s from the best remaining parts of the original structure of several Canadian Hurricanes, available at that time. Without any specific history or identity it assumed the identity of CCF c/n 72036, being the number on the airframe quoted by Stephen Grey and confirmed by the late Graham Trant in 1988. The plate is no longer carried within the aircraft but this is not unusual, indeed neither LF363 nor PZ865 carry their identity plates on the fuselage structure any longer having both been rebuilt in recent years.

Both RCAF 5711 and RCAF 5424, the two Hurricanes which can be identified as having contributed in some way

to the airframe of G-HURI, had significant wartime histories with the RCAF in Canada. 5711 served on the east coast in Nova Scotia, within Eastern Air Command, probably with No. 123 Sqdn at Debert, and Nos. 127 and 129 Sqdns at Dartmouth, between August 1943 and May 1944, then served during May-November 1944 with No. 1 Advanced Tactical Training Detachment, an offshoot of No. 1 OTU, based at Greenwood, Nova Scotia. 5424 served on the west coast in British Columbia with No. 135 Sqdn at Patricia Bay, Vancouver, from October 1942 to August 1943, serving with Western Air Command squadrons possibly until May 1944, when No. 135 Sqdn re-equipped with Kittyhawks, and remaining in Western Air Command until February 1945, when transferred to No. 2 Air Command on the prairies, not for anti-balloon-bomb defence but to await disposal.

With the development of The Fighter Collection the Hurricane was delivered to Duxford in January 1988 and much work was seen to have been done since its arrival in the UK some five years earlier. It was soon ensconced in a hangar and Paul Mercer continued to oversee the restoration process, assisted by Peter Rushen and other engineers from The Fighter Collection. During the next few months the final systems were installed and when it made its first flight, on 1 September 1989, it was seen to be painted in RAF markings as 'Z3781', coded 'XR-T' of No. 71 'Eagle' Sqdn – although the serial was partly obscured by the fighter band around the rear fuselage. This squadron had been equipped with the Hurricane IIA and IIB from April-August 1941 when based at Martlesham Heath and North Weald. The original Z3781, after transfer to No. 133 'Eagle' Sqdn, had been destroyed in a fatal accident in bad weather on 8 October 1941 near Maughold, Ramsey, Isle of Man whilst on a transit flight from Fowlmere near Duxford to Eglinton, Northern Ireland, which took the life of Connecticut-born P/O Andy Mamedoff (a flight commander in No.133 Sqdn). His grave is in Brookwood Military Cemetery.

G-HURI flew in these markings until 2004 when it emerged from an 18-month-long overhaul at Duxford in new markings representing 'Z5140', a Gloster-built Hurricane IIB flown by No. 126 Sqdn during the siege of Malta June 1941-March 1942. The identity was chosen as it could carry the squadron code letters 'HA-C', the initials of the Historic Aircraft Collection, which had acquired the aircraft in August 2002 in exchange for a Hawker Nimrod Mk I, S1581

(G-BWWK). The original Z5140 arrived at Malta on 6 June 1941 during Operation Rocket, having flown off HMS *Ark Royal*. The Malta squadrons were desperate to receive any aircraft regardless of colour, including Hurricanes delivered in the northwest European temperate camouflage scheme. Early Hurricanes delivered to Malta in summer 1940, originally intended for Egypt, were in desert camouflage. In September 2005 the 'new' Z5140 became the first Hurricane to return to Malta since World War 2. It flew there together with HAC's Spitfire, BM597, as part of the 'Merlins Over Malta' project.

In August 2012, this remarkably active and much-flown old warrior undertook an epic long-distance flight to Russia and back, to participate in the centenary celebrations of the Soviet Air Force, at Ramenskoye airfield, southeast of Moscow. In successfully fulfilling this mission, 'HA-C' became the first Hurricane to fly in Russian skies since approximately 3,000 of them were supplied via hazardous Arctic convoys to the Soviet Air Forces from 1941 onwards. On this occasion, G-HURI was flown at Ramenskoye before President Putin by serving RAF instructor and display specialist F/Lt Dave Harvey. He then ferried her home via Lithuania, Poland, Germany and Belgium, displaying the aircraft at the Belgian Zoersel air base en route. During this ambitious flight G-HURI flew 18 sorties and completed some 21 operational hours before Dave returned it to its long-time home at Duxford, Cambridgeshire.

In the early days of aircraft restoration, it was not considered important to present a machine in its original detail specification, but during their years of ownership the Historic Aircraft Collection has gone to great lengths to reintroduce authentic equipment. This has even included the installation of a brand-new unused Merlin 29, Air Ministry serial number A265386. It is a measure of the owner's persistence in returning the aircraft to its original specification that the perfectly good Merlin initially fitted was removed and replaced by this correct specification power unit. An original period gun sight is also installed. In fact G-HURI's only modern equipment comprises the radio, the seat harness and long-range fuel tanks fitted discreetly into the wing gun bays to enhance the aircraft's versatility, as amply demonstrated by its ground-breaking forays to Malta and Moscow.

During the winter of 2014-2015 G-HURI underwent some refurbishment, part of which was a change of colour scheme. Bearing in mind that 2015 is the 75th anniversary of the Battle of Britain the markings chosen are those of 'P3700 / RF-E' which was flown by No. 303 (Polish) Sqdn and abandoned by Sgt Kazimierz Wünsche over Poynings, Kent, on 9 September 1940 having sustained damage from a Bf 109 during combat over Beachy Head.

Unidentified

Although some of the preceding aircraft have only been tentatively identified there are still others where it has not been possible to establish formal identity. They are, therefore, listed by location.

Canada, Darrell Brown, Oshawa, Ontario

Darrell Brown has the centre section of the third ex-Soviet Hurricane sold by Ed and Rose Zalesky to John Norman. When John sold off the parts he no longer required for the restoration of AM274 (qv) the two hulks were acquired by Brian Davis of Hamilton, Ontario. Brian retained Z2330 (qv) and passed the remains of the other on to Darrell Brown. It has Gloster Aircraft Co. Ltd plates attached and would seem to have been a Mk I which was not converted to a Mk II Srs I but there is no other identification on the structure. Darrell will use this as the basis of a long-term static restoration project.

(John and Heather Norman)

Russia, Central Museum of the Great Patriotic War, Moscow

This museum has a static display of aircraft which have been recovered from the tundra and restored for static exhibition. The Hurricane was initially displayed outside in Victory Park as a bare fuselage skeleton under camouflage netting but over the years it has been 'restored' and is now displayed under cover. It is painted in grey green camouflage with Soviet red stars and the code number '11' in white on the fuselage sides. It is believed that much of the structure has been mocked up using modern replacement parts.

(Ken Duffey)

Russia, Revda, Lovozero Murmansk Region

A Hurricane painted to represent 'BM959' was unveiled as a war memorial at Revda, 200 miles from Murmansk in northern Russia on 1 September 1989. The aircraft had been recovered from a crash site near Lovozero on the Kola Peninsula, renovated and placed on a concrete plinth with the inscription 'To the Fighting Brotherhood of the Allies in the struggle against Fascism during WWII and in the memory of the pilots who did not return from combat and who died in the tundra, mountains, lakes and swamps of the Russian North'. The aircraft was discovered with a Merlin XX engine, four 20mm cannon and a tropical filter.

(*Author's Collection*)

UK, The Fighter Collection, Duxford, Cambs

The Fighter Collection holds in store the bulk of the second ex-Soviet Hurricane which was recovered with that now displayed at Duxford as 'Z2315' and believed to be BE146 (qv). When the Imperial War Museum had completed their static restoration the second airframe was stored. The Fighter Collection has no immediate plans for this airframe. The best parts from both airframes were used in the construction of 'Z2315' so the stored airframe is a combination of parts from both.

(*Author's collection*)

USA, National Museum of the US Air Force, Wright-Patterson AFB, Dayton, Ohio

Bob Schneider of RRS Aviation, Hawkins, Texas, rebuilt two static display Hurricanes from parts of five acquired from Jack Arnold of Brantford, Ontario, Canada, in the 1980s. Both of these featured welded square section steel fuselage frames, incorrect cowling profiles and an incorrect fin shape. One is exhibited in the Pima Air and Space Museum at Tucson, Arizona, and is claimed to be RCAF

5662 – although this is highly doubtful – the other was exchanged for a Lockheed C-130A and was displayed at the National Museum of the US Air Force from 1990 onwards. Following several years on display the aircraft – claimed to be 'RCAF 5390' – was dispatched to Hawker Restorations in January 2001 who rebuilt it all over again at Earls Colne, Essex. The welded steel tube fuselage was replaced with one using non-airworthy tubing from other recoveries, cowlings of the correct profile were fitted and a replacement fin installed before the aircraft was returned to Wright-Patterson in August 2002 where it is displayed as 'Z3174 / XR-B'. The real 5390 was lost at sea off Tofino on the west coast of Vancouver Island, BC, on 7 February 1944 and was not recovered.

(*US Air Force Museum*)

Other Projects and Relics

Although some of the preceding aircraft could be considered as incomplete projects they are included due to the fact that they will probably remain in their current form for the foreseeable future. There are other aircraft in the pipeline, some just in the form of a recovered identity plate, which in due course may be promoted to full entries. These include the following.

L2005, Hurricane Mk I, Hawker Restorations Ltd, Milden, Suffolk, UK

Hawker Restorations have the identity plate from L2005 of No. 151 Sqdn, North Weald, which was shot down in flames on 28 August 1940; the pilot, P/O J N E Alexander, bailed out but was badly burned. His aircraft crashed into a bungalow at Millthorpe, Godmersham, at 1630 hours. The crash site was excavated in the 1970s and various items, including the identity plate, were recovered. This may become the basis of a restoration project in due course.

Z2892, Hurricane Mk IIB, Brian Davis, Hamilton, Ontario, Canada

In addition to his other projects Brian Davis has the identity plate from Z2892 which served with No. 87 Sqdn and crashed on 27 October 1941 whilst engaged in Turbinlite operations. It had been delivered as a Hurricane IIA in March 1941 and served with Nos. 249 and 601 Sqdns before being converted to a IIB at No. 18 MU in June 1941 before joining the night fighters of No. 87 at Charmy Down on 24 June 1941. This may become the basis of a restoration project in due course.

Z3571, Hurricane IIC, Malta Aviation Museum, Ta'Qali, Malta

The Malta Aviation Museum holds the rear fuselage of Z3571 in its collection at Ta'Qali, having recovered substantial remains from a farm where it crashed on 27 January 1942 resulting in the death of P/O Alex Mackie. Mackie, of 1435 (night fighter) Flight at Ta'Qali, was the first of several Hurricanes preparing to take off at dusk for test flights following the installation of long-range tanks for intruder duties over Sicily. As Mackie took off in Z3571 'J',

six Messerschmitt Bf 109s appeared from the direction of Rabat, three of them breaking off after Mackie's Hurricane and the other three strafing the airfield. Mackie hit a dry stone wall as he attempted to force land his stricken Hurricane but was thrown out of the cockpit and died of his injuries two days later. Parts from Z3571 were used in the restoration of Z3055 (qv) and the rest is displayed as a bare frame.

(Phil Glover)

Midland Aircraft Recovery Group

This group are said to be building a static Hurricane project, which may be the one to which Phil Lawton donated the remaining parts of G-RLEF at the end of 2014.

Paul Linsell, Norfolk, UK

Paul is working on a Hurricane project at his home in Norfolk. It utilises parts from a number of crash-site recoveries.

Technical Museum, Zagreb, Croatia

The Technical Museum in Zagreb, Croatia, has the rear fuselage and tail assembly of a Hurricane on display, together with a Rolls-Royce Merlin III fitted with a de Havilland 'bracket' propeller. During 1938, the Yugoslav government purchased 12 Hurricane Mk Is for the Royal Yugoslav Air Force and followed this up with an order for another 12 together with a manufacturing licence to allow production of the fighter at the Rogozarski (orders for 60) and Zmaj (orders for 40) factories. These plants, together with the Ikarus concern, had been designing and manufacturing sporting and training aircraft since the 1920s. Production was expected to reach eight per month from each assembly line by mid-1941. In the event, by the time of the German onslaught of April 1941, which put an end to further production, Zmaj had delivered 20 Hurricanes but Rogorzarski had delivered none. It is assumed that the engine was from one of the Mk I Hurricanes but the rear fuselage is unidentified and may be from a British Mk I, a licence-built aircraft or even one which had served in the Balkans at the end of the Second World War

(Phil Glover)

St Petersburg, Russia

Phil Lawton has confirmed that several Hurricanes remain stored in the St Petersburg area of Russia but it is becoming more difficult to secure export permits for them and they are likely to remain there for the foreseeable future.

India

A Hurricane is known to exist at a military location in India. No identity has been found but efforts are being made to secure it for the Indian Air Force Historic Flight.

Ant Whitehead, Worcestershire, UK

Ant is working on a Hurricane cockpit project at his home in Worcestershire. It utilises parts from a number of crash-site recoveries.

(Ant Whitehead)

Rumours

Over the years various lists of surviving Hurricanes have been published in print and on the internet which include a number of aircraft not mentioned in this book. The reason for this is simple, unless there is definite proof, either in the form of a photograph or recent first-hand testimony, then the aircraft cannot be included. The majority of these are aircraft claimed to have been recovered by the late Jack Arnold but of which no trace can be found as they were probably sold as parts and their identities lost. For the sake of completeness the aircraft which fall into this category are listed below.

Serial	Comments
L1606	Purchased back by Hawkers and used for propeller development as G-AFKX, cancelled from register on 4 May 1941 as permanently withdrawn from use. Was never a survivor.
P2725	Parts including engine recovered from crash site for television programme, only small engine parts remain on display at RAF Museum, Hendon. Remainder melted down to make Hurricane models for sale.
Z3176	Parts may have been recovered from Russia but used as spares in other projects.
BH229	Crash site recovery from Russia, any remaining parts shipped to New Zealand with P3351/DR393 in 1995. Believed used as spares.
BW835	Jack Arnold, no evidence of recovery or continued existence.
BW841	Jack Arnold, no evidence of recovery or continued existence.
BW847	Jack Arnold, no evidence of recovery or continued existence.
BW873	Jack Arnold, no evidence of recovery or continued existence.
5380	Jack Arnold, no evidence of recovery or continued existence.
5392	Possible recovery by David Maude, Victoria, BC, Canada, no evidence.
5409	Parts only, used in restoration of 5667, no longer extant.
5424	See G-HURI, page 206.
5450	Project registered as G-TDTW, not proceeded with, believed used as spares.
5455	Parts used in 5447, remainder used as spares, no longer extant.
5590	Unknown owner, Ontario, no evidence of continued existence.
5625	Moore Aviation Restoration, Ontario, no evidence of continued existence.
5627	Tiger Boys, Ontario, no evidence of continued existence.
5715	Les Fairn recovered the wreckage of this aircraft from the bed of Gaspereau Lake, Nova Scotia, during the summer of 1984. At the time he offered it for sale as parts but no trace of its continued existence can be found.
?	Kap Aeronautical Collection, Ontario, two airframes, no evidence of recovery or continued existence.

Typical of the problems faced in attempting to identify many of the Canadian recoveries is this example seen at Jack Arnold's storage area in 1980. The number spray-painted on the hulk is not a CCF constructor's number and gives no clue as to the identity of this very substantial relic. Its fate is unknown. *(Don Bradshaw)*

The Ones That Got Away

Although this book is about surviving Hurricanes there are a number which have been lost in recent years due to various reasons and others which survived well into the 1960s before succumbing to the scrapper's torch or axe. This section aims to remember the most significant examples of these Hurricanes that have now disappeared for ever. They are listed in date order with the most recent losses first.

RCAF 5385 / G-RLEF

The most recent example of a Hurricane to have been lost is the ex-Maurice Bayliss project, G-RLEF, which was removed from the UK Civil Aircraft Register in September 2014 by owner Phil Lawton. The identity RCAF 5385/ CCF 42020 was officially given for this project when it was placed on the register in March 2007 but it is believed to have been made up of the spare components left over when Paul Mercer completed the restoration of 5711/G-HURI for Stephen Grey. Much new tubing was made for this project over the years but when it was examined by Phil Lawton and Bruce Ellis of Phoenix Aero at Thruxton they came to the conclusion that it was not to airworthy standard. As a consequence the entire tail section was used in the reconstruction of G-CBOE and the rest was donated to a static Hurricane project being constructed in Kenilworth, Warwickshire. This may be the project being assembled by the Midland Aircraft Recovery Group. G-RLEF was 'permanently withdrawn from use' by the UK Civil Aviation Authority on 10 September 2014 and the identity 5385 no longer exists.

RCAF 5589 / G-HURR

This aircraft, which was made up from the components of a number of Canadian Hurricanes which were left over from Harry Whereatt's restoration of RCAF 5447 (qv), crashed at Shoreham on 15 September 2007 with the loss of its pilot, Brian Brown. The remains were bought from the insurance company by Phil Lawton for possible use as a parts source for his other Hurricane projects. In the event the parts proved to be too badly damaged to be of any use and, as included in the agreement with the insurers, they were destroyed to prevent the identity being used again. The only part that remained was the Merlin engine block which was sold to be converted into a coffee table.

(Darren Harbar Photography)

Z3176

Recovered from Russia, parts of this Hurricane were acquired by Hawker Restorations but have been utilised as spares and the identity no longer exists.

Z5053

This Hurricane was recovered from a crash site at Welikoe, Oneshakji, on the Kola Peninsula and 'restored' using many wooden and other parts to form a passable static representation of 'Z5252' for a Russian museum. It was sold to the UK but on arrival it became obvious that it was not the genuine article. As a consequence any usable components were stripped by Hawker Restorations Ltd for use in other projects including P3717 / G-HITT and the remainder was scrapped. In October 2014 all that remained was part of the outer starboard wing.

(Peter Dimond)

BD736

This was one of several aircraft recovered from Russia – the parts were acquired by the Cambridge Fighter and Bomber Society for use in the restoration of L1639 (qv).

Z2505

This Hurricane Mk IIA served with No. 310 Sqdn and crashed in Loch Oich, Scotland on 31 August 1941. A large amount of airframe material was recovered from the loch during the 1990s but it is believed that this was sold off as components and souvenirs and the identity no longer exists. It is, of course, possible that the identity plate may still be in a private collection and could form the basis of a new aircraft but there is no evidence of this.

RCAF 5377 / C-GCWH

This was the first privately-restored flyable Hurricane, having been rebuilt at Carman, Manitoba, by Bob Diemert as RCAF 5585/CF-SMI and flown as early as 1966. It was brought to the UK in June 1967 and used in the film *The Battle of Britain* as it was one of just three airworthy Hurricanes available worldwide. Re-registered as G-AWLW it was sold to Samuelson Film Services in July 1969 and then to Sir William J D Roberts who had it fully restored at Strathallan, Scotland, and repainted as 'P3308/UP-A'. The poor handling qualities of this aircraft were commented on by many of its pilots – including Hawker Siddeley's chief test pilot Duncan Simpson – and was due to an incorrect aerofoil section being used for the ailerons. Once these were exchanged with those from a static museum aircraft it flew perfectly. Acquired by the Canadian Warplane Heritage in 1984 the aircraft flew from Hamilton, Ontario, as 'P3069 / YO-A' until it was destroyed in a hangar fire on 15 February 1993. The undercarriage legs were all that remained and they are fitted to a full-scale static replica owned by CWH.

(Robert Rudhall Collection via Peter R Arnold)

BW854

This CCF-built Hurricane served with No. 126 (F) Sqdn at RCAF Station Dartmouth, NS, Canada, in 1942 and was coded BV-X. It was destroyed in a Category A forced landing in Pine Lake, NS, after engine failure during formation practice, on 8 February 1943. The wreckage was salvaged by the Atlantic Canada Aviation Museum, using a Canadian Coast Guard Bell 212 helicopter, and stored until 1988 when it was sold to Matt Sattler of Carp, Ontario. It is believed that it was included in the sale of various Hurricane wrecks to Tony Ditheridge some years later and was used for spares. The radiator was taken off the wreck by Ken Beanlands for use on RCAF 5708 (qv).

(Mark Peapell)

Iranian Air Force 2-15

A Hurricane bearing the serial 2-15 was held by the Imperial Iranian Air Force Museum at Ghale Morghi, Tehran, but is understood to have been destroyed following the overthrow of the Shah of Iran in February 1979.

South Shore Demolition Company, Lytham St Annes, Lancs

During the late 1960s the aircraft preservation movement in the UK was still in its infancy and at the forefront were the Historic Aircraft Preservation Society, based in southeast London, and the Northern Aircraft Preservation Society, based in Stockport, Greater Manchester. At that time there were still significant amounts of military aircraft scrap to be found in yards around the country which was left over from the mass scrapping of World War 2 vintage aircraft which had taken place throughout the 1940s and 1950s. One such yard was the South Shore Demolition Company of Lytham St Annes, Lancashire, which contained the mortal remains of at least ten Hurricanes. The damaged and rusted fuselages would today be considered ripe for restoration but at that time it was impossible to find them a home. The members of the Northern Aircraft Preservation Society did what they could to recover them but in the end they had to sell all but two of them on to another scrap merchant as only one other group was prepared to consider them. That group (Reflectaire Ltd) eventually collapsed and their two frames were also scrapped. The serials of the aircraft found were: LE834, LF330, LF563, LF678, LF746, PG552, PG590, PZ751, PZ778 and PZ813. The identity plates of all of these aircraft were removed and are in the possession of one of the founder-members of NAPS.

(Lloyd P Robinson/The Aeroplane Collection)

V6846, Bihta Air Force Base, Patna, India

Rumours of the continued existence of this Hurricane Mk I continue to surface from time to time and its identity has frequently been linked to the Hurricane displayed in the Indian Air Force Museum at Palam. V6846 had a distinguished wartime career which included a forced landing near Dalton in Furness, after running out of fuel on 15 October 1940 when being flown by S/Ldr Jan Ambrus who was leading Yellow Section of No. 312 Sqdn on a dusk patrol from their base at Speke, Liverpool. It was not badly damaged and after repair it served with Nos. 3 and 247 Sqdns. At 2340 hours on 22 July 1942, V6846/ZY-W was being flown by a Free French pilot, S/Lt Hélies, of No. 247 Sqdn, then based at Exeter as a night-fighter unit, when he shot down a Ju

88 – a remarkable feat in an old eight-gun Hurricane Mk I. V6846 was eventually dispatched to India as a training airframe and was discovered in a semi-derelict state on the Indian Air Force base at Bihta, Patna, in August 1966 by Steve Simms, who took the photograph reproduced here. The RAF roundels were still visible beneath the wings and the serial was confirmed at that time. When Steve returned to Patna the following year it had gone and despite rumours of it being displayed outside a tea shop in the area it can safely be assumed that it was scrapped on site in 1966/67.

(S N Simms)

Unidentified Mk IV, Waterkloof, South Africa

The photograph reproduced here is evidence that at least one Hurricane Mk IV was still in existence at Waterkloof during the mid-1960s. It is safe to assume that it was scrapped shortly after this photograph was taken.

(Dave Rautenbach)

PG499 / 5500M, R J Coley's Yard, Hounslow, UK

Hurricane IIC PG499 (5500M) was to be found in the yard of R J Coley and Son (Hounslow) Ltd as late as 1964, having been delivered there from Dunsfold after it had donated parts to the Science Museum's Mk I, L1592 (qv), which was restored by Hawker Aircraft Ltd in 1960-61. It is thought to have been displayed near Chester for a time before moving to Castle Bromwich and then on to an RAF dump. When Hawkers requested parts to assist with the restoration of L1592, PG499 was delivered to Dunsfold. When Kevin Patience visited the yard and took the photograph reproduced here he was offered the aircraft for £25, but unfortunately he had nowhere to store it and it was subsequently scrapped.

(Kevin Patience via Peter R Arnold)

Index